Music for the Listener

Music for

Roland Nadeau
and William Tesson
NORTHEASTERN UNIVERSITY

the Listener

ALLYN AND BACON, INC.   BOSTON

to Beverly

to Jennifer

Preface

In *Music for the Listener* we are going to give you a background — the essential workings of music — that will prepare you to listen to any music with a discerning ear. You will not have to *read* music — although you will quickly learn to *follow* music through the SCORE PROFILES. You will have to listen — often and hard — just as you would have to concentrate often and hard to understand French, Shakespeare, or baseball.

The special feature of this text, the SCORE PROFILE (**SP**), is not basically an original idea. The presentation of the *leading compositional idea* of a musical work as it evolves has been used before for various reasons. In the field of musical theater or the night club, the conductor often uses a "lead sheet," which is a diagram of the *melody* or the *"leading" voices* at any given moment. Perhaps, in its simplest form, our SCORE PROFILE is really a "lead sheet." But we hope it is more than that. Our idea of a SCORE PROFILE is that it is similar to a topographical map. We try to give not only the contours of the main ideas, but a little of the elevation too, as it were. This we try to do in several ways. The first is by showing the manner in which the various instruments are combined. If they are in unison, the instruments are shown on a single line: VL, CL, OB. If they differ in register, the relationships of the registers are shown: VL

CL

OB

Thus, the violin is above the clarinet is above the oboe. Second, the SCORE DETAILS, beginning in Part One, may also be regarded as a "blow-up" illustration. Special details of the original full score

v

are magnified in order to enhance the understanding of a musical work.

Music for the Listener contains a great many musical examples in addition to several full SCORE PROFILES. There may be some who feel that this is too much to present to those who do not read music. But to this objection there are two answers:

1. It is not necessary to *read* music on the page to perceive important aspects of its meaning. *Following* SCORE PROFILES, using specific techniques explained in the Introduction, is enough for the beginning listener.
2. Almost all basic appreciation texts use musical examples to a greater or lesser degree. *Music for the Listener* goes to the logical conclusion: if musical examples of a few measures are a help to the reader, longer musical examples most certainly are not a hindrance.

Music for the Listener is planned so that the "hows" of music in the first two parts—"*Theory*" and "*Performance*"—lead to the "whys" of music in Part Three, "*History*." In addition to learning basic vocabulary, theory, and how to follow music using the SCORE PROFILES, you will learn about the composers and the times and conditions that affected their music.

We want you to be enlightened about music—not only entertained by it. To achieve this you must participate. Great music will affect you in direct proportion to the extent of your participation.

Note: Important technical terms in the text are in ***boldface italics***, except in the Introduction, where they appear in *italics*, and may be found in three separate places in the book:
   (1)   within the text itself
   (2)   in the GLOSSARY-INDEX
   (3)   at the end of each pertinent chapter in a special listing: FOR REFERENCE AND REVIEW.
When these terms are not immediately defined, find the definition in the GLOSSARY-INDEX.

We wish to thank the following people for their help: Dr. Colleen Bicknell of Northeastern University for making helpful suggestions in certain portions of the text, and Clinton Arrowood for his enthusiastic cooperation in the selection and creation of the sketches. We also wish to express our gratitude to the staff of Allyn and Bacon: Nelson Jansky, Roger Powers, Susan Prindle, and Virginia Safer for exemplary guidance of the authors; and a special kind of thanks to Malcolm Bessom for extremely careful scrutiny of the music manuscript.

Contents

PART TWO: PERFORMANCE MEDIA

PART THREE: HISTORY

INTRODUCTION

The eye and the score

THE DISCUSSION of theoretical materials in this section is brief and synoptic. Its purpose is to launch the reader immediately into following SCORE PROFILES, which are a special feature of this text. As you continue to listen and to follow the SCORE PROFILES, you will need to explore music theory more deeply. The chapters in Part One cover this material in detail.

The score

A complete score may include any number of *staves*, depending on the number of instrumentalists or singers involved in its performance. Following are the first four measures of a complete score as the conductor sees it.

The beginning of a full conductor's score is shown in Example 1.

The score profile

A Score Profile extracts the primary melodic elements from the complete score and represents them on one staff, occasionally more. Its purpose is to allow the listener to see the direction and

Example 1   Symphony No. 1, Opus 21, Beethoven

shape of the primary melodic elements while listening to the whole.
The beginning of a Score Profile is shown in Example 2.

Example 2

Following a Score Profile is not equivalent to reading music. Being able to read music means that one can either hear, identify, or reproduce precise pitches in the correct time in a musical flow. This requires applied musical training in depth over a considerable span of time.

To follow a Score Profile, the listener is required only to keep his place in the music. Then, by observing certain characteristics on the printed page, he gains added insights into the music that are not always possible in ordinary passive listening. By looking as well as listening he focuses on the main points of interest in the music. He finds *melodic contour* and *climax*, changes of *instrumentation*, varying *rhythmic patterns*, *tempo* changes, special *articulations*, and *dynamic* levels.

Strictly speaking, learning to follow a score is not essential for gaining a love of music. But it does hasten music appreciation and most certainly deepens it. When the listener grafts a topographical knowledge of a score to the pure listening experience, he gains a new dimension of appreciation: the "how" of music composition. He learns how the piece of music is constructed: its *form*, its design. When he perceives that music has shape, direction, unity, contrast, and continuity, his appreciation of the composer's solutions to musical problems grows enormously.

THE ESSENTIALS OF FOLLOWING A SCORE PROFILE

The following step-by-step directions will use musical examples from the first movement of Beethoven's Symphony No. 1, in C major, Opus 21. This movement is found in Score Profile at the end of this chapter.

The Staff. Music is ordinarily notated on five-line *staves*. Each line and each space represents the letter name of a *pitch*. In general, the higher the note on the staff, the faster the vibrations of the pitch, and therefore the higher it will sound to the ear. Example 3 shows a staff with rising pitches.

Example 3

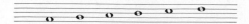

Clefs.   In Example 3 no *clef* is used. A clef is placed on the music staff to specify exactly what pitch name each line and space is given. In Chapter 1, pitch identification by means of clef is fully explained. For the purpose of this chapter and for score following in general, only the basic role of the three clefs need be explained.

The clefs are: The G clef, 𝄞 ; the F clef, 𝄢 ; the C clef, 𝄡 .

A G clef means that pitches on the staff will be played or sung by high-sounding instruments or voices and is used, for example, in music for *soprano voices, flutes, trumpets,* and *violins.* When this clef (Example 4) is used, its staff is called *treble.*

Example 4

G clef ——— { Treble staff

The F clef is used for low-pitched instruments or voices such as the *tuba, contrabass, bassoon* and *baritone voice.*The resulting staff is called *bass* (Example 5).

Example 5

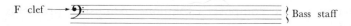

F clef ——→ { Bass staff

The C clef is used for middle-range voices or instruments such as the *viola, trombone,* and *cello.* These instruments use other clefs as well. If the C clef straddles the middle line of the staff, it is called *alto* (Example 6). If the C clef straddles the second line from the top of the staff, it is called *tenor* (Example 7).

Example 6

C clef ——→ { Alto staff

Example 7

C clef ——→ { Tenor staff

The important thing to remember in following a score is that a staff with a G clef placed upon it is used for high-sounding pitches; one using an F clef is used for low-sounding pitches; and one using a C clef is used for pitches in the middle range.

When the melody line jumps from low to high instruments, the appropriate clef will be seen on the staff. In the following example from the Beethoven Symphony No. 1, the clef changes as the melody is tossed back and forth from high to low instruments.

For the time being, do not be concerned with differing note values and *rests*, which will be explained later. Each measure has the same number of beats regardless of indicated durational values (Example 8).

Example 8

Tempo Indications. At the beginning of each Score Profile, various tempo indications, such as *Allegro, Andante, Presto*, will be seen. *Allegro* means fast tempo; *andante* means walking tempo; *presto* means very fast. These terms tell the listener at approximately what rate of speed the music is moving and consequently how fast his eye must move on the page to follow the melody. Tempo indications are often written in Italian, but may be seen in any language. Often, different tempo indications are introduced during the course of the music. Notice that the Beethoven symphony in Example 9 begins in measure 1 with the tempo indication *Adagio molto* — very slow.

Example 9   Symphony No. 1, Opus 21, Movement 1, Beethoven

But then, at measure 13 (Example 10), a new tempo is given, *Allegro con brio* — fast, with brilliance.

Example 10   Symphony No. 1, Opus 21, Movement 1, Beethoven

The listener watches for tempo changes such as this one and adjusts his eye movements accordingly.

TIME SIGNATURES

At the beginning of each Score Profile and occasionally elsewhere in the music, there is a fraction-like figure called the *time signature*.

Typical time signatures are: $\frac{4}{4}$ $\frac{3}{4}$ $\frac{6}{8}$ $\frac{2}{2}$.

Time signatures tell the listener what the *meter* of the music is. The numbers indicate precisely how many and what kind of counts there will be between strong natural *accents* in a musical flow. For practical purposes, however, only the upper number is vital in following a Score Profile. It indicates how many beats there are in each measure of music. A measure of music is marked off on the staff by vertical *bar lines*.

For instance, if the Score Profile is headed by a three-four time signature, the listener knows that he must count or feel three beats for each measure. The first count always occurs immediately to the right of the bar line. This strong count in the measure is called the *downbeat*.

Exceptions: In fast tempo, if the upper number is 6, 9, or 12, it is to be divided by three. The resulting number is the number to be counted:

$\frac{6}{8}$—two counts per measure

$\frac{9}{8}$—three counts per measure

$\frac{12}{8}$—four counts per measure.

The symbol **C** is equivalent to a four-four time signature. The symbol **¢** is equivalent to a two-two time signature.

C = $\frac{4}{4}$ or, four counts per measure

¢ = $\frac{2}{2}$ or, two counts per measure.

A complete explanation of the theory of time signatures, meter, and durational values is found in Chapters 1 and 3.

USING THE SCORE PROFILE

The Score Profile, as you have seen at the beginning of this introduction, is a compression of the essentials of a full score. It is designed in such a way that you can easily and quickly locate any of its important elements.

The leading melodic line is most often found on a single staff. When two important melodic lines are sounding together, they will be seen either on the single staff or on two.

On the top of the staff will appear names of instruments and tempo indications only. Abbreviations side by side indicate that the melodic line is played by instruments in unison. Abbreviations in vertical position show the melodic line played by instruments in different octaves. Below the staff will appear all other performance indications, as well as analyses of the music by the authors. *Every* measure is numbered.

Occasionally, a Score Detail will be seen. These will always be located at the bottom right of the page. These show in greater depth important portions of the score.

To the left of the first page of the Score Profile will be found pertinent data on the music. There you will see a brief commentary on the music, a legend of instrumental abbreviations, and the type of formal structure used.

How To Start.   (Use the Score Profile following.)

1. Look at the tempo indication. This will tell how fast the notes will be played and how fast you must count to keep your place on the Score Profile. Notice what clef is used to start.
2. Look at the time signature. The *upper* number will tell you how many counts there are in each measure.
3. Listen to the beginning of the music without the Score Profile. Feel exactly what the tempo actually is. Count the correct number of beats in each measure while listening to the music.
4. Now follow the Score Profile all the way through, again counting out loud each beat. Each time you say "one," place your finger on the first note after the bar line.
5. Repeat the above process several times, each time noticing more and more details on the Score Profile. After two or three times you will not need to count out loud and can concentrate on important structural features of the composition. Notice what instrument is playing. Watch for dynamics and signs indicating fluctuations of tempo. Notice whether the notes go up or down. Climaxes usually occur high on the staff.

Once you are familiar with every detail of the Score Profile and can keep your place with ease, you will be prepared to study each new Profile in depth. As you learn about the basics of music and about musical ideas in Part One, "Theory," refer constantly to their visual and aural representation through the Score Profiles. For example, as you become acquainted with musical forms in Chapter 7, search out these forms in the Profile of that chapter as well as in those of other chapters. When you encounter *modulation*, follow each Score Profile and compare the different manners in which that device is handled by the masters. If you do this consistently, you will possess a firm and pertinent knowledge of the theory of music. Then, Part Two, "Performance media," and Part Three, "History," will have a valid meaning for you, for it will be based on an *applied* knowledge of theory.

Example 11   Symphony No. 1, Opus 21, Movement 1, Beethoven

There are four beats in each measure.
In general, high-sounding instruments will be heard.

Symphony No. 1, Opus 21, Movement 1, Beethoven

Written in 1799–1800, this work harks back in style to Haydn and Mozart, but also shows much originality. The introduction, with the first cadence in the subdominant rather than in the tonic, is quite original, and surprised many when it was first heard.

Orchestra:

2 Flutes (FL)
2 Oboes (OB)
2 Clarinets (CL)
2 Bassoons (BN)

2 French Horns (HN)
2 Trumpets (TR)

2 Timpani (TIMP)

Violins (VL 1, 2)
Violas (VA)
Violoncellos (VC)
Contrabasses (CB)

Form: Sonata-allegro with introduction and coda.

SCORE PROFILE

PART ONE

Theory

MUSIC EXISTED as a natural expression of man long before it was ever set down on paper. The essence of music was understood naturally long before it was ever expounded. The notation of music came about only when it was necessary. When it was necessary, it was also possible. The notation of music, the theory of music, and learned essays on the art of music all had to wait upon the creation of music. That theory follows practice is now only too well known, but throughout the history of music there have been many times that the theorist has forgotten he was a theorist and instead thought he was an arbiter of taste, and an authority on what music should be.

The composer is the first authority and the audience is the last authority. Nevertheless, we may grant that a body of theory has arisen without granting that it takes the place of the composer's work itself.

The substance of the first part of this book is this body of theory. Grasping the essentials of this theoretical knowledge, we are in a position to appreciate and evaluate what has been done by the composer. But remember that the composer will write, the theory will follow.

1

The notation of pitch and duration

IF A PEBBLE is dropped into a pool of water, the disturbance of the water is visually apparent in the ripples that extend outward from the point of impact. If this same pebble is dropped on the floor, the impact sets up a disturbance in the air, and the "ripples" are spoken of as **vibrations**. **Sound** consists of the impact of these air vibrations on the eardrum. You may easily demonstrate for yourself the disturbance of the air by clapping your hands close to your ear. You will feel the disturbance of the air as well as hearing the sound. When the vibrations are irregular, the sound is referred to as noise. When the vibrations are regular, musical tone is the result.

Pitch

WHAT IS PITCH?

Pitch is the term used to designate the "highness" or "lowness" of a particular sound. We speak of a woman's high-pitched voice; we speak of the low-pitched fog horn. And, of course, there are the high-pitched piccolo and the low-pitched tuba. Technically, pitch refers to the *number of vibrations per second* of a particular

"We speak of a woman's high-pitched voice; we speak of the low-pitched foghorn. And, of course, there are the high-pitched piccolo and the low-pitched tuba" (p. 19).

musical tone. The more vibrations per second, the higher pitched is the tone; the fewer vibrations, the lower pitched. The number of vibrations per second is more compactly spoken of as the *frequency*. For example, the frequency of "orchestra *A*" (the pitch to which an orchestra tunes) is 440, that is, 440 vibrations per second. This pitch is commonly referred to as "*A 440*."

The musician, however, does not usually refer to pitches by their frequencies. His terminology is based upon a system of letter names that designate relative pitches.

KEYBOARD ORIENTATION

A look at the Octave Reference Chart (page 22), which illustrates the piano keyboard, shows us the system of letter names in use that designate musical tones. Only seven letters of the alphabet are necessary to designate the various pitches. These are repeated in series, ABCDEFG, starting with the lowest tone of the piano, A_4, and reading from left to right, ending with the highest tone of the piano, C^4. The ear recognizes that any *A*, whether it is low or high, "seems to" sound the same in spite of the difference in register. The same is true for the pitches represented by each of the other letters. The acoustical reasons for this will be made clear later.

The term *octave*, abbreviated *8ve*, refers to a span of eight notes. Thus, C^2 is spoken of as being an octave higher in pitch than C^1. The 88 keys of the keyboard consist of white keys and black keys. The black keys are in alternating groups of twos and threes and serve to orient the eye as well as the fingers of the pianist.

Thus, finding the position of middle *C* on the keyboard as the white note directly to the left of the two-black-key group, one may locate all of the *C*'s on the keyboard. All *F*'s may be located in the same manner, being the white keys directly to the left of the three-black-key groups.

During the time in history when music was improvised or handed down by word of mouth and a given piece consisted of only a single melody, no system of writing music was necessary. But when it became necessary for music to be written for others to read, i.e., when there was more than one melody, a system of notation had to evolve. Thus, today we have what amounts to a graph that shows simultaneously the exact pitch of a tone and its proportionate duration.

THE STAFF

Various musical graphs have been used. At one time the pitch aspect was represented by four lines and their adjacent spaces. The

Figure 1   Octave Reference Chart

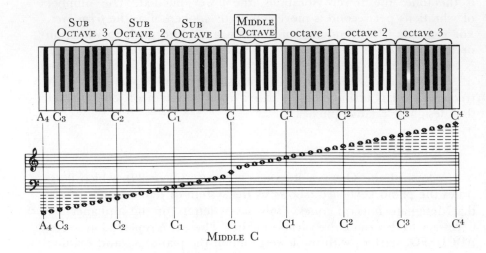

It is understood that in this chart, in naming the octaves, the eighth note of each octave is not included, so that technically only seven letters are included. But it would only be confusing to be correct. Other more scientific systems of measuring would not present this problem; only in music does one count *both* the starting point and the stopping point in measuring *from* something *to* something.

The above system of naming the octaves of the keyboard and the Great Staff departs from the system used by certain other texts. However, we feel it is the most practicable for orientation to both the keyboard and the Great Staff because of its features of symmetry.

musical graph in use today consists of five lines and the adjacent spaces. This is known as the ***staff***. As briefly mentioned in the Introduction, a staff may be used for high, middle, or low register voices or instruments with the use of the proper clef.

In the evolution of notation, an 11-line staff evolved for keyboard instruments, because of their great range. Visual orientation to 11 lines and their spaces was difficult, however, and the necessity for something simpler resulted in the system that is in use today. It is a modification of the 11-line system. The middle line of the 11 is left out except when the note on that line is needed, and then only a short segment of the line is used: enough on which to write the note. This short line is called a ***leger line.*** Leger lines and their adjacent spaces are used above or below any of the staves when it is necessary to extend the staff. Thus, we have the ***Great Staff*** (Example 12), which is used to notate music for the piano, the organ, and the harp as well as the harpsichord, clavichord, and celeste. It is also used in music for mixed voices, as seen in songbooks and hymnals.

Example 12   Great Staff

CLEF SIGNS

Clef signs evolved historically as reference points. They were letter designations of a note placed upon a line of the staff (Example 13).

Example 13

G clef locates G above MIDDLE C → { TREBLE STAFF

── MIDDLE C

F clef locates F below MIDDLE C → { BASS STAFF

The **G clef** and the **F clef** shown in their proper positions on the Great Staff are stylized versions of the actual letters G and F. These are the two clefs most commonly in use today, but there is a third clef that is used in orchestral scores in writing for instruments in the middle register. This is the **C clef** (Example 14), and locates **middle C.** It is used with two different five-line staves, the alto staff and the tenor staff.

Example 14

MIDDLE C → { ALTO STAFF

MIDDLE C → { TENOR STAFF

Its relationship to the Great Staff shows that it is not that the C clef sign moves, but that there is a different selection of five lines from the Great Staff (Example 15). Each clef designates a specific staff of five lines that may be used separately, depending upon the range of a specific instrument or voice (Example 16).

At one time, music for voices was written on all four of these staves (as well as others no longer common). But facility with clef reading has diminished, and most music is written on the treble and bass staves only. Perhaps this was inevitable with the growing popularity of the piano, on which the player need only read the treble and bass staves.

Example 15

C clef locates MIDDLE C →   { Alto staff

C clef locates MIDDLE C →   { Tenor staff

Example 16

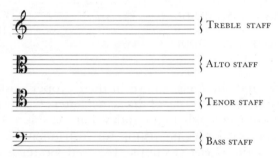

{ Treble staff

{ Alto staff

{ Tenor staff

{ Bass staff

The chief purpose of using a particular staff is to avoid the writing of numerous leger lines. The center of an instrument's register, and originally of a particular voice's register, was the specific deciding factor in choosing the staff and clef to be used. Thus, music for a soprano voice or instrument would be written on the treble staff, for an alto voice on the alto staff, and so on. This, of course, avoided the extensive use of leger lines, saved the copyist much time and effort, and reduced the possibility of error. It also saved the reader from encountering numerous leger lines, which, in manuscript especially, are obviously more difficult to read than notes on the staff.

The Great Staff covers the normal span of female and male voices. But in writing for certain instruments, it may be expanded by the use of leger lines. However, if too many leger lines are involved for facility in reading, the sign *8va*, for the Italian *ottava,* may be used to signify that the notes so designated sound an octave higher than written (Example 17). In the same manner, *8va **bassa*** may be used to signify notes sounding an octave lower than written.

In songbooks and hymnals, the parts for women's voices, soprano and alto, are written on the treble staff; the parts for men's voices,

Example 17

tenor and bass, are written on the bass staff. In larger choral works, however, where a separate staff is used for each of the different voices, an anomaly exists in the writing for the tenor voices. The tenor part, instead of being written on the bass staff as in songbooks, is written on the treble staff an octave higher than its actual sound. Since the tenor part often goes to the *G* above middle *C*, and sometimes higher, this does save the use of leger lines (Example 18). Sometimes no indication

Example 18

is made that the actual sound is an octave lower; but the more acceptable practice of putting an 8 under the G clef (Example 19) specifically

Example 19

indicates that the entire part sounds an octave lower, the figure 8 below the clef standing for *8va bassa*. Another method of indicating the same octave transposition is the use of two G clefs side by side (Example 20).

Example 20

Either of these clef symbols is acceptable, but preference should be given to the former for its correct simplicity. However, there is a third sign in use, which consists of combining the G clef and the C clef (Example 21) in an attempt to show that the third space *C* of the treble staff really sounds as middle *C*. This usage should be discouraged, because the C clef in correct usage always designates middle *C* as being on a line.

Example 21

SHARPS, FLATS, NATURALS

The Octave Reference Chart shows that the lines and spaces of the staff coincide with the white notes of the keyboard. The distance between any two adjacent notes on the keyboard, *considering both black and white notes*, is a **half-step** (also called **semitone**). In Figure 2 the half-steps are shown by the arrows. The distance between two adjacent white notes is a **whole step** (also called a **whole tone**), with the exception of *E* to *F* and *B* to *C*.

Figure 2

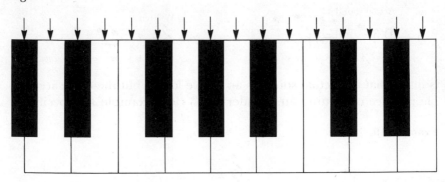

When it is desired to raise the pitch of a tone by a semitone, a **sharp,** ♯, is placed in front of the note (Example 22). When it is desired

Example 22

to lower the pitch of a tone by a semitone, a **flat,** ♭, is placed in front of the note Example 23).

Example 23

On the keyboard, *C*-sharp and *D*-flat are the same black key: the one that stands between *C* and *D*. Continuing this procedure, we find that each black key has a double name. Although not as common, it is also possible for a white key to have another letter name. If we raise the pitch of *E* a semitone (Example 24), *E*-sharp is the white key that is also

Example 24

E   E-sharp

called *F*. By the same procedure, we find that *B*-sharp and *C* are the same white note. Experiments with lowering tones will produce similar results.

ENHARMONICS

When one pitch has two designations, such as *C* ♯ and *D* ♭, either of these designations is the **enharmonic** of the other. Composers use enharmonics to facilitate notation during modulation, or to simplify certain key signatures. An example of the latter is Beethoven's use of key signatures in his Piano Sonata No. 2, Opus 27 ("Moonlight"). The first and third movements have key signatures of *C* ♯ minor. The middle movement has the key signature of *D* ♭ major, instead of the more theoretically correct *C* ♯ major.

At certain times in the course of a composition, it is necessary to raise by a semitone the pitch of a tone that is already sharped. For this, the **double-sharp, ✕**, is used (Example 25). *F* double-sharp is the enhar-

Example 25

F-sharp   F-double-sharp

monic of *G*. To lower a note that is already flatted, the **double-flat, ♭♭**, is used (Example 26).

The natural, ♮, cancels the effect of any sharp or flat, including

Example 26

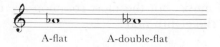

A-flat   A-double-flat

double-sharps and double-flats, returning the note to its pitch un-sharped or unflatted.

On occasion it is desired to return a double-sharp or a double-flat to a single sharp or a single flat. In this case, the natural and the single sharp or flat are combined (Example 27).

Example 27

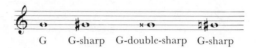

G G-sharp G-double-sharp G-sharp

Duration

PROPORTIONS

The notation of the durational value of a musical tone or its equiv-alent *rest* (silence) is based upon a proportional system in which any value is divisible by two. No value may be divided in any other way. Thus, the whole-note may be divided into two half-notes. Each half-note may be divided into two quarter-notes, and so on. Example 28

Example 28

NOTES			RESTS
	○	whole	▬
♩ or ♩		half	▬
♩ or ♩		quarter	𝄽
♩ or ♪		eighth	𝄾
♩ or ♪		sixteenth	𝄿
♩ or ♪		thirty-second	𝅀
♩ or ♪		sixty-fourth	𝅁

shows the note values most commonly in use and their equivalent rests. The note values shown indicate relative duration only. The actual duration will be established by the tempo indication. Thus, any of the note values are of longer duration in a slower tempo than in a faster one.

Any of the note values shown above may be used as the *basic unit beat* of a piece of music, but the most common are the half-note, the quarter-note, and the eighth-note.

The various portions of a note, the "diacritical marks," as it were, are referred to as the ***notehead,*** the ***stem,*** and the ***flag*** or ***beam,*** as shown in Example 29. The notehead may be open, as in the whole-note

Example 29

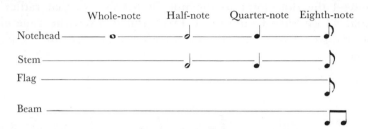

and half-note, or it may be closed, as in all other notes. There is no stem on the whole-note; on the half-note the stem symbolizes a splitting of the whole-note in two. Thus: ♦=♩♩ . Further divisions are symbolized by the flag or beam. Each flag or beam divides by two the note value that would exist without it (Example 30).

Example 30

THE TIE AND THE DOT

The binary system of the division of note values does not contain within itself any way to denote a duration three quarters of the given value of a particular note. If three quarters of the length of a whole-note is desired, this problem in notation is solved by joining a half-note and a quarter-note by means of a *tie* (Example 31). In the evolving

Example 31

"shorthand" of notation, the tied quarter ultimately became a *dot*. See Example 32. The dot in this case equals a quarter-note, which is half the value of the half-note preceding. In certain English and other editions of music, this shorthand dot representing the tied quarter is

Example 32

still written with the spacing shown in Example 32, but modern usage
has moved the dot closer to the note it follows, so that rather than
Example 33 we have Example 34. From this evolved the general rule
that *the dot placed after any note or rest adds to it half its value.* Thus; see
Example 35.

Example 33

Example 34

Example 35

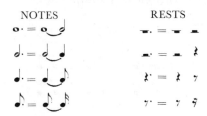

TRIPLETS AND DUPLETS

As in poetry, where there are duple and triple divisions within
main accents, so in music. In a system of notation that is binary in its
divisions, a triple division is taken care of by a special notation. When
three notes are wanted in place of two, a **triplet** is written and bracketed
as shown in Example 36. The triplet takes the same length of time as

Example 36

the two notes that it replaces (Example 37).

Example 37

Similarly, we find that when two notes are wanted in place of three, a *duplet* is written and bracketed as shown in Example 38.

Example 38

TIME SIGNATURE

As time in our everyday lives may be measured by any system that uses equal segments of duration such as seconds, minutes, hours, days, or even "moons," the system of musical notation uses wholes, halves, quarters, eighths, and so forth.

At the beginning of each piece of music, a *time signature* is placed on the staff (directly after the key signature) to show the method of measuring for that particular piece of music.

Vertical *bars* (or *bar-lines*) placed on the staff throughout the piece divide the music into *measures*. The lower number of the time signature designates what note value is to be the measuring unit; the upper number designates how many of these will be in each measure. Thus, the time signature $\frac{2}{4}$ ("two-four") specifies that a quarter (note or rest) is the measuring unit, and that there are two in each measure. No bar-line is necessary at the beginning (Example 39). Any combination of note

Example 39

values or rests that equal two quarter-notes may, of course, appear in each measure (Example 40).

Example 40

The table following presents the signs and symbols most commonly in use in music.

Signs and Symbols

	TERM	MEANING	USAGE OR PLACEMENT
∙	staccato mark	note so indicated played shorter than its value	dot placed above or below note
stacc.	staccato	same as above, but applying to several notes	above notes at point of usage
˄	"wedge" mark	not as short as staccato and accented	above or below note
˃	accent	note so indicated to be accented	above or below note
marc.	marcato	"marked," a slightly lighter accent than preceding entry	above notes at point of usage
⌢	legato	notes to be connected without separation; to be played smoothly	above or below notes
⌒	tie	two notes of same pitch to sound as one continuous tone	connects notes separated by bar-line, or of unequal values
‾	tenuto mark	hold note full value, or even slightly longer; sometimes also means "slightly pressing"	above or below note
'	comma	short breathing space: it may or it may not interrupt the rhythmic pace	between two notes, especially between phrases
//	pause	short pause of silence	at end of phrase
𝄐	pause, fermata, hold	longer pause of silence or sound	over bar-line (silence), over note (sound)
G.P.	grand pause, general pause	silence for all instruments	over a measure of rest in all parts

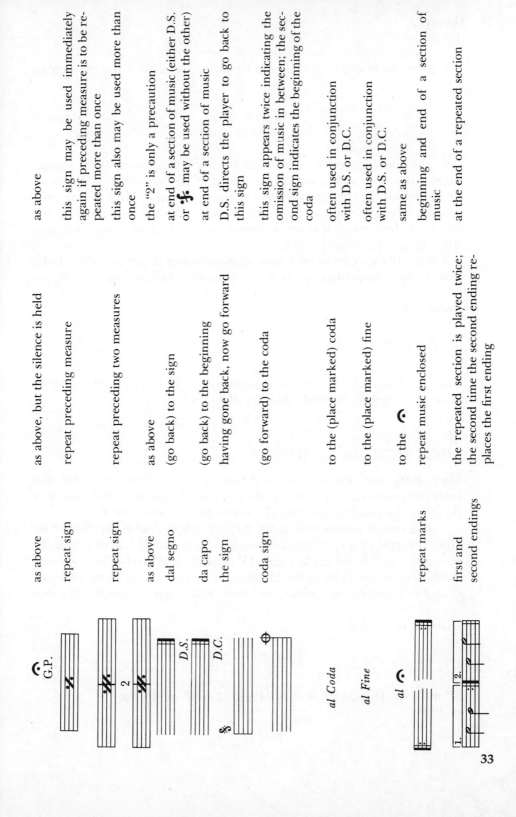

Symbol	Name	Description	Notes
𝄐 G.P.	as above	as above, but the silence is held	as above
𝄎	repeat sign	repeat preceding measure	this sign may be used immediately again if preceding measure is to be repeated more than once
2	repeat sign	repeat preceding two measures	this sign also may be used more than once
	as above	as above	the "2" is only a precaution
D.S.	dal segno	(go back) to the sign	at end of a section of music (either D.S. or 𝄋 may be used without the other)
D.C.	da capo	(go back) to the beginning	at end of a section of music
𝄋	the sign	having gone back, now go forward	D.S. directs the player to go back to this sign
⊕	coda sign	(go forward) to the coda	this sign appears twice indicating the omission of music in between; the second sign indicates the beginning of the coda
al Coda		to the (place marked) coda	often used in conjunction with D.S. or D.C.
al Fine		to the (place marked) fine	often used in conjunction with D.S. or D.C.
al 𝄌		to the 𝄌	same as above
	repeat marks	repeat music enclosed	beginning and end of a section of music
	first and second endings	the repeated section is played twice; the second time the second ending replaces the first ending	at the end of a repeated section

Thus, to emphasize, the time signature designates for each measure:

$_2$—how many
^{4}—what kind.

The time signature is in effect until a change is desired, whereupon a new time signature will be placed at the beginning of the measure in which the change takes place. Very often there is only one time signature for a whole movement or section of a work, but much of the music of the twentieth century shows the use of constantly changing time signatures within a work.

With the exception of a time signature that designates the whole-note as the measuring unit, as in Example 41, which is now exceedingly

Example 41

rare, the lower number of the time signature is never an odd number because, to repeat, the only division of notes is by twos.

Other signs and symbols

Many signs and symbols are used that are not technically within the realm of notation; that is to say, they are not notes on a staff. But they do affect the reading of notes, the repetition of notes, etc.

The end of a section of music is marked by a ***double-bar***. See **SP m. 16a.** The end of a movement is marked by a double-bar in which the second vertical bar is thicker. See **SP m. 178.** This particular "heavier" double-bar is also used at the beginnings and ends of sections of music that are repeated, including two dots with each (Example 42). See

Example 42

SP m. 1, m. 16, also **SP m. 57, 64** and also **SP m. 65, 72.**

Symphony No. 6, Opus 74, Movement 2, Tchaikovsky

Written and first performed in 1893, this is Tchaikovsky's last complete symphony. It is known by the name "Pathetique," although the title was not originated by the composer. It stands, with Tchaikovsky's Fourth and Fifth Symphonies, as among the most popular of orchestral works. The first performance in St. Petersburg was conducted by the composer.

Orchestra:

> 3 Flutes (FL)
>   including Piccolo (PIC)
> 2 Oboes (OB)
> 2 Clarinets (CL)
> 2 Bassoons (BN)
>
> 4 French Horns (HN)
> 2 Trumpets (TR)
> 3 Trombones (TB)
> 1 Tuba (TU)
>
> 3 Timpani (TIMP)
>
> Violins (VL 1, 2)
> Violas (VA)
> Violoncellos (VC)
> Contrabasses (CB)

Form: Ternary, with coda.

SCORE PROFILE

Listen to effect of pizzicato strings against melody in woodwinds.

The distinctive triplet is missing in the brass version of the theme.

The triplet returns

Pedal point continues in lower instruments to measure 95

con dolcezza e flebile

Pedal point concludes

Pedal point resumes on D and continues to the end of the movement.

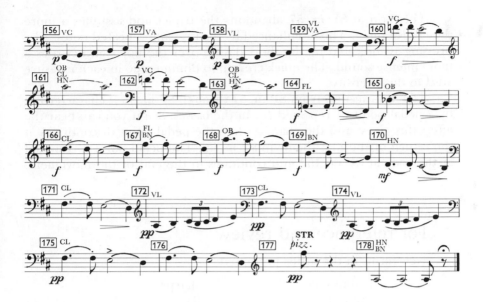

Listening notes

The accents in $\frac{5}{4}$ are usually grouped in either of two ways: 3 + 2, or 2 + 3. The two strong accents in each measure would be shown

then as | | | | | or | | | | |

(1 2 3 1 2) (1 2 1 2 3)

The accent is cleverly disguised in **SP m. 1** and in alternate measures thereafter by the placement of a triplet exactly in the middle of the measure. If this figure were continued, the effect would be that of five beats without a duple pulsation, but in **SP m. 2** and in later measures the accent of | | | | | is clearly established.

Note how the uneven duple rhythm gives an interesting lilt to the movement. This "con grazia" rhythmic pulse and the key of D major provide excellent contrast to the first movement in B minor.

Note the extra sparkle given to the texture by the violins and violas in **SP m. 33** playing pizzicato in octaves above the theme now being played by all of the woodwinds.

In **SP m. 49** the theme is "straightened out" by the trumpets and trombones in ascending octaves as the upper strings move into a countermelody. But the strings take over again in **SP m. 53** to end this section with the original distinctive figure.

The Trio at **SP m. 57** abandons the triplet and assumes a more thoughtful mien. This is enhanced by the pressing repeated notes. The pressing is indicated by the short dashes over the notes and creates a more intense sound. The quick crescendo-diminuendo in each measure adds to the intensity.

The Trio section from **SP m. 57** through **SP m. 95** is characterized by a pedal point of repeated *D*'s in the basses. See if you can hear the effect this gives, and the change when the pedal point discontinues at the return of the first theme in **SP m. 96**. The pedal point is resumed at the coda at **SP m. 152** and continues to the end of the movement.

For reference and review

New terms in the order presented:

vibrations	sharp
sound	flat
pitch	enharmonic
frequency	double-sharp
A 440	double-flat
octave	natural
8ve	rest
staff	basic unit beat
leger line	notehead
Great Staff	stem
clef	flag
G clef	beam
F clef	tie
C clef	dot
middle C	triplet
8va	duplet
ottava	time signature
8va bassa	bars
half-step	bar-lines
semitone	measures
whole-step	double-bar
whole-tone	

The terms from the table of signs and symbols are not reproduced here.

2

Intervals,
scales,
and tonality

Intervals

When two instruments, even of different families, sound a tone of the same pitch, the ear recognizes the similarity, even though the **timbre** of the two instruments may be different. This sounding of the same tone by different instruments is called a **unison**, that is, *sounding as one.* Moreover, when the two instruments sound two tones, one an octave above the other, the ear hears these two tones as very similar.

There is an affinity between two tones an octave apart that is recognizable in every country or culture. One tone sounds as if it were a reinforcement of the other. The difference is there, but the similarity is apparent. Thus, when men and women sing the same tune, in their normal voice registers, the ear recognizes the "sameness," even though the men sound "lower" than the women or, conversely, the women sound "higher" than the men. Both the difference and the similarity are due to a natural acoustical fact: the upper tone of the octave has twice as many vibrations as the lower tone. Thus every other vibration of the upper tone occurs simultaneously with *each* vibration of the lower tone. For example, the ratio of the vibrations of *A* 440 to A^1 an octave above it, with 880 vibrations, is 1:2. It is this simple ratio that accounts for the similarity between two tones an octave apart. Other pairs of tones have different ratios. This is explained in the text accompanying the Chart of the Overtone Series at the end of this chapter.

It is often necessary to speak of the difference in the number of vibrations between tones. As the phrase "difference in the number of vibrations" is correct but cumbersome, the following equation proves useful:

difference in the number of vibrations
equals
difference in frequency
equals
difference in pitch
equals
distance.

We may now state the definition of an *interval* very simply and clearly. *An interval is the distance between two tones.*

NAMING THE INTERVALS

An interval may have a generic name and a specific name. The generic name of an interval is found by counting all of the letter-names of the notes in the span covered from one note to the other, including both of these notes. Thus, the generic name for the interval *C* to *E* is *third* (Example 43), the letters in the span being *C, D, E*. Example 44

Example 43

Example 44

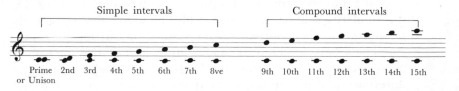

shows the generic names for the most common intervals. *C* is arbitrarily chosen as the lower note.

A *simple interval* is that of an octave or less; a *compound interval* is one that is larger than an octave.

Now note that *C* to *E* and *C* to *E*♭ (Example 45) are both intervals

Example 45

Third   Third   Third   Third

of a third, but the distance from one note to the other in the first interval is two whole-steps, whereas the distance in the second interval is only one and a half steps. All intervals may vary in size in similar fashion, either because they contain one or both of the white-note half-steps (*E-F* and *B-C*) or because they are affected by accidentals or key signature.

These variations in the size of an interval are expressed by the specific name added to the generic.

GENERIC NAMES	SPECIFIC NAMES
1 = prime (or unison)	P = perfect
2 = second	M = major
3 = third	m = minor
4 = fourth	° = diminished
5 = fifth	⁺ = augmented
6 = sixth	°° = doubly diminished
7 = seventh	⁺⁺ = doubly augmented
8 = octave	

The specific name of an interval may be found by applying the following statements. Using *C* as a keynote in the ascending white-note pattern:

1. The interval from the keynote to any other note is ***major*** except the ***prime***, fourth, fifth, and octave, which are ***perfect***. See Example 46.

Example 46

P1   M2   M3   P4   P5   M6   M7   P8

2. All major and perfect intervals increased in size by a semitone are ***augmented*** (Example 47). (The lower note may be lowered, or the upper note may be raised.)

Example 47

3. All major intervals decreased in size by a semitone are *minor* (Example 48).

Example 48

4. All minor and perfect intervals decreased in size by a semitone are *diminished* (Example 49).

Example 49

The following two statements refer to intervals that are less common.

5. All augmented intervals increased in size by a semitone are *doubly augmented.*
6. All diminished intervals decreased in size by a semitone are *doubly diminished.*

The preceding six statements are summarized in Figure 3. Note

Figure 3

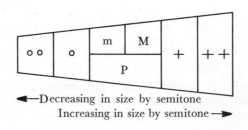

that perfect intervals cannot become major or minor. Note also that
there cannot be a diminished prime. Statement 4 specifies that perfect
intervals decreased in size by a semitone are diminished. The perfect
prime cannot be made smaller.

The terms *perfect, major, minor, augmented,* and *diminished* not only
refer to the specific size of an interval, but are used as terms to denote
the **quality of the interval.** Thus, the quality of an interval may be major
or minor, or any of the other specific terms which apply.

The quality of each compound interval is as if it were a simple
interval. See Example 50.

Example 50

M 9   M 10   P 11   P 12   M 13   M 14   P 15

TRANSPOSITION

All of the foregoing information concerning intervals has been in
relation to *C* as the keynote or lower tone. By *transposing* the white-
note pattern of eight notes from any *C* to the *C* an octave higher, any
other tone may be taken as the lower note of an interval.

Transposition is the exact reproduction (in writing or in sound) of
any pattern of tones at a different pitch level. Thus, this pattern

Example 51

may be transposed to

Example 52

or

Example 53

and so on. The intervallic relationships between the tones of the original pattern must be strictly adhered to in the transposition.

THE INTERVAL FINDER

The Interval Finder was devised as a method of checking empirically your calculated results. It is lined up to show the names of intervals from *C*. Thus, *C* to *C* ♯ is an augmented prime; *C* to *D* ♭ is a minor second. To use it with any other note, cut it out of the book along the line shown by the arrow. Place P1 at the circle on the lower note. The circle on the upper note will be adjacent to the name of the interval. The Interval Finder may also be used with an actual piano keyboard. It is urged that you not only use it visually with the representation of the keyboard, but use it at the piano and sound the tones you are checking. This will be of definite value to you as you continue your listening experiences.

DIATONIC AND CHROMATIC INTERVALS

The Greek word **diatonic** means *across the tones,* and refers in practical usage to the letters of the tones as they stand in succession, omitting none and repeating none. The white-note pattern *C D E F G A B C* is a diatonic pattern. Thus, a diatonic semitone consists of an interval that uses two letters that stand in succession. *E* to *F* and *B* to *C* are diatonic and semitones as well as minor seconds. Further, *C* to *D* ♭ and *F* ♯ to *G* are diatonic semitones (and minor seconds). *C* to *C* ♯, however, is a **chromatic** semitone, and is not a minor second but an augmented prime. *Chroma,* also from the Greek, means *color;* and so the term *chromatic* has been applied to the alteration of a tone by raising or lowering it with the application of an **accidental.**

An accidental is a sharp, flat, or natural that alters the pitch of a tone standing in a diatonic succession.

The distance between two tones sounded together is referred to as a **harmonic interval.** When the two tones are sounded in succession, the distance is referred to as a **melodic interval.**

INTERVAL INVERSION

The **inversion** of an interval takes place when the positions of the two notes on the staff are reversed so that the lower note becomes the upper. This is accomplished by raising the lower note, or lowering the upper note, the distance of an octave. Thus, the interval $\frac{C}{F}$ becomes $\frac{F}{C}$.

The Interval Finder

Figure 4

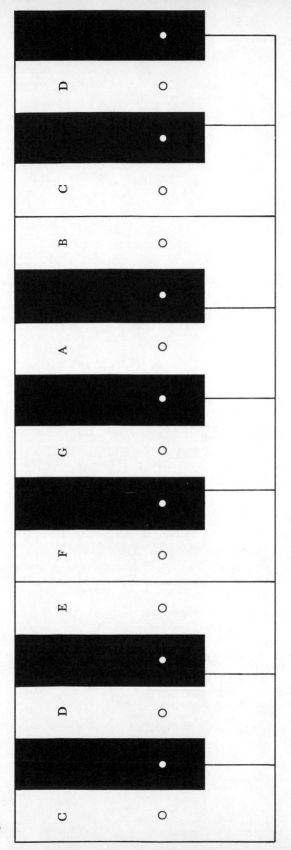
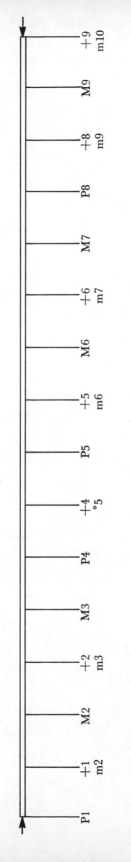

Example 54

At the same time, the quality of the interval changes, as shown in Figure 5.

Figure 5

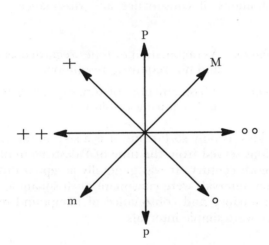

THE QUALITY OF INTERVALS WHEN INVERTED

In Figure 5 we see that, when inverted, any *major* interval becomes *minor*, any *minor* interval becomes *major*, and so on. Note that *perfect* intervals remain *perfect*.

The number of an interval plus the number of its inversion always gives the sum of nine, for intervals of an octave and smaller.

Example 55

This may be used as a check in figuring intervals and their inversions.

INTERVALS AS CONSONANCE AND DISSONANCE

The dictionary definitions are:

> *consonance.* A combination of tones regarded as pleasing and not requiring resolution.

> *dissonance.* A combination of tones regarded as displeasing and requiring resolution.

The terms "pleasing" and "displeasing" are misleading. They are qualitative, implying that consonance is better than dissonance. Let us recast the definitions of consonance and dissonance given above as follows:

> *consonance.* A combination of tones regarded as stable and not requiring resolution.

> *dissonance.* A combination of tones creating tension and requiring resolution.

This still gets us only so far, but it is a step in the right direction. These definitions served from the time of Palestrina until near the end of the nineteenth century. It was generally accepted during this 400-year period that intervals were consonant or dissonant as shown below. Note: The dissonance and consonance of compound intervals is the same as if they were simple intervals.

INTERVAL	ITS INVERSION	CONSONANT	DISSONANT
P1	P8	X	
m2	M7		X
M2	m7		X
m3	M6	X	
M3	m6	X	
P4		sometimes	sometimes
	P5	X	
+4	°5		X

Note that the perfect fourth is listed as sometimes consonant and sometimes dissonant. Whether it is consonant or dissonant depends upon the context. When the lower tone of the perfect fourth is in the bass (the lowest part), as in Example 56, the interval is dissonant. In all other cases it is consonant.

Example 56

THE USES OF CONSONANCE AND DISSONANCE

Composers in every age have used dissonance to create tension. The proportions of dissonance and consonance have varied not only with the period, but with each composer within a period. Similarly, each listener's reaction to consonance and dissonance depends upon his milieu, his listening habits or experience, and his temperament.

Consonance and dissonance in their varying degrees may be compared to the spices used in preparing food. Some are bland and some are bitter, some sweet, and some sour. But we cannot really classify some flavors as pleasing and others as displeasing. It is a matter of taste. But as tastes in food can be acquired or developed, so can tastes in music.

It was in the music of Debussy that the traditional concept of consonance and dissonance began to be blurred, although there were earlier instances. The newer concept regarded consonance and dissonance as relative, and also began to abandon the idea that dissonance required resolution in the usual manner. Consonance and dissonance in varying degrees were now pitted against each other in the context of structures or masses of sound. Tension and resolution still existed, but the concept was more encompassing. Combinations of sound included varieties of dissonance in which the lesser dissonance sounded consonant. Other factors now became more important in the creation and dissipation of tension.

It will be better for our purposes in trying to broaden our appreciation of music in *all* periods to consider consonance and dissonance as relative rather than immutable. The amount of consonance or dissonance of an interval may be rated according to the ratios of the frequencies of any two tones. The simpler the ratio, the more consonant the interval, as shown in the table below. The column labeled "Subjective Description" means just that, although there has been *some* agreement about some of the terms. But if you disagree with these, mildly or violently, you are urged to devise your own adjectives based upon what the sounds suggest to you.

Intervals and Their Ratios

INTERVAL	RATIO	SUBJECTIVE DESCRIPTION
P1	1:1	Pure
P8	1:2	Almost pure
P5	2:3	Less pure, somewhat bare
P4	3:4	Less bare, harder, a little "hollow"
M6	3:5	Bland
M3	4:5	Open, bright, stable
m3	5:6	Not as bright
m6	5:8	Slightly unstable
m7	5:9	Quietly vibrating
M2	8:9	More vibrating
°5	5:7	Unstable, uncertain
+4	7:10	Vague
M7	8:15	Intense, creates tension
m2	15:16	Strident, creates more tension

Presenting consonance and dissonance in a table only partially represents their effect when used in a piece of music. Although in theory the dissonance of a compound interval is equated with the dissonance of its counterpart within the octave, in actuality compound intervals are less dissonant than their equivalent simple intervals. Although this is rarely mentioned in texts, composers are aware of it. When they wish to soften a dissonance, they separate the notes of the dissonant interval by one or more octaves. In addition to "enlarging" the interval by an octave, there are other ways of changing the effect of a dissonance.

1. A dissonance sounds stronger after a bland texture.
2. A dissonance sounds stronger when isolated.
3. A dissonance sounds stronger when produced by instruments of the same family.
4. A dissonance sounds weaker after a harsh texture.
5. A dissonance sounds weaker when the space between the two notes is filled.

Example 57

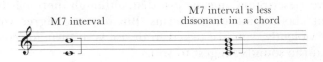

M7 interval

M7 interval is less dissonant in a chord

The point does not need to be labored. It is similar to the use of color. Orange is more striking against areas of blue than it is against areas of brown.

THE TRITONE

The interval of the augmented fourth, and its inversion, the diminished fifth, has been an important one throughout the history of music. Because of its instability it was used carefully and sparingly in early music, and was referred to as the *diabolus in musica.* In music of the major-minor period its instability was used as a driving force in the resolution of chords that contained it. In impressionistic music, and later in Stravinsky, the two tones of the interval became interchangeable as roots of chords. The intervals divide the octave in half. Every jazz musician knows this. Today either the augmented fourth or the diminished fifth is conveniently spoken of as the *tritone*, as each note is three whole-tones away from the other on the keyboard. The actual letter-names of the notes are disregarded.

Scales

When as children we first learned to sing or whistle a tune, we were certainly aware of the melody and knew "how it went," but we probably could not have arranged the tones of the tune in an abstract orderly pattern any more than we could have constructed the alphabet out of the words we used in speaking.

We learned the alphabet later as a theoretical abstraction. And it was as an abstraction that the alphabet was originally formed from the language already in existence. A *scale* is a theoretical abstraction of the tones used in a piece of music. Named from the Italian word *scala*, meaning ladder, it is an arranged series of notes in stepwise order. The normal scale consists of the diatonic tones used in a particular *mode.* Scale and mode are often equated, especially in attempts to be brief, as in certain dictionaries of music. But *mode* properly refers to the music itself, and the aural impression it makes upon us. A scale is but the theoretical enumeration of tones that are the basis—the "base of operation," if you will—of a musical work.

The music came first. By analyzing a particular piece of music, the diatonic tones may be arranged in stepwise order, and thus the scale is formed. Thus, we say that a piece of music is "in the minor mode"; we do not say that it is "in the minor scale."

SCALES AS INTERVALS

There are many different scales representing different modes, each gaining its individuality by the differences in the intervals between the successive scale steps. In most scales the intervals are whole-steps or half-steps, but certain scales contain other intervals.

If we examine the following spiritual in Example 58, we discover

Example 58   "Nobody Knows the Trouble I've Seen"

that there are only five different tones. The concluding tone is the ultimate resolution tone and is shown at the beginning of our scale for this piece of music (Example 59). These are the scale tones of the

Example 59

pentatonic mode with G as the central tone.

If we investigate the vocal, unaccompanied music of many seemingly different cultures, we find the pentatonic mode as the base for many tunes. Many Scottish songs are pentatonic; "Auld Lang Syne" and "The Campbells are Coming" are but two. We find the pentatonic mode in the musical culture of the American Indian, in the Orient, and many other places.

The relationships of tones of the pentatonic scale are as shown:

Figure 6

Notes	1	2	3	4	5
Distance by Tones		1	1	1½	1
Interval		M2	M2	m3	M2

Let us transpose the pentatonic scale of *G* so that the starting tone is *C*. Remember that the intervallic relationship between each two tones must remain the same. It will look like Example 60 on the staff.

Example 60

If you transpose the pattern to *F*♯ or *G*♭, you will find that the black notes of the keyboard conform to the pattern.

MODES

Music during the Middle Ages and the Renaissance, until about 1600, was written in what are called the **church modes.** Each of these modes may be represented by a **diatonic scale** that uses only the white notes of the piano keyboard, and is represented by the lines and spaces of the staff. The names of the modes were determined chiefly by the tone that concluded the music which was called the **final.** Each final designated two corollary modes, the **authentic mode** and the **plagal mode**, differentiated from each other by their respective ranges and their "**dominants.**" These differences were clear in **monophony**, but in **polyphony** the authentic mode prevailed.

There were originally four authentic modes — the Dorian, Phrygian, Lydian, and Mixolydian — to which were added the Aolian, Locrian, and Ionian. It can be seen in Example 61 that the distinguishing feature of each mode depends upon the particular arrangement of the whole-steps and half-steps.

However, certain chromatic changes began to be introduced by the singer. Example 62, in the Dorian mode, shows the *C* raised to *C*♯ in a final **cadence.**

MUSICA FICTA

The term **musica ficta** is used to describe these chromatic changes. They were not written into the music, but were made according to the practice of the time. An illustration of this may be seen in "L'Homme Armé," which is in the Mixolydian mode. The origin of this French chanson is unknown, but it was used as a theme in many masses by composers in the fifteenth and sixteenth centuries. The two *F*♯'s shown in Example 63 were not written into the music, but show where the singer made the chromatic alteration.

Example 61

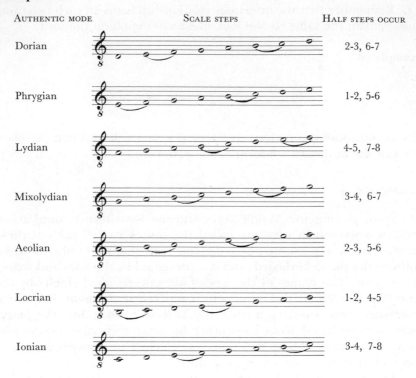

Authentic mode	Scale steps	Half steps occur
Dorian		2-3, 6-7
Phrygian		1-2, 5-6
Lydian		4-5, 7-8
Mixolydian		3-4, 6-7
Aeolian		2-3, 5-6
Locrian		1-2, 4-5
Ionian		3-4, 7-8

Example 62

MAJOR AND MINOR MODES

With the constant changing of pitches by the application of accidentals and the "growing art" of harmony, the Ionian and Aolian modes emerged to become the two modes that since have been the basis of harmony of Western music until the twentieth century, when their hegemony began to diminish.

With only two modes in common usage, the old mode-distinguishing names gradually went out of general use, and the two modes were referred to by the specific difference in pitch of the third scale-step as related to the tonic. Thus, the Ionian mode became the ***major***

Example 63   L'Homme Armé"

mode, and the Aolian mode became the ***minor mode.***

The older church modes modulated little, but with the advent of equal temperament, major and minor modes were possible from any of the 12 different tones. Thus, on the keyboard, 12 different scales of each mode are possible. In writing music there are 14 scales in common use, the two additional scales being possible because of enharmonic spelling. Theoretically, even more are possible—but certainly not practical.

TETRACHORD

The scale for the major mode may be divided into two four-note patterns, each called a ***tetrachord,*** and distinguished as lower and upper (Example 64).

Example 64

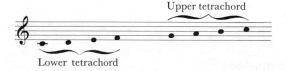

Note that the intervallic relations of one tetrachord are the same as those of the other. This similarity of tetrachords makes it possible for us to introduce each new scale systematically. Thus, the upper tetrachord may become the lower tetrachord of a major scale starting on *G*. The new upper tetrachord must be adjusted so that the last two notes are a semitone apart Therefore, the *F* is raised a semitone by the application of a sharp (Example 65).

Example 65

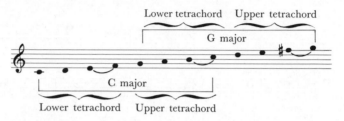

KEY SIGNATURES

In a piece of music that is written in the key of G, the *F* ♯ is normal to the key and would constantly be used. To avoid writing the sharp each time it occurs, it is placed at the beginning of the music directly after the clef, on the fifth line of the treble staff and on the fourth line of the bass staff, as shown in Example 66. This is the *key signature* for

Example 66

the key of G, and specifies that all *F*'s within that staff throughout the piece of music are sharped, in any octave.

The upper tetrachord of G major may now become the lower tetrachord of a new scale, D major. The seventh scale-step will again have to be raised (Example 67). The key signature for D major is

Example 67

shown in Example 68.

Example 68

Major Scales, Keys with Sharps

KEY OF		KEY SIGNATURE SPECIFIED AS
C	C D E F G A B C	—
G	G A B C D E F♯ G	1 sharp
D	D E F♯ G A B C♯ D	2 sharps
A	A B C♯ D E F♯ G♯ A	3 sharps
E	E F♯ G♯ A B C♯ D♯ E	4 sharps
B	B C♯ D♯ E F♯ G♯ A♯ B	5 sharps
F♯	F♯ G♯ A♯ B C♯ D♯ E♯ F♯	6 sharps
C♯	C♯ D♯ E♯ F♯ G♯ A♯ B♯ C♯	7 sharps

Major Scales, Keys with Flats

KEY OF		KEY SIGNATURE SPECIFIED AS
C	C D E F G A B C	—
F	F G A B♭ C D E F	1 flat
B♭	B♭ C D E♭ F G A B♭	2 flats
E♭	E♭ F G A♭ B♭ C D E♭	3 flats
A♭	A♭ B♭ C D♭ E♭ F G A♭	4 flats
D♭	D♭ E♭ F G♭ A♭ B♭ C D♭	5 flats
G♭	G♭ A♭ B♭ C♭ D♭ E♭ F G♭	6 flats
C♭	C♭ D♭ E♭ F♭ G♭ A♭ B♭ C♭	7 flats

The procedure, continuing throughout the sharp keys, may be shown now without using the staff. The new sharp always occurs at the seventh scale-step so that 7-8 becomes a half-step.

The following table shows all of the sharp keys in succession as originally derived from the pattern of the C major scale. To find the flat keys in the order of adding flats, we may start again with the two tetrachords of the C major scale. This time the *lower tetrachord* becomes the *upper tetrachord* in forming each new scale. The new flat always occurs at the fourth scale-step so that 3-4 becomes a half step.

Each major scale has a **relative minor** scale starting a minor third below the major scale to which it is related. The relative minor is so called because it has the same key signature as its **relative major.** The relative minor has the same notes as well, although in a different order. Example 69 illustrates *A minor*, the relative minor of *C major.* It is shown

Example 69

A minor (pure form)

in its **pure** form. Note that the half-steps occur between 2 and 3 and between 5 and 6.

In *harmonic cadences* the seventh scale tone is consistently raised, in whatever part of the chord it occurs, so that there is a half-step relationship between scale-steps 7 and 8. From this practice is derived the **harmonic minor** scale (Example 70).

Example 70

A minor (harmonic form)

In ascending stepwise *melodic patterns* in minor, both the sixth and the seventh scale-steps are raised a semitone, but in descending patterns both the seventh and the sixth scale-steps usually revert to the pure form of the minor. This results in the **melodic minor** scale (Example 71).

Example 71

A minor (melodic form)

The key signatures of all the major keys and their relative minor keys may be illustrated in the Circle of Fifths (Figure 7). The

Figure 7   Circle of Fifths

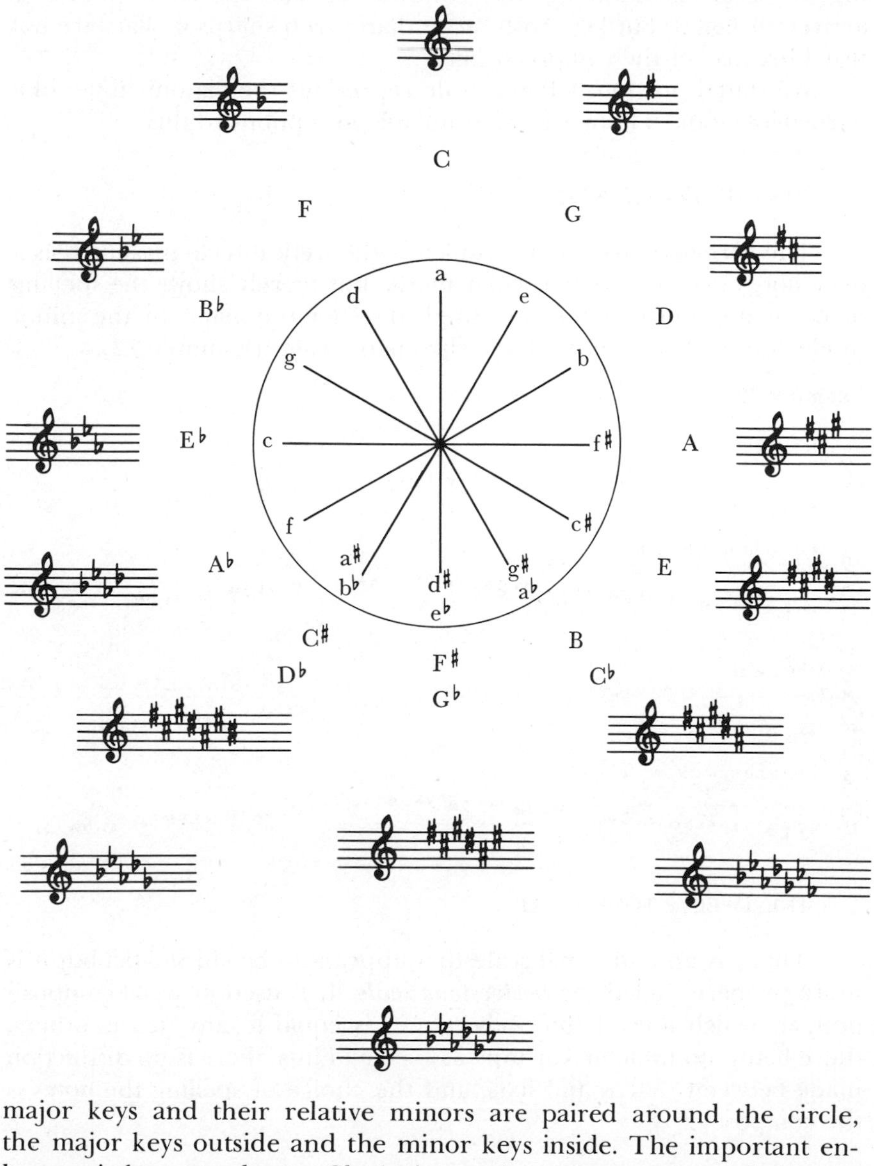

major keys and their relative minors are paired around the circle, the major keys outside and the minor keys inside. The important enharmonic keys are shown. Clockwise motion represents key relations in ascending perfect fifths; counterclockwise, in descending perfect fifths. Proceeding around the circle of fifths clockwise from C shows the sharp keys in succession, with each succeeding key note a perfect fifth higher than the preceding one. Proceeding from *C* counterclockwise shows the flat keys in succession, with each key note a perfect fifth lower than the preceding one. Note that exact opposites are a tritone apart. Proceeding in either direction we may continue around the circle until *C* is arrived at again, but keys with more than seven sharps or flats are not usual because of their impracticality.

We stated previously that a scale represents the diatonic tones of a particular mode. There are three notable exceptions to this.

THE CHROMATIC SCALE

The *chromatic scale* is a completely theoretical scale inasmuch as it does not represent any particular mode, but merely shows the spelling of chromatic tones as they are used in either the major or the minor mode. Thus, there are two basic chromatic scales (Example 72).

Example 72

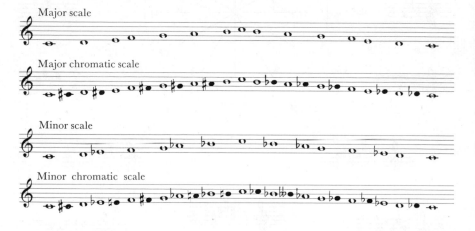

THE TWELVE-TONE SCALE

There is an additional scale that appears to be chromatic, but it is more properly called the *twelve-tone scale*. It is used in serial composition, in which any of the twelve tones is equal to any of the others, there being no tonic or key-tone as a rule. Thus, there is no distinction made between sharps and flats, and the choice of spelling the notes is the composer's.

THE WHOLE-TONE SCALE

The *whole-tone scale* is a synthetic scale that was explored in impressionistic music. Debussy used it as one device among many in a search for new colors and new effects. Its use has not been extensive because, by its very similarity of intervals throughout, it loses in any attempt at contrast. Without any half-step relationships, there is no tension and release. There are only two actually different whole-tone scales, one on *C* and one on *C* ♯ or D♭ — the spelling no longer matters. All others sound like portions of these two, as there is no real tonic (Example 73).

Example 73

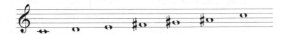

SCALE DEGREES

Each step of the major or minor scale is spoken of as a **degree**, and is designated by a Roman numeral. In addition, it is given a name that shows its importance as a tonal factor (I, IV, V), or its position in relation to the tonal factors. C major is used as an example in Example 74. Thus, in the ascending pattern of the C major scale, we have the

Example 74

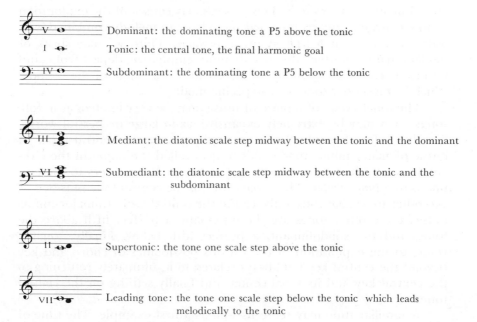

Dominant: the dominating tone a P5 above the tonic

Tonic: the central tone, the final harmonic goal

Subdominant: the dominating tone a P5 below the tonic

Mediant: the diatonic scale step midway between the tonic and the dominant

Submediant: the diatonic scale step midway between the tonic and the subdominant

Supertonic: the tone one scale step above the tonic

Leading tone: the tone one scale step below the tonic which leads melodically to the tonic

degrees shown in Example 75.

Example 75

Degree numeral: I   II   III   IV   V   VI   VII
       Tonic   Supertonic   Mediant   Sub-   Dominant   Sub-   Leading tone
                                      dominant   mediant

       Texts differ on the use of the term *sub-tonic*, but in this text it is reserved for the seventh scale-step that is a whole tone below the tonic, with the term *leading tone* always referring to the seventh scale-step that lies a semitone below the tonic, whether in major or minor. This distinction is important in referring to music either of the Renaissance or of the twentieth century in which the whole tone below the tonic is often used *cadentially.*

Tonality

Tonality embraces the concept of key or mode, but it is not synonymous with either. It is a larger concept. It is perhaps best to think of tonality as a *process*, which, with one single tone as the central tone, constantly departs from it in exploration of other tones and their relationship to it and ultimately returns to it. This process may consist of the exploration of tones through unaccompanied melody or in melody combined with other sounds as in *polyphony* or *homophony*. Thus, we may speak of modal tonality, in which the melody notes emphasize, depart from, and ultimately converge upon and find rest in the last note of the melody, which is the central tone of the specific mode.

       The tonal range of a piece of music may be very limited, as in folk songs, or it may be extremely expansive, as in large orchestral works. Tonality refers first of all to one single tone as the central tone. In music of major-minor modes this tone is called the *tonic*; in the Gregorian modes it is called the *final*. Further, tonality refers to the emphasis of a *tonal center*. This tonal center is the central tone plus one or two other tones that constantly lead to the central tone. In major-minor music, these other tones are the dominant, a perfect fifth above the tonic, and the subdominant, a perfect fifth below. Finally, tonality refers to the exploration of the various possibilities of chord and key beyond the central key but always related to it, ultimately returning to the central key and its tonal center and finally settling on the central tone.

       A familiar tune may serve us well as a first example. The tune of "My Country 'Tis of Thee" begins by sounding the tonic twice and then circling around it, passing through it, and in the sixth measure settling again on it (Example 76). Note that the tonic note itself occurs during

Example 76

seven and a half quarter beats of the eighteen quarter values that there are in these six measures. There are other emphases of the tonic as well: in measure 3, the two *B*'s are part of the tonic chord, and in measures 5 and 6, the bass notes of the cadence are IV, V, I, strongly confirming the tonic feeling of the entire six-bar phrase. At the beginning of the next phrase, the melody leaps up to the dominant and, through the melodic emphasis of the dominant in measures 7 and 8, and the dominant chords of measures 9 and 10, shifts the center of interest momentarily away from the tonic (Example 77). The dominant

Example 77

as a secondary focal point is very strong in all major-minor literature. The strength of the fifth scale-step as a point of interest next to the tonic seems to arise from the relation of the perfect fifth (the third note of the series) in the overtone series to the fundamental tone. The first overtone of the series is but an "affirmation" of the fundamental. The first really different sound is the next overtone of the series, a perfect fifth higher. Also note that the dominant is the root of the penultimate chord in the true final cadence in the majority of major-minor literature.

In the final four measures of "My Country 'Tis of Thee" the center of interest shifts back to the tonic in measures 11 and 12, and the IV-V-I emphasis in both the melody and the accompanying harmony in measures 13 and 14 completely reaffirms *G* as the tonal center (Example 78).

Example 78

In the comparative simplicity of the melody and harmony of this tune, it may be argued that what has been discussed illustrates "keyish-ness" or "tonicity" more than tonality. However, tonicity is at the beginning of tonality, and the range of tonality cannot exist without the establishing of tonicity. If you wish to reserve the term *tonality* for musical structures with a wider scope of harmonic content, it will only serve to emphasize that the concept of tonicity is certainly included in tonality, but it is only the beginning of the larger scope of tonality.

In the tune of "My Country 'Tis of Thee" the supportive harmony is not needed to establish G as the tonal center and the mode as major. The melody alone does this. But the harmony in this case does support and affirm the implications of the melody. In pure *monophonic* music, of course, the melody itself must clearly establish the tonality. In the same manner that the melody of "My Country 'Tis of Thee" has a tonic-dominant interplay and final affirmation of the tonic, so does the modal melody in Example 79 establish the tonality. In the church modes, the

Example 79   Old English Melody

tonal center is called the *final*, and indeed the central tone must be the final tone. Only with the advent of harmony could the final melodic tone of a piece of music be other than the central tone.

MODULATION

Modulation is the process of moving from one key center to an-other (see Chapter 5). It may be done suddenly or gradually, strikingly or subtly, but it must be convincing. The ear recognizes a modulation in retrospect. It is only after the listener has heard enough of the tones in the scale of the new key that he realizes that a modulation has taken place.

A simple explanation of modulation may be stated this way. A piece that has begun in the key of C major may modulate to the key of F major by the constant substitution of $B\flat$ for $B\natural$, and by the emphasis on F as the new tonic through the melodic design and the harmonic emphasis, which will now be upon C and $B\flat$ as the dominant and subdominant. Usually it is not until this harmonic emphasis is felt that the new key center is really established.

CLASSICAL TONALITY

The essence of tonality in the classical period is that the key center may shift while the basic tonal center remains unchanged. In other words, there may be modulation to closely related or distantly related keys, *but the exploration of these keys is always in relation to the basic tonal center*, which ultimately returns. This is true not only throughout a symphonic movement, but throughout the entire symphony. There is always the connecting thread between even the most distant key center and the basic tonal center. The new key center amounts to an exploration or a side excursion. The concept of tonality embraces the idea that there will be a return to the basic tonal center.

The course of the tonality of a symphonic work in classical literature may be likened to a journey — or, better still, a quest — in which one central, all-pervading thought is always present. Musically, this central thought is the basic tonal center at the heart of the central key, which is always returned to, in spite of various peregrinations that take the traveler away from the main course. Each peregrination is only part of the main quest, and though at the time it may seem to be leading somewhere else, the main purpose, or course, is always returned to.

A diagram of the first movement of Mozart's Symphony No. 41 will illustrate this (Figure 8).

Note that the basic key center is adhered to for slightly more than half of the first section, and then that the dominant becomes the key center throughout most of the second and third sections until the repeat sign, which is the end of the exposition. The strong relationship of the dominant to the tonic is illustrated by the fact that upon repetition of the exposition no modulation of any kind is needed. The dominant just "falls into" the tonic.

In the recapitulation, there is a brief excursion into the subdominant. And then back onto the main road, the basic tonality, until the end of the movement. Inspection or analysis of the other movements should only make it clearer that Mozart's Symphony No. 41 in C major is not in the key of C major, but in the "tonality of C major." That is to say, C as the central tone and major as the mode provide the tonal center for the entire work. Note that Sir Donald Francis Tovey speaks

70

Figure 8 Symphony No. 41 ("Jupiter"), K. 551, Movement 1, Mozart

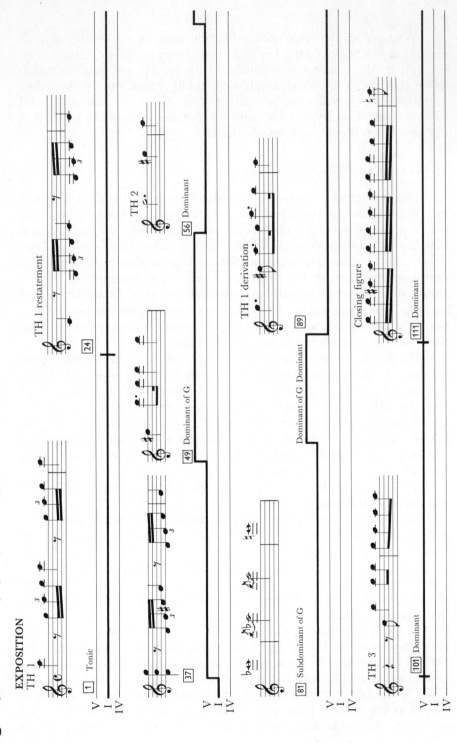

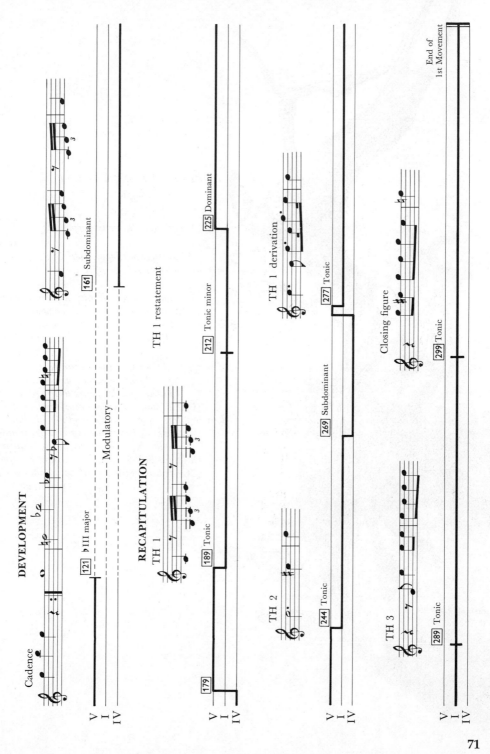

DEVELOPMENT

Cadence

121 ♭III major

161 Subdominant

Modulatory

V
I
IV

RECAPITULATION

TH 1

TH 1 restatement

189 Tonic

179

212 Tonic minor

225 Dominant

V
I
IV

TH 2

244 Tonic

269 Subdominant

277 Tonic

TH 1 derivation

V
I
IV

TH 3

289 Tonic

Closing figure

299 Tonic

End of
1st Movement

V
I
IV

L'APRÈS-MIDI D'UN FAUNE
Èglogue
LE FAUNE

Ces nymphes, je les veux perpétuer.

Si clair,
Leur incarnat léger, qu'il voltige dans l'air
Assoupi de sommeiles touffus.

Aimai-je un rêve?
Mon doute, amas de nuit ancienne, s'achève
En maint rameau subtil, qui, demeuré les vrais
Bois mêmes, prouve, hélas! que bien seul je m'offrais
Pour triomphe la faute idéale de roses.
Reflechissons . . .
Ô bords siciliens d'un calme marécage
Qu'à l'envi de soleils ma vanité saccage,
Tacite sous les fleurs d'étincelles, contez,
"Que je coupais ici les creux roseaux domptés
"Par le talent; quand, sur l'or glauqe de lointaines
"Verdures dédiant leur vigñe à des fontaines,
"Ondoie une blancheur animale au repos:
"Et qu'au prélude lent où naissent les pipeaux
"Ce vol de cygnes, non! de naiades se sauve
"Ou plonge . . . ."

L'Après-midi d'un faune

of Schubert's String Quartet in C major as "one of the greatest of all essays in tonality." Whatever the analogy—an essay, a journey, a quest—the point is that tonality is at the core of an experience that lasts a certain length of time.

Not all expressions of tonality are so clear cut as that which we have just seen. The classical period was the essence of unity, and one of the ways of achieving unity was the emphasis on a basic tonal center. Even in the classical period, however, a basic tonal center is not always the *sine qua non*. In opera, for example, there are too many other considerations, not the least of which are the length of the opera and the demand that would be put upon the listener if he were to be required to keep in mind a basic tonal center. Even in a symphony the composer helps the listener recognize the tonal center by various means: thematic recurrence, certain essentials of form, similarities in orchestration. Composers usually do not write for other composers, but even if they did, the other composers as listeners would need something beyond the fact of a return to a tonal center in order to recognize it. Otherwise they would need a musical memory similar to what is spoken of as "total recall." This kind of musical memory is commonly called **perfect pitch**. Perfect pitch may be a blessing, but like all blessings it is somewhat rare even among musicians.

Tonality as a way of organizing music continued, albeit with change of emphasis and purposeful ambiguities, throughout the nineteenth century. Even today, in spite of the inroads of atonality, there are composers whose music is spoken of as being **tonal**—within the concept of tonality.

But the romantic composers were interested in mood, and thus became more interested in certain kinds of sound for the subjective uses to which they could be put. Tonality was there, but color began to be sought for its own sake. Liszt, Wagner, and others started emphasizing shifting tonal centers. Debussy began the actual breakdown of tonality.

THE OVERTONE SERIES

It is one of the phenomena of nature that when any musical sound is produced there are present, in addition to the basic tone, **overtones** that, although not distinguishable separately by the human ear, do add further color to the sound. They are called "overtones" because they are higher in pitch than the fundamental tone. Any single tone sounded by an instrument or voice is a fundamental tone, with a certain number of the overtones sounding with it. The number of overtones sounded varies with the instrument.

In Example 80, C_2 is chosen as the fundamental, and the remainder

Example 80

of the notes shown (number 2 through number 16) represent the pitches of the overtones. The series illustrated is referred to as the *overtone series*, the *series of partials*, or the **harmonic series**. Also, because this series represents a natural phenomenon, it has been referred to as the **chord of nature**. The series actually continues on, in ever-decreasing intervals between each two succeeding tones.

It is not possible to represent on the musical staff the exact pitches of the notes in the series. This may be done with a graph. The most noticeable deviations in pitch from what can be shown on the staff are represented by the blacked-in notes. All of the blacked-in notes are lower in pitch than their representations on the staff indicate. The single arrow represents a moderate discrepancy between the actual pitch and its representation; the double arrow indicates a greater discrepancy. To put it in other terms: the notes having a single arrow are definitely lower in pitch, but are still recognizable as the tone that the note indicates; the notes having the double arrow are so low in pitch that the actual pitch is not recognizable as the tone that the note indicates. As it is a mathematical fact that each tone in the series lies halfway between the note that precedes it and the note that follows it, with respect to the number of vibrations, it may be seen that the notes having double arrows cannot even be approximately designated.

The ratio of the number of vibrations of any one tone to the number of vibrations of any other tone in the series is as the two tones stand in the series numerically. Thus, the ratio of the vibrations of the first two tones represented in the series is $1:2$; of the second and third, $2:3$, and so on. The difference in the number of vibrations between any two tones is referred to by musicians as the *interval* between two tones. Thus, the musician's, rather than the scientist's, definition of an interval is that it is the *distance* between any two tones. "Distance," of course, refers to the visual as seen on the keyboard or the staff, but it means the difference in vibrations heard by the ear. However, it is less cumbersome for purposes of discussion, and certainly legitimate as long as it is kept in mind that the term "distance" is a convenience.

Finally, the ratio of the tones of any interval in the overtone series is the ratio of that interval *at any other pitch*. The second and third tones in the series form a perfect fifth, and have the ratio $2:3$. This is the ratio of all perfect fifths.

The overtone series can be demonstrated empirically at the piano. Using the series illustrated above, with C_2 as the fundamental:

1. Depress slowly, without sounding the tone, the key representing the second note in the series, C_1.
2. Strike the key representing the fundamental tone. Let go of it immediately.
3. Listen carefully, and you will hear the strings of C_1 sounding in sympathetic vibration.

This demonstration may be performed with any of the overtones in the series.

Prélude à "L'Après-midi d'un Faune," Debussy

This *Prélude* was to have been the first of three sections of a work originally titled, *Prélude, Interlude, et Paraphrase Finale pour "L'Après-midi d'un Faune,"* but Debussy abandoned the second and third sections, which had not gone beyond some initial sketches. The entire work had been planned for a concert early in 1894, but Debussy, extremely meticulous, withdrew it for revision. Finally, in December of that year, the *Prélude* was performed. Its success was immediate.

Orchestra:

> 3 Flutes (FL)
> 2 Oboes (OB)
> 1 English Horn (EHN)
> 2 Clarinets (CL)
> 2 Bassoons (BN)
>
> 4 French Horns (HN)
>
> 2 Antique Cymbals
> 2 Harps (HARP)
>
> Violins (VL 1, 2)
> Violas (VA)
> Violoncellos (VC)
> Contrabasses (CB)

Form: Free, suggestive of ternary.

SCORE PROFILE

Score Detail: m. 1–2

Outlining the tritone C♯–G suggests vagueness and instability. In the older, or traditional, tonal sense, it could suggest a resolution to D. In m. 3, however, Debussy makes the first reference to E major as the basic tonality.

Score Detail: m. 11

The first note of the melody is the seventh degree of the D major scale. Note the effect of different harmonizations used later in the composition.

Score Detail: m. 26

A fresh harmonization of the flute melody. Listen for the harps in the background.

Score Detail: m. 55–56

Note the melody in the woodwinds, pentatonic in color, set against a tritonic bass line.

Score Detail: m. 62–63

In the woodwind melody at m. 62, note the use of the whole-tone scale.

Listening notes

The tonal center of *L'Après-midi* is E major, but this is not apparent in the opening two measures of the work. Note that the unaccompanied flute solo outlines an interval, G-C♯, that does not exist in the scale of E major. Also, it is the tritone, the interval of instability. Whatever suggestions of resolution there may be in this interval are not carried out, and in **SP m. 3** the G♮ is cancelled and the tonic chord of E major is stated. Not until **SP m. 13**, however, does Debussy reinforce this harmonically.

Note that in various restatements of this opening theme it is accompanied by varied harmonizations. For example, in **SP m. 11** the roots of the chords are *D* and *G*, a plagal alternation suggesting the key of D major. In **SP m. 26** the accompanying harmony shows a dominant ninth chord on *E*. The *E* "evaporates" as a root, and the harmony then shows alternating *minor triads with added major sixth* on the roots *B* and *C*. In **SP m. 94–95** the harmony alternates between dominant structures with *E* and *C* as their roots. These different harmonizations of the tritonic melodic outline add to the nebulous effect of the harmony. The tritone is further emphasized in the bass line in **SP m. 55–56** against the pentatonic melody in the woodwinds.

The work remains tonally based, however, through strong cadences that reinforce the key of E. In **SP m. 29–30** the melody (confirmed by the harmony) cadences to *B*, the dominant of the home key.

Finally, at **SP m. 105–106** may be seen the strong dominant-to-tonic cadence that harmonically brings the work to a close.

Thus does Debussy, through musical means, evoke the dreamlike atmosphere of Mallarmé's poem, which depicts the "sensuous, passionate" faun, half-man and half-animal with cloven hoof.

For reference and review

New terms in the order presented:

timbre
unison
interval
simple interval
compound interval
major
prime
perfect
augmented
minor
diminished
doubly augmented
doubly diminished
quality of the interval
transposition
diatonic
chromatic
accidental
harmonic interval
melodic interval
inversion
consonance
dissonance
diabolus in musica
twelve-tone scale
whole-tone scale
scale degree
sub-tonic
leading tone
tonality
homophony
tonic

tonal center
tritone
scale
mode
pentatonic mode
church modes
diatonic scale
final
authentic mode
plagal mode
dominant
monophony
polyphony
cadence
musica ficta
major mode
minor mode
tetrachord
key signature
relative minor
relative major
pure minor
harmonic minor
melodic minor
chromatic scale
modulation
perfect pitch
overtones
overtone series
series of partials
harmonic series
chord of nature

3

Rhythm and meter

A S NATURAL CREATURES of the universe, we consider some experiences normal and others abnormal. Those that seem normal are those that recur. That seems abnormal which is a distortion or exaggeration of the usual, such as a man eight feet tall or one four feet tall, or which is only occasional, such as an August frost. Those things which occur regularly we take for granted and accept, sometimes without thinking about it, as a normal part of our existence. Our heartbeat, in diastolic movement, is perhaps our closest connection with the movement of life. When we live at a normal pace, it beats regularly and at a certain speed. This is so taken for granted that the doctor uses its regularity and its speed as one check on our health. When we are excited or exert ourselves, it beats faster. When we sleep, it beats more slowly. From these facts of nature has arisen the theory that our heartbeat gives to us the feeling of what is normal in the **pulse** or **beat** of music.

Thus, if a person's pulse beats 80 times per minute, a piece of music with 80 pulses or beats per minute will seem to be the norm or median with which all other pulses may be compared. Slower or faster pulses will seem less normal. Very fast pulses will feel exciting; very slow ones will feel numbing. Pulse in music, the regular occurrence of beats at various speeds, can then be considered as a basic ingredient underlying all musical movement. It is a strong sign of musical life and is the result of the powerful, energizing force underlying all music—*rhythm.*

Rhythm

In the broadest possible sense, musical rhythm can be said to include everything pertaining to the duration of musical sound. More specifically, though, rhythm refers to time spans separating successive musical impacts. In effect, it is that element in music that sometimes causes us to tap feet, snap fingers, or set our whole body moving in sympathetic motion.

Note that the first statement uses the term *sound*, not *pitch* or *tone*. Though rhythm is usually inextricably bound up with **melody** and **harmony**, which in turn are themselves dependent on pitch and tone, it can exist without them. In the field of art music, especially that written in our day, pitchless or near-pitchless compositions exist. One example is the "Geographical Fugue" by Ernst Toch, written for speaking **chorus** (Example 81). And many will have heard a jazz drummer "take a chorus" on his battery of percussion instruments, none of them pitched.

Despite there being no pitch or tone involved, both the above types of music can elicit from an audience emotional or aesthetic responses. If, as we said before, pulse is a strong sign of musical life, the very stuff of musical movement, then rhythm must be its breath and energizing power.

For rhythm to become meaningful in a musical composition, two essential aspects of duration come into play: **accent** and **repetition**. One element of repetition, pulse, has already been discussed.

ACCENT

In the world around us, accent is very important. A good speaker accents certain words or syllables in an artful way, resulting in clearer meaning and better communication. Verse systematizes accent so that it comes regularly and expectedly as in metered verse or sporadically as in blank verse. A woman will accent her costume of subdued color with a scarf or a bag in a vivid hue. In all accent, selected elements from among many are emphasized and made to stand out in one way or another. This is turn gives definition and meaning to the whole.

In music, accent comes about in many ways. Some of these are: **dynamic accent, melodic accent, intervallic accent, agogic accent**, and **metric accent**.

Example 81   Geographical Fugue, Ernst Toch

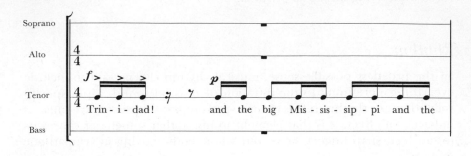

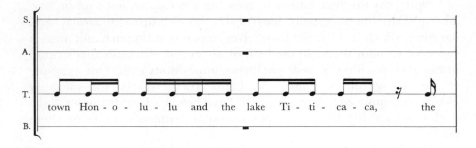

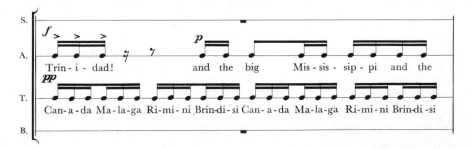

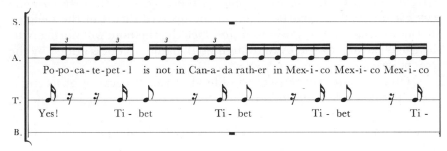

"Geographical Fugue" by Ernst Toch. Copyright © 1950 by Mills Music, Inc. (Used by permission)

One common kind of accent occurs when a tone or chord is played louder than those around it. This is dynamic accent. Many signs exist in musical notation to indicate this. Example 82 shows but a few.

Another type is natural melodic accent, shown in Example 83. The

Example 82   Arabesque No. 2, Debussy

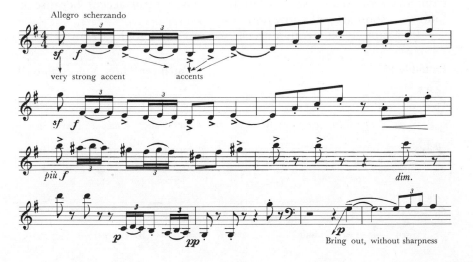

Example 83   Sonata Opus 10, No. 2, Movement 1, Beethoven

circled note seen in the first theme is the highest within the **melodic contour** and is the climactic object of the upward thrust of the melody. Because of its relative position in the melody, the note will normally be heard as having accent, even though no dynamic accent is added by the composer.

Often a note will possess considerable accent because of its intervallic position relative to others before it. In the following Example 84,

Example 84   Die Fledermaus, Act II, Johann Strauss, Jr.

from *Die Fledermaus*, Adele's "high C" has natural accent because it follows so soon after the low note.

In Example 85, from Purcell, we can see agogic accent at play.

Example 85   Catch for Three Voices, Purcell

Agogic accent occurs when a longer note is preceded or followed by shorter ones. The notes with asterisks are generally of longer duration than the others. They therefore will stand out and possess agogic accent. In addition to this agogic accent, they are also often placed in the measure in such a way as to achieve *syncopation*.

A powerful kind of accent occurs when the several kinds converge on one note at the same time, as in Example 86. The chord with the

Example 86   Sonata No. 8 Opus 13 ("Pathetique"), Movement 3, Beethoven

asterisk not only is played suddenly very loud but also is approached by a leap. The net result here is dramatic accentuation—a characteristic of the music of Beethoven.

Musical accent is thus the result of various kinds of stress occurring at certain points in the flow of the music. When these stresses are repeated regularly, two important elements of rhythm occur: rhythmic pattern and meter.

RHYTHMIC PATTERN

A rhythmic pattern occurs when a varied group of note values is repeated enough in a composition to become one of its unifying, structural elements. The rhythmic pattern in Example 87 has been

Example 87

isolated from its melody, shown in Example 88.

Example 88   Piano Concerto No. 3, Opus 37, Movement 1, Beethoven

Note that the symbols involved in the raw rhythmic pattern itself (Example 87) are those representing durational values only. Rhythmic

pattern, then, is closely related to agogic accent, which pertains only to duration.

To understand the essential character of a rhythmic pattern it is not at all necessary to consider pitch, an element usually associated with it in a complete musical composition. It is obvious, though, that ultimately both of these must be considered together if the whole musical structure is to be understood.

If we isolate the durational values from the American song, "Clementine" (Example 89), we arrive at Example 90. Within this series is

Example 89   American Folk Song, Clementine

Oh, my   dar-ling, oh, my   dar-ling, oh, my   dar-ling, Cle-men-

tine! Thou art   lost and gone for-ev-er, Dread-ful sor-ry,   Cle-men-tine.

Example 90

heard a distinct pattern Example 91), which provides the basic rhyth-

Example 91

mic organization for the whole. In fact, the pattern occurs five times, providing strong rhythmic cohesion.

Example 92

Certain musical structures, especially those of a simple nature like the above, will be dominated by one rhythmic pattern. One very celebrated theme by Paganini (Example 94), used as the basis for extended compositions in the variation form by Schumann, Brahms, Liszt, Rachmaninoff, and Blacher, is based entirely on the rhythmic pattern illustrated in Example 93.

Longer compositions will usually contain several rhythmic patterns. These will contrast with one another and easily be identified

Example 93

Example 94   Caprice No. 24, Paganini

as they return in the working out of the composition. Example 95

Example 95   Symphony No. 3, Opus 55 ("Eroica"), Movement 1, Beethoven

shows three basic rhythmic patterns from the first movement of the
"Eroica" Symphony by Beethoven. Note how the rhythmic pattern
from theme 2 (Example 96) is easily recognized in the passage Example
97) from the middle section of the first movement despite the melodic
contour's being totally different.

Example 96

All of the examples given above are taken from melodies. But it
should be remembered that rhythmic patterns are also heard in supportive elements, particularly in ***accompaniment patterns***.

Example 97   Symphony No. 3, Opus 55 ("Eroica"), Movement 1, Beethoven

In the *aria* in Example 98, the rhythmic pattern in the bass staff is

Example 98   Carmen, Act I, Bizet

repeated constantly and gives the music a dance character, in this case that of the Habanera.

Examples 99–103 illustrate several other well known supportive patterns consistently heard in the dance.

Example 99   Polonaise

Suggested Listening: Tchaikovsky, Polonaise from *Eugene Onegin*; Beethoven, Finale from Triple Concerto, Op. 56

Example 100   Bolero

Suggested Listening: Chopin, Bolero, Op. 19; Ravel, Bolero

Example 101   Cakewalk

Suggested Listening: Debussy, "Golliwog's Cakewalk" from *The Children's Corner*

Example 102   Waltz

Suggested Listening: Ravel, La Valse; Verdi, Drinking Song from *La Traviata*

Example 103   Mazurka

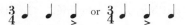

Suggested   Listening: Chopin, Mazurkas; Szymanowski, Mazurkas, Op. 50

   Meaningful rhythmic patterns, then, can be found on different levels of a musical structure, different ones often being heard simultaneously, as was seen in Example 98. There may be few or many; and once they are firmly established as important structural entities, they will tend to return in a composition, providing unity and cohesion.

Meter

Music is said to be metered when certain pulses are accented on a regular, predictable basis. These accented pulses are felt as primary **strong beats** and distinguished from several intermediary **weak beats**. The two primary characteristics of **meter** are:

1. Alternation of strong and weak beats.
2. Strong beats occurring regularly and often predictably.

   Let us re-examine the song, "Clementine," to see how the feeling of meter arises from a simple melody. We assume that whoever first played or sang this melody felt accents on certain pitches, and therefore emphasized them. Anyone can feel the song's natural accent empirically by simply singing it strongly and rhythmically. When he does, he will feel what can be seen in Example 104, the arrow over a

Example 104   "Clementine"

note indicating a natural metric accent.
   A glance at the rhythmic patterns underlying the melody (Example 105) provides further understanding of why these particular pitches

Example 105

feel as if they should be accented. The circled notes are longer than the rest and therefore have a natural, agogic accent of their own. The boxed notes also have agogic accent because of their relation to the previous shorter note values. Underlying the whole, of course, is pulse. This pulse can be felt by singing the words while tapping on certain syllables.

If we again sing the song, this time accenting sharply every third tap starting on the first syllable of the word *darling*, we unmistakably feel meter and regular metrical accent. In this instance, because we have felt a regular accent every three pulses, the meter is called ***triple***.

Example 106 again shows "Clementine" with an arrow over each

Example 106

note of the melody that receives a strong metric accent. The equal-duration values below the melody represent the unit of pulse in the given system of notation. These can be counted thus: one – two – three; one – two – three; or tapped as before.

Note that, between accents, the durational values of the melody itself will vary considerably; *they are not equal*. These *differences* in note duration are absolutely necessary for meaningful, rhythmic patterns to occur. The counts or taps representing the beat or pulse, however, are *steady* and *equal* in duration.

MEASURES AND BAR LINES

A convenient way for the composer to indicate precisely where the first strong metric beat occurs throughout a piece of music is to place a vertical **bar line** on the staff immediately before it. The distance from one bar line to the next is said to be a **measure**. The first beat of each measure is called the **downbeat**; the last one in the measure, the **upbeat** (Example 107).

Example 107

Bar lines are placed in the score to facilitate the task of the performer or musical analyst. He is constantly reminded where strong metric beats are located and in rehearsal with other performers can quickly locate specific measures.

The useful nature of bar lines can be fully appreciated by examining Example 108, where a tangle of black notes greets the eye.

Example 108   Adagio in D minor, Arr. J. S. Bach from Marcello

The bar lines give the performer who is reading the music for the first time a quick knowledge of where the strong metrical beats are located. Where the composer has given no bar lines as in Example 109,

Example 109   Old and New Duets for Two Flutes, Sweelinck

TYPE OF METER	BEATS PER MEASURE	TIME SIGNATURES
Simple { duple	2	$\frac{2}{1}\ \frac{}{2}\ \frac{}{4}\ \frac{}{8}\ \frac{}{16}\ \frac{}{32}$
Simple { triple	3	$\frac{3}{1}\ \frac{}{2}\ \frac{}{4}\ \frac{}{8}\ \frac{}{16}\ \frac{}{32}$
Common*	4	$\frac{4}{4}$ also: **C**
Compound†	6 or 2	$\frac{6}{1}\ \frac{}{2}\ \frac{}{4}\ \frac{}{8}\ \frac{}{16}\ \frac{}{32}$
	9 or 3	$\frac{9}{1}\ \frac{}{2}\ \frac{}{4}\ \frac{}{8}\ \frac{}{16}\ \frac{}{32}$
	12 or 4	$\frac{12}{1}\ \frac{}{2}\ \frac{}{4}\ \frac{}{8}\ \frac{}{16}\ \frac{}{32}$
Asymmetrical**	5 or combinations of 2's and 3's	$\frac{5}{1}\ \frac{}{2}\ \frac{}{4}\ \frac{}{8}\ \frac{}{16}\ \frac{}{32}$
	7 or combinations of 3's and 4's	$\frac{7}{1}\ \frac{}{2}\ \frac{}{4}\ \frac{}{8}\ \frac{}{16}\ \frac{}{32}$
Mixed	Alternating combinations usually of 2's, 3's or 4's	$\frac{3}{4} + \frac{2}{4}$ (typical)
Polymeter	Any number of beats, but heard simultaneously with different beat groups	$\frac{6}{8}$ (typical) $\frac{3}{4}$
Changing	According to the measure of the moment	Any combination at any time

*Meters in 8 are usually multiples of common meter.
†Compound meters can have higher beat numbers: 15, 18, etc.
**1) Higher beat numbers are possible: 10, 11, 13, etc.
　2) Inner combinations—other than 3's or 4's—are possible:

Ex.:

EXAMPLE	SUGGESTED LISTENING
$\frac{2}{4}$ ♩♩│♩ │ ♫♫│♩. │♩. ♪│♩ ‖	Beethoven, Movement 4, Symphony No. 1 meter: $\frac{2}{4}$
$\frac{3}{4}$ ♩ ♩│♩♩♩│♩♫♩│♩. ♪♩ ‖	Tchaikowsky, Movement 3, Symphony No. 5 meter: $\frac{3}{4}$
$\frac{4}{4}$ ♩♩♩♩│♩ ♩│♫♫♩│ o ‖	Beethoven, Movement IV, Symphony No. 5 meter: **C** ($\frac{4}{4}$)
$\frac{6}{8}$ ♩. ♩.│♩♪♩.│ ♫♫♩♪│♩ ♩. ‖	Brahms, Movement 1, Symphony No. 1 meter: $\frac{6}{8}$
$\frac{9}{8}$ ♩. ♩. ♫♫│♫♫♩♪.│♩. ♩. │♩. ♩. ‖	Tchaikowsky, Movement 1, Symphony No. 4 (Moderato con anima) meter: $\frac{9}{8}$
$\frac{12}{8}$ ♩. ♩. ♩. ♩.│♫♫♩. ♫♫♩.│♩. ♩. ‖	Tchaikowsky, Movement 2, Symphony No. 5 meter: $\frac{12}{8}$
$\frac{5}{8}$ ♫♩♫♫│♩. ♫│♫♫♩♫ ‖	Ravel, General Dance, from Suite No. 2, *Daphnis and Chloe* meter: $\frac{5}{4}$
$\frac{7}{8}$ ♫♫♫♫│♩. ♫♫♫│♩ ♫♩ ‖	Prokofiev, Movement 3, Piano Sonata No. 7 meter: $\frac{7}{8}$
$\frac{3}{4}\frac{2}{4}$ ♩♩♩│♩♩│♩. ♪│♩│♩│♩.│♩│♩♫♩ ‖	Bartok, *Mikrokosmos*, Vol. 6, Bulgarian Dance No. 1 meter: $4 + \frac{2}{8} + 3$
$\frac{6}{8}$ ♫♫♩.│♩♪♫♫│♩. ♩. ‖ $\frac{3}{4}$	Mozart, Ball Scene, *Don Giovanni* meters: $\frac{3}{8}$ $\frac{2}{4}$ $\frac{3}{4}$
$\frac{3}{4}$ ♩♩│♩♩♩│$\frac{2}{4}$♩♩│$\frac{3}{1}$ o o o│$\frac{3}{8}$♫♫│$\frac{4}{4}$♩♩ ‖	Bartok; Music For Stringed Instruments, Percussion and Celesta, Movement 4 meter: varied

the performer relies strictly on the numerical values of the notes and the counts for finding strong and weak beats.

TIME SIGNATURES AND METER

The performer, in addition to the visual aid he gets from the recurring bar lines, finds further help through the *time signature*. We have seen in the several examples from the song "Clementine" that it has a natural metric accent occurring every three beats. We therefore call its particular meter *triple*, and see bar lines placed on the staff to mark off each metric group.

In addition to this, the notation of "Clementine" will show fraction-like figures at the beginning of the music, telling the performer ahead of time precisely what the meter will be (Example 110). This time signa-

Example 110

ture stands either for the whole piece or until a new signature is introduced.

For the purposes of understanding meter itself, only the top number of the signature need be considered. It tells the performer how many beats he will encounter in the music for each metrical group.

$\frac{3}{4}$ – music to be felt in threes
$\frac{2}{1}$ – music to be felt in twos
$\frac{7}{8}$ – music to be felt in sevens
$\frac{5}{16}$ – music to be felt in fives

It has been stated earlier that the number on the bottom tells the player about relative durational values. Remember that it signifies exactly what durational value each beat will have. Arithmetical considerations dealing with durational values, such as quarter-notes, sixty-fourth-notes, dotted notes, etc., fall into the area of musical notation, a subject already explored in Chapter 1.

SIMPLE AND COMPOUND METERS

Numbers most often found at the top of the signature are 2, 3, 4, 6, 9, and 12. The first three indicate *simple meters*; the last three, *compound meters*. In the case of the simple meters, the upper number given indicates precisely how many beats there are.

When the upper number in the time signature is 6, 9, or 12, however, the situation is more complicated. Taken at face value, a signature of ⁶₈ clearly indicates six beats to a measure. Thus, one would normally expect, in the famous theme from the Horn Concerto K.447 by Mozart (Example 111), to feel six even beats. This is true, and we can indeed

Example 111   Horn Concerto, K.447, Movement 3, Mozart

Counts: 6   1 2 3 4 5 6   1 2 3 4 5 6   1 2 3 4 5 6   1 2 3 4 5

feel six beats. However, a metric grouping of six beats tends also to be felt in two groups of three beats rather than the one of six—especially in quick tempo. To experience this one need only count six beats several times over, placing a slight emphasis on the counts one and four. Therefore, the Mozart theme, which moves along at a lively pace, will not only be felt in six very fast beats as in Example 111, but also in two, as in Example 112.

Example 112

Count ⟶ 1   2   1   2   1   2   1   2

Thus, compound meter is aptly named. Beats can be felt and counted in two ways. Meters in 9 and 12 will also subdivide easily into fewer but longer beats per measure. To see this, one simply divides the top number by three. Thus, a 6 meter can be felt in 2, a 12 in 4, and a 15 in 5. The faster the pace of the music, the more easily this subdivision can be felt.

ASYMMETRICAL METER

Meters other than those discussed above are termed *asymmetrical*. We have seen how compound meters can be subdivided into combinations of threes: a 6 meter into a combination of two threes; a 12 meter into a combination of four threes, etc. (Example 113). In all compound meters, the normal subdivided grouping is the same—in threes. They therefore feel even. Asymmetrical meters such as 5, 7, etc., can also be

Example 113

subdivided into combinations. But as can be seen in Example 114, the groupings are not the same. The whole, therefore, feels uneven.

Example 114

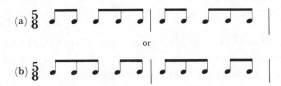

In Example 115 we see the time signature $\frac{5}{4}$ used by Tchaikovsky

Example 115   Symphony No. 6, Opus 74 ("Pathetique"), Movement 2, Tchaikovsky

Example 116

for the second movement of his "Pathetique" Symphony. While listening, we can count five beats fairly easily. But without considerable practice, it is possible to lose the downbeat and miss the count. We actually feel more comfortable counting one-two; one-two-three; one-two; one-two-three, as is indicated in Example 117. What we are feeling here, of course, is duple and triple meter alternating on a regular basis. It is interesting to note that both compound and asymmetrical meters ordinarily subdivide into the two basic meters, duple and triple. In fact, all meter consists of either simple duple or triple, or their combinations. Meters with one beat are notated, but do not actually

Example 117

Count ➝ 1 2 1   2 3   1   2   1 23   1 2 1   2 3   1   2   1 2 3

function musically as such on a consistent basis. One-beat measures are actually heard in multiples, either in twos or threes.

> *Suggested Listening:* The "General Dance" from Ravel's *Daphnis and Chloe, Suite No. 2* for asymmetrical meter $\frac{5}{4}$.

MIXED METER AND POLYMETER

Mixed meter occurs when measures in different meter alternate. These will usually be indicated by adjacent time signatures, as in Example 118.

Example 118   Variations on a Hungarian Song, Opus 21, No. 2, Brahms

Polymeter is heard when two or more meters occur simultaneously. This term is used in the same sense as are the terms *polychord* and *polytonality*. Both of these define different chords or keys sounding simultaneously. Therefore, when discussing simultaneous meters, the term *polymeter* is much more exact than the usual but highly ambiguous *polyrhythm*.

Example 119, from the opera *Don Giovanni* by Mozart, shows no less than three meters occurring at the same time.

The Waltz, Opus 42, in A♭ major by Chopin exemplifies a unique

Example 119   *Don Giovanni*, Act I, Mozart

example of implied polymeter (Example 120). The melody in the

Example 120   Waltz, Opus 42, Chopin

pianist's right hand actually sounds in $\frac{6}{8}$ meter (two beats to the measure) but is notated within a $\frac{3}{4}$ metrical signature (Example 121). When this is

Example 121

superimposed on the bass line, which itself is in a $\frac{3}{4}$ meter, a striking effect is achieved. Chopin might well have metered this section of the Waltz as shown in Example 122.

Example 122

CHANGING METER

Changing meter occurs when time signatures change often enough so that regular downbeats do not come at the same place each time as expected (Example 123). When this occurs consistently as may be seen,

Example 123   Metrical Changes in Stravinsky's *The Rite of Spring*

it can be questioned whether metrical accent really happens at all. Predictability, one of the basic facts underlying the principle of meter, obviously is not present. Though pulse remains, these changing meters serve more to produce varying accent than meter as such.

SYNCOPATION

Syncopation is to regular meter what dissonance is to traditional harmony. It provides momentary excitement in the expected and regular flow of beats in normal meters. Simple syncopation occurs when expected weak beats are accented. Example 124 shows an expected weak beat, in this case the second in a four-beat meter, strongly accented. This is common in music and is often encountered in Beethoven (Example 125).

Example 124   Symphony No. 44 ("Trauer"), Haydn

Example 125   Variations on a Theme of Diabelli, Opus 120, Theme, Beethoven

Strong syncopation is felt when an expected strong beat is replaced by a rest (Example 126), or when a note is tied or held over from a

Example 126   Symphony No. 3, Opus 55 ("Eroica"), Movement 1, Beethoven

weak beat to a stronger one (Example 127). Syncopated accent can also

Example 127 Symphony No. 5, Opus 64, Movement 1, Tchaikovsky

sound between beats. These may occur every few measures (Example 128), or sometimes on a regular basis, within each beat (Example 129).

Example 128 Carmen, Act II, Bizet

Example 129 Variations on a Theme of Handel, Opus 24, Brahms

In each case, these are called *accented offbeats.*

Jazz, perhaps more than other kinds of music, uses much syncopation—especially that produced by accented offbeats. Accents are placed at various points between beats consistently, with the last third of the beat favored. Underlying everything is unflagging and steady pulse, much of the time organized in the meters $\frac{4}{4}$ or $\frac{2}{2}$. The result of regular but varied offbeat accents constantly set against an orderly flow of metered beats can be very exciting and lively.

Tempo

Tempo deals with the pace of the beats and nothing else. One sometimes hears the phrase ". . . in a fast rhythm." This is incorrect. What is meant is ". . . in a fast tempo," the phrase suggesting that the beats heard follow one another quickly. The field of rhythm includes the

"I got him to make me one" (p. 108).

study of tempo as one important element, but the term *rhythm* should not be used when *tempo* is meant.

At the beginning of a piece or movement there is usually a *tempo indication*. These, written in any language, give approximate tempos. Thus, a tempo direction *Lebhaft* in a Schumann piano piece tells the pianist to play in a lively tempo. The term *Lent* in a Debussy prelude will indicate a slow pace. These will apply to the whole piece unless different tempo indications are later introduced.

The tempo given at the beginning of the Score Profile of Beethoven's *Leonora* Overture No. 3, accompanying this chapter, is *Adagio* (very slow). This applies only until measure 37, when the term *Allegro* (fast) is seen. Later, at measure 514, Beethoven indicates that the music is to be played *Presto* (extremely fast).

Table of Common Tempo Indications

ITALIAN

Allegro – Moderately fast
Vivace – Fast with vivacity
Allegro con brio – Fast with brilliance
Allegro con spirito – Fast with spirit
Presto – Extremely fast
Andante – Walking tempo
Moderato – Moderate
Allegretto – Not quite as fast as Allegro
Lento – Slow
Grave – Slow and solemn
Adagio – Slow and calm
Largo – Slow and broad

FRENCH

Animé – Animated
Moderé – Moderate
Lent – Slow

GERMAN

Lebhaft – Lively
Mässig – Moderate
Langsam – Slow

It can readily be seen that terms for tempo are only general indications, helpful though never precise. There have been many attempts to find a system that would be accurate and constant in specifying the speed of a particular piece of music. Thomas Jefferson was concerned with this problem, as the following quotation shows:

I got him to make me one. I find the pendulum regulated to Largo vibrato, 52 times in a minute; Adagio vibrato, 60 times in a minute; Andante, 70 times in a minute; Allegro, 95 times in a minute; Presto, 135 times in a minute. Everyone, therefore, may make a chronometer adapted to his instrument. For a harpsichord, the following occurs to me: In the wall of your chamber, over the instrument, drive five little brads, as 1, 2, 3, 4, 5, in the following manner. Take a string with a bob to it, of such length, as that hung on No. 1, it shall vibrate fifty-two times in a minute. Then proceed by trial to No. 2, at such a distance, that drawing the loop of the string to that, the part remaining between 1 and the bob, shall vibrate sixty times in a minute. Fix the third for seventy vibrations, etc., the chord always hanging over No. 1, as the centre of vibration. A person playing the violin may fix this on his music stand. A pendulum, thrown into vibration, will continue in motion long enough to give you the time of your piece.

THE METRONOME

The most successful solution to the problem of precise tempo indication was that of the German inventor, Johann Maelzel, who introduced in Paris in 1816 the **metronome**, which is still in use today. It consists of a weighted pendulum. The weight may be moved to any numbered position on a graduated scale, the numbers of which designate the number of beats per minute. This number may then be used at the beginning of a piece instead of, or in conjunction with, the verbal tempo indication (Example 130).

Example 130

M.M. signifies "Maelzel's Metronome." half-note = 120 signifies that there are 120 half-notes per minute as established by the metronome. The metronome weight is set at the graduation of 120, and then a few ticks of the pendulum are enough to establish the pace of the basic beat. The performer or the conductor ultimately memorizes some of the more common tempos and uses the metronome as a check.

If no metronome is available, the following chart may be used as a rough guide to establish the correct rate of speed.

M.M.	PHYSICAL ACTION	POSSIBLE ITALIAN TERM
140	Jogging, or polka tempo	Presto
120	Marching	Allegro
100	Walking	Moderato
80	Strolling	Andante
60	Counting seconds	Lento

Taken on face value, tempo indications, both arithmetical and verbal, would seem to suggest a very steady pulse. This is often true, especially in the Allegros of the baroque and classical periods. Obvious, though, is the fact that not all music is meant to be played in strict, inflexible tempo. Music in which the pace of the beats varies considerably is said to be in the **rubato** style, the term *rubato* taken as it applies to nineteenth-century romantic music. In earlier periods, it applied more to deviations from notated durational values than to fluctuations of pulse.

Beats gradually increasing in pace are indicated by the term **accelerando** (acc.); **ritardando** (rit.) indicates the reverse. Other terms indicating tempo adjustments are:

> **A tempo**— In the established tempo of the piece
> **Tempo 1 (tempo primo)**— In the first tempo given
> **Ritenuto, rallentando**— The same as ritardando

Various other terms and signs:

> cut time ⎫
> Alla Breve ⎬ $\frac{2}{2}$
> ¢ ⎭

Leonora Overture No. 3,
Opus 72a, Beethoven

Written in 1806, this overture is one of four written by the composer for his only opera, *Fidelio.* It was first used with the opera in March, 1806. It now is played primarily as a concert overture, the overture called *Fidelio,* Op. 72b prefacing modern performances of the opera.

Orchestra:

2 Flutes (FL)
2 Oboes (OB)
2 Clarinets (CL)
2 Bassoons (BN)

4 Horns (HN)
2 Trumpets (TR)
3 Trombones (TB)

Violins (VL 1, 2)
Violas (VA)
Violoncellos (VC)
Contrabasses (CB)

Form: Sonata-allegro, with introduction and coda.

SCORE PROFILE

Score Detail: m. 27

While the violins are sweeping up the scale and then down, the rest of the orchestra is holding an A♭ major chord with flutes on top and the contrabass anchoring the whole on the bottom.

(cont.)

Rhythmic pattern in
trumpets and timpani

(cont.)

TUTTI

Rhythmic pattern in TR, HN

Score Detail: m. 278–280

Background figures in the strings under the theme in the woodwinds.

Rhythmic pattern in strings, later in winds

continues

Score Detail: m. 606−613

Note the powerful sequence of chords leading to the searing diminished 9th chord at m. 610. Note the dynamic indicated *fff* — extremely loud.

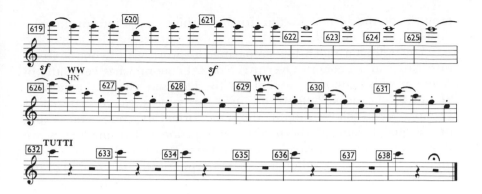

Listening notes

Rhythmically, this composition is one of the most exciting Beethoven ever wrote. Syncopation is very prominent.

Note how the syncopated rhythmic pattern,

underlying the main theme of the allegro, **SP m. 37**, crops up in so many places: **SP m. 106** — where a dynamic accent, sfp, underscores the syncopation, **SP m. 254** — in the winds, as background to the theme in the strings, **SP m. 546** — where the rhythmic pattern is completely isolated from the original melody, **SP m. 614** — where a dynamic accent is placed on a different note of the rhythmic pattern than before,

Other exciting syncopated passages can be heard beginning at measures 169, 360, 452, and 570.

Another important rhythmic pattern, this time of a nonsyncopated nature, occurs in the trumpet solo section beginning at **SP m. 278**. The pattern

is used as background in the strings and bassoons to the theme in the winds. It is interesting to note both the derivation and later usage of this rhythmic pattern. It is taken from the first few notes of the trumpet call itself,

SP m. 272. Later it re-enters in the timpani, **SP m. 481**, as quiet background for the section leading to the rushing scales introducing the final Presto, **SP m. 514**.

You will gain much by comparing this work with Leonora Overture No. 1 and Leonora Overture No. 2. Leonora 1 has very little in common with Leonora 3, except for the Florestan theme (Leonora 3, **SP m. 9**). Leonora 2, however, uses the same melodic material as Leonora 3 and follows roughly the same formal structure. You should first acquaint yourself thoroughly with Leonora 3, using the Score Profile, and then compare it to the others. You will then see a "case history" of musical evolution and metamorphosis that was typical of the work of Beethoven.

For reference and review

New terms in the order presented:

pulse	downbeat
beat	upbeat
rhythm	time signature
melody	simple meter
harmony	compound meter
chorus	asymmetrical meter
accent	mixed meter
repetition	polymeter
rhythmic pattern	polychord
dynamic accent	polytonality
melodic accent	accented offbeats
intervallic accent	tempo
agogic accent	tempo indication
metrical accent	lebhaft
melodic contour	lent
syncopation	adagio
accompaniment pattern	allegro
aria	presto
polonaise	metronome
bolero	rubato
cakewalk	accelerando
waltz	ritardando
mazurka	a tempo
strong beat	tempo 1
weak beat	tempo primo
meter	ritenuto
triple meter	rallentando
bar line	cut time
measure	alla breve

4

Melody

O F THE THREE ELEMENTS of music, *rhythm* and *harmony* are
far easier to discuss separately than *melody*. Melody, the most
evanescent of the three, the most indefinable, is nevertheless the
element that through the ages has captured the fancy first and
foremost. This may be partially explained by spot-lighting a
certain fallacy in discussing rhythm, harmony, and melody as
three totally separate elements.

Rhythm may exist totally by itself, but usually cannot be a
part of a musical work until it is adorned with musical *tone*. Harmony hardly exists without being intimately interwoven with both
rhythm and melody. Note that when a succession of chords is
played separately, even with no consideration of melody or
rhythm, the listener always regards the notes that are the highest
in *pitch* as constituting the melody, and will also strive to find an
underlying rhythmic pulse.

But we may say that melody can exist totally by itself, because
it contains within itself both rhythm and harmony. Melody in its
forward flow establishes its own rhythm. It does this by its varying
note values, the accents inherent in longer tones and higher or
lower tones, its repetitions of patterns, its cadences. It can be as
free as free verse, or it can be as rhythmically strict as a limerick.
Also, in its leaps and falls, and in its accents, melody suggests or
outlines chords or harmony, and in its cadences it suggests or
emphasizes *tonality*.

125

But what is its mystique? What is it that entrances us? In its unfolding, artless or complex, it gradually becomes more than rhythm and suggested harmony. In its unfolding it is becoming itself. And it is not itself until it is complete. Also, upon its completion it no longer exists — except in the memory. And thus we go back to hear it again. If it is simple, a few times will do; if it is more than simple—and we do not necessarily mean complex—we go back more often, if possible. If it has qualities of greatness—whatever these may be—we go back again and again.

When we say melody we now mean not only *tune*, but the entire *melodic content* or compositional idea of a work and the entire emotional aura that it establishes. This aura is its personality, so to speak; this is its *melos*.

The shaping of melody may be a tortuous task, or it may seemingly flow from the pen. It varies from composer to composer, and with a single composer the facility with which he writes may vary from day to day. But the one sure fact remains: the shaping of melody is a planned, controlled act—an act of the highest creative order.

What is melody?

There are many kinds of melody. From early times to the present day there have been as many different melodic styles on the part of the composer as there have been different tastes for melody on the part of the listener. But there are structural principles underlying these melodic styles that can be perceived in all periods of music.

Melody cannot be divorced from rhythm. Notice, for example, that if we separate a well known melody from its rhythmic pattern (Example 131), the melody becomes difficult to recognize. But it is equally

Example 131

difficult to identify the same melody through its rhythmic pattern alone (Example 132). If we now combine the melodic tones given above with

Example 132

the rhythmic pattern given we have the familiar melody in Example 133.

Example 133

What, then, is melody? A simple definition would be: the succession of single tones in time. For the time being we will consider the succession of single musical tones without specific reference to rhythmic patterns.

Direction and distance

A tone may be repeated (Examples 134 and 135). A tone may move to

Example 134   My Country 'Tis of Thee

Example 135   **SP m. 1**, Brahms

a higher pitch, by step (Examples 136 and 137), or change to a lower

Example 136   Frère Jacques

Example 137   **SP m. 88**, Brahms

pitch by step (Examples 138 and 139), or leap up an interval of a 3rd (Example 140) or more (Example 141), or leap down an interval of a

Example 138   Welsh Air

Example 139   **SP m. 63–7**, Brahms

Example 140   Symphony No. 3, Opus 55, Movement 1, Beethoven

Example 141   Symphony No. 4, Opus 36, Tchaikovsky

3rd (Example 142) or more (Example 143).

Example 142   **SP m. 222–6**, Brahms

Example 143   None But the Lonely Heart, Tchaikovsky

    Having looked at the several intervallic and directional possibilities inherent in only two notes, it is clear that the prospects for variety in a melody lasting through many measures are manifold.

Melodic contour

As a melody spins itself out, it begins to assume an individuality of its own that could only be guessed at from the opening few notes. It now assumes what is variously called shape, profile, contour. The ***shape of a*** *melody* may be seen by looking at the music as it is printed on the staff. In the well known melody from Tchaikovsky's Fifth Symphony in Example 144, notice the essentially rising character of the line until the

Example 144   Symphony No. 5, Opus 64, Tchaikovsky

high point, or **climax**, is arrived at in measure three. This type of melodic shape may be seen more clearly in Example 145. Further

Example 145

abstracted, the shape of the melody looks like Example 146.

Example 146

This shape is very often found in melody: its **gradual rise and sharp fall** may be represented by the symbol shown in Example 147. It

Example 147

can be seen in the familiar melody in Example 148. The ascending

Example 148   My Country 'Tis of Thee

character of this melodic line is essentially the same as that of Example

144 in spite of the small changes of direction within the total contour. The various dips in the melody in no way impede the gradual rise of the line to the climax in measure 13.

Other melodic shapes often found are:

1. *Gentle rise, gradual decline* (Example 149).

Example 149   Bolero, Ravel

Special permission granted for reprint Durand and Cie, Paris, France; Copyright owners—Elkan-Vogel Co., Inc., Agents.

2. *Rise and fall of approximate equal length* (Example 150).

Example 150   Violin Concerto No. 4, K.218, Mozart

3. *Fall and rise of approximate equal length* (Example 151).

Example 151   Concerto No. 1, Opus 25, Piano and Orchestra, Mendelssohn

These four melodic shapes are not the only ones possible: many variants occur. But no matter what the shape, the listener should try to hear the important high and low points of a melody. Further, these shapes may be combined and altered in many ways, especially in melodies of greater length. The greater the length of the melody or section of music the more possibilities there will be for variety of contour and for subsidiary climaxes leading ultimately to the high point.

Example 152   **SP m. 113–126,** Brahms

MELODIC RANGE

In considering melodic style in relation to **range** it will be noted that melodies that are meant to be sung or based upon the vocal style often stay within a relatively small range. Gregorian chant, for example, falls within a very small range (Example 153). The theme that

Example 153   Dies Irae

Beethoven used as the basis for the choral section of his Ninth Symphony has a range of only an octave (Example 154). In the last movement of Brahms' First Symphony the main **theme** (Example 155) is not sung, but is based on a vocal "chorale" style and thus has a relatively small range.

Instruments have more range and flexibility than the voice, and composers have taken advantage of this in expanding the range of melody and in developing greater variety of contour (Examples 156 and 157).

Example 154   Symphony No. 9, Opus 125, Beethoven

Example 155   Symphony No. 1, Opus 68, Movement 4, Brahms

Example 156   Also Sprach Zarathustra, Opus 30, Strauss

Example 157   Symphony No. 2, Opus 36, Beethoven

CONJUNCT AND DISJUNCT MELODIC MOTION

It will be noticed in the examples given above that vocal music uses step-wise or *conjunct motion* predominantly. On the other hand, instrumental melodies more often use leaps: *disjunct motion.* Notice the interplay of conjunct and disjunct motion in certain melodies. In

Example 158, the predominant conjunct motion is neatly balanced by

Example 158   Symphony No. 40, K.550, Mozart

two sets of leaps strategically placed in the contour. In Example 159
the opening disjunct motion in the first four notes is balanced by several
measures of conjunct motion.

Example 159   **SP m. 129–132**, Brahms

Academic Festival Overture, Opus 80, Brahms

"Will you write us a Doctoral Symphony for Breslau? We expect a Festal Ode at the very least."

This question was contained in the letter of congratulations Brahms received from Breslau University several days after it had conferred upon him a doctoral degree. In the following year, 1880, he informed the University that he had completed the *Academic Festival Overture*. Brahms spoke of the *Overture* as a medley of student songs.

Orchestra:

1 Piccolo (PIC)
2 Flutes (FL)
2 Oboes (OB)
2 Clarinets (CL)
2 Bassoons (BN)
1 Contrabassoon (CBN)

4 French Horns (HN)
3 Trumpets (TP)
3 Trombones (TB)
1 Tuba (TU)

3 Timpani (TIMP)
1 Bass Drum (BD)
1 Cymbal (CYM)
1 Triangle (TRI)

Violins (VL 1, 2)
Violas (VA)
Violoncellos (VC)
Contrabasses (CB)

Form: Modified Sonata-Allegro, with Coda.

SCORE PROFILE

Score Detail: m. 17−18

While the flutes are holding a long, soft A♭, the clarinets are articulating a broken chord. Also note the arched figure of the cellos.

Score Detail: m. 63–70

The brass begins quietly, trumpets only. The other brass are gradually added —note the horn and trombone entrances. By m. 72 all the brass are playing and the flutes and oboes as well become part of the wind sound.

Score Detail: m. 174–178

While the bassoons take the original folk song, the violins play its free inversion above.

Listening notes

Although Brahms spoke of the *Academic Festival Overture* as a medley of tunes, it is less than a medley. It is also more than a medley —much more. It is less than a medley because it does not straightforwardly present a collection of songs or tunes with slight transitional or modulatory material between them. It is more than a medley because Brahms has incorporated the student songs into a cohesive whole. Certain thematic *ideas* of the songs are subject to development and mixture, and become integrated within the total concept.

The first figure of the opening theme, in C minor **SP m. 1–13**, is reminiscent of a portion of the "Rakoczy March" of Berlioz in its rhythmic pattern Example 160), and it establishes the moderate tempo

Example 160   Rakoczy March, Berlioz

associated with ceremonial music. But as well, its vigorous rhythm suggests the joy of the festive day. This is superseded by the theme in C major, beginning at **SP m. 64**, which is based on the Thuringian folk song (a nod to a German Students' Association of the time), "Wir hatten gebauet" (Example 161). The basis of the theme beginning in

Example 161   Wir Hatten Gebauet

Wir hat - ten ge - bau - et ein statt - lich - es Haus,

SP m. 129 is "Der Landesvater" (Example 162). The brisk theme in

Example 162   Der Landesvater

Hört, ich sing das Lied der Lie - der hört es, mei - ne

deut - schen Brü - der, hall es, hall es wie - der fro - her Chor!

"Brahms did not respond to the request for a Doctoral Symphony with a pompous, inflated work . . ." (p. 144).

G major that is begun by the bassoons at **SP m. 157** may be compared to the original version of the "Fuchslied" (Example 163). Brahms re-

Example 163   Fuchslied

turns to the opening key, C minor, at **SP m. 241**, but reverses his thematic materials in a quasi-recapitulation. The key changes to C at **SP m. 290** and fragments of the three songs are incorporated into the texture, with the final reference to the "Fuchslied" bringing us directly to the "Gaudeamus Igitur" (Example 164), which may be termed a coda

Example 164   Gaudeamus Igitur

but is more in the manner of a concluding symbolic statement, an apotheosis of the freedom of youth.

Brahms did not respond to the request for a Doctoral Symphony with a pompous, inflated work that might have impressed the faculty and the officials at Breslau, but chose instead to write what he termed a medley in the manner of von Suppé. The spirit of freedom — especially from the students' point of view — evidently appealed to Brahms. Note the text of "Gaudeamus Igitur."

> Let us now in youth rejoice,
> None can justly blame us;
> For when golden youth has fled,
> And in age our joys are dead,
> Then the dust doth claim us.

For reference and review

New terms in the order presented:

rhythm
harmony
melody
tone
tonality
pitch
note values
tune

melodic content
melos
shape of a melody
climax
range
theme
conjunct motion
disjunct motion

5

Chord structure
and chord connection

RHYTHM ENERGIZES music; melody and form give it definition; *harmony* provides it with depth and color.

Rhythm sets music in motion. It affects us kinesthetically. It propels the musical idea forward. Harmony, while also providing forward motion through *chord progression*, fleshes out the sound by providing for several tones to occur simultaneously. It can be defined as the simultaneous occurrence of three or more tones resulting in *chords*, and the relationships between these chords.

Though music does not actually exist in space, it is sometimes useful to think of it in terms of high, low, up, down, horizontal, vertical. When we discuss *horizontal* aspects, we refer to melodic elements that are represented in notation as going from left to right along the staff. This is also called the *linear* element of music. Tones occurring *simultaneously* from lower to higher parts of a staff or from lower to higher staves are said to represent *vertical* aspects.

Chords, of course, need not always be lower than the melody. They may be above it (Example 165), or both above and below it (Example 166). But regardless of where the chords are located relative to the melody or melodies—top, middle, or bottom—they are enormously powerful agents used by the composer to affect mood and atmosphere. Indeed, the plainest kind of tune can be metamorphasized by the subtle use of chords.

Example 165   Preludes, Opus 28, No. 22, Chopin

Example 166   Intermezzo, Opus 16, Brahms

The well known melody, "God Save the King," is harmonized very simply by Beethoven in his keyboard variations of 1804 (Example 167),

Example 167   Seven Variations on the National Song, Theme, God Save the King, Beethoven

though not as simply as it can be heard in its American version, "My Country 'Tis of Thee" (Example 168). In the coda to the variations,

Example 168   My Country 'Tis of Thee

Beethoven not only changes the contour of the melody, but completely transforms the harmonic scheme from one of routine expectedness to one replete with poignant chords (Example 169).

Example 169   Coda, Seven Variations on the National Song, God Save the King, Beethoven

Tertian harmony

Though it is true, as we said before, that *any* three or more sounds occurring simultaneously can be termed chords, it is also true that certain fixed intervallic relationships between the notes of certain chords have been more common than others in the history of music. One particularly common system of harmony, which has underscored Western music for centuries, is called **tertian**. It is based on the interval of the third.

The tertian harmonic system also is inextricably bound up with **tonality**, the whole system intuitively appearing to the great majority of people as being at the very wellspring of music itself. The cornerstone of the tertian system is the **triad**.

A triad is a three-note chord built in thirds. Simple triads accompanying tonic-oriented, diatonic melodies seem to many to be as eternal and normal as air and clouds, the color spectrum, indeed anything experienced simply but surely in nature itself. The aural comfort and expectedness of tertian harmony may well have a basis in the physical acoustical laws regulating tone itself. It can be shown, for instance, that the three tones of a basic triad (Example 170) are identical with the first

Example 170

five partials of the overtone series (Example 171). If it is true that the overtone series (see Chapter 2 for detailed discussion) is deeply imbedded in human aural experience, it follows that triads, tertian har-

Example 171

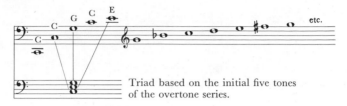

Triad based on the initial five tones
of the overtone series.

mony, and the whole tonal system have been and perhaps for some time
to come will be fundamental to musical experience.

TRIADS

Triads may be constructed on any note on any staff, including
notes with accidentals (Example 172). We have said that triads are

Example 172

constructed in thirds. Visually, this can be ascertained by noting that all
three notes of the triad in fundamental position are either on spaces or
on lines. The intervallic distance of adjacent lines or adjacent spaces is
always a third (see Example 172). The lowest note of the triad is
termed its **root**, and the triad takes its letter name from it (Example
173).

Example 173

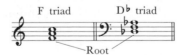

F triad   D♭ triad

Root

DOUBLINGS

Chords often will consist of more than three tones. The chord in
Example 174 has seven tones, but only three *different* notes. It can
quickly be seen that the note on top and the three notes on the bottom
are repetitions in different octaves of the bracketed triad. This chord,
then, is simply a consonant triad with its basic tones doubled.

Example 174

EXTENDED CHORDS

Chords will often be made up of four or more *different* notes. These are called **extended chords** because the intervallic construction —in thirds—is extended beyond the limits of the three-note triad itself. In other words, triads that consist of paired thirds can be extended simply by adding extra thirds above (Example 175). In Example 176

Example 175

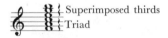

Example 176

not one of the seven notes is the same. The interval between the lowest note, *F*, and the fourth one up, *B*, is an augmented fourth (Example 177); the interval between the third tone up, *A*, and the second from

Example 177

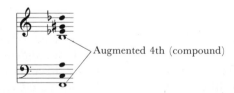

the top, *G*-sharp (Example 178), is that of a major seventh. Both are

Example 178

Major 7th

strong dissonances and cause the chord basically to be dissonant. But despite the dissonant character of the chord, it is, in fact, a derivation and extension of the simple triad represented by its lower three notes. The notes in Example 179b are precisely those of 179a, but rearranged

Example 179

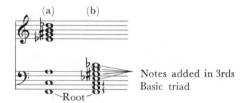

Notes added in 3rds
Basic triad

so that the chord is in *fundamental, close position*. Seen in this formation, each added note is a third above the previous one. The whole extended chord, then, is but a series of superimposed thirds with a triad anchoring the whole, and therefore falls within the tertian system.

All extended chords in fundamental position are numbered according to the intervallic distance between the root and the uppermost note. The chord described above (Example 180) is called a thirteenth chord.

Example 180

Interval of a 13th

The quite common seventh chord consists of only four notes and, again, is numbered according to the intervallic distance between the top and bottom notes (Example 181).

Example 181

Interval of a 7th

INVERSION

The root of a chord is not always at the bottom (Example 182).

Example 182

When the lowest note of any chord—called the **bass**—is one other than the root, the chord is said to be **inverted**. Chords are inverted both for the value of their sound and for interesting bass lines that can result.

Example 183 shows a Beethoven phrase with a melodically effec-

Example 183   Sonata, Opus 14, No. 2, Movement 2, Beethoven

tive bass line. The chords with asterisks are inverted. A reharmonization of this theme using only root-position chords not only would result in a duller bass line but would end in bland chordal sounds as well.

Example 184

ACCIDENTALS AND CHORDS

All of the principles discussed above are valid regardless of whether accidentals are present in the chords or not. In other words, sharps and flats do not affect their basic structure but affect their color, just as in scales or melodies. Example 185 shows what color effects

Example 185

result from the addition of accidentals to a simple major triad built on the note *F*. It can be imagined to what degree interesting chordal color can be achieved through added or subtracted accidentals in extended chords.

CHORDS AS TEXTURE

Chords, regardless of their basic intervallic structure, assume manifold additional textural effects through the *spacing* and dispersement of the given notes.

Close Position. Chords are said to be in *close position* when the interval between any two of their adjacent notes is no more than a fourth. This applies to chords in fundamental and root positions as well as to inversions and extended chords (Example 186).

Example 186   Chords in Close Position

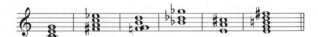

The effect of chords in close position, depending on the performance forces and on *tessitura*, tends to be thick and "blocky." Indeed, these are often called *block chords* by musicians.

Open Position. *Open position* occurs when any two tones are more than a fourth apart (Example 187). Because of the disposition of

Example 187   Chords in Open Position

partials in the overtone series itself, with the open spacing close to the fundamental and close spacing higher up, chord tones themselves have a tendency to be spaced according to register. Chords to be played in the bass register seldom are seen in close position. When this happens, as in Example 188, the composer deliberately exploits the gruff,

Example 188   Sonata, Opus 13, Movement 1, Beethoven

growling sound that inevitably results when thickly clustered chord tones are heard in the bass. Chords in open spacing are seen in all ranges, but sound particularly good in the bass.

Broken Chords.   Chord tones that are not sounded simultaneously but are close enough to one another to be heard as one chordal entity are called either *arpeggios* or *broken chords*. Broken chords, as the term implies, are simply chords with the tones played separately instead of simultaneously. These can be either precisely notated with appropriate durational values (Example 189) or loosely suggested with

Example 189

certain symbols (Example 190).

Example 190

CHORDS AND MELODY

When basic triads are placed on the degrees of ordinary diatonic scales (Example 191), their relationship with melody becomes apparent.

Example 191

I II III IV V VI VII
(leading tone triad)

It can readily be seen that each scale note is present not only as the root of the triad placed upon it, but also as the third or fifth in other triads. Thus, the fifth scale (circled) step is present in triads built on V, I, III. The fifth scale step, when found as part of a simple diatonic melody, could then easily be harmonized by either V, I, III (as shown in Example 192).

Example 192

I V I III V

Though the scale upon which these triads are placed in Example 191 is of a single type, the triads themselves contrast in color. This can be pragmatically ascertained by simply playing on the piano the tonic, submediant, and leading tone triads in Example 191. Each sounds different. The tonic triad is major; the submediant, minor; and the leading tone, diminished. This color contrast between certain triads occurs because of the intervallic structure of the diatonic scale, which is not uniform itself.

It will also follow that chord types will vary according to the particular diatonic scale used whether it be major or one of the several forms of the minor or one of the ancient modes. Example 193 shows four common scales: major, natural minor, harmonic minor, and mixolydian, with triads placed on each scale step. Note how the resulting triads are predominantly major and minor, with but few occurrences of the dissonant diminished and augmented triads.

Example 193

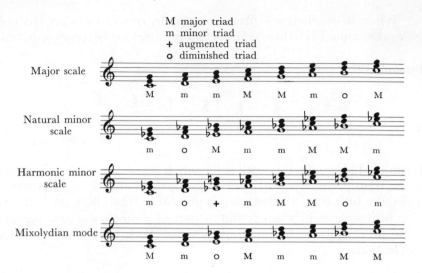

Chord connection

Heard singly, chords can be striking by themselves. But just as a single variety of flower seldom makes a garden, neither does the single chord make music. Harmony results only when two or more different but interrelated chords are present in a composition.

The manner in which these chords are connected is vital. Harmony textbooks refer to chord sequence as *progression*. The jazz musician speaks of *changes*. But whatever it is called, logical, natural chord connection is to homophony what syntax is to language. Just as certain ordered words make sense while others result only in gibberish, chords go well together only in certain patterns. These patterns follow principles of chord progression that are consistent and logical.

To see this, one need only compare the melody in Example 194

Example 194   Old Folks at Home, Foster

above, harmonized with a simple but appropriate set of chords, with the same melody in Example 195 harmonized with chords that do not

Example 195

follow well. Though in any given musical situation any triad can connect with any others, certain triads connect much more smoothly than
others. For example, a chord built on V (Key of C major, Example 196)

Example 196

V

will naturally lead to a chord built on I (Examples 197 and 198), and a

Example 197

I

Example 198

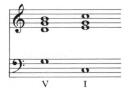

V   I

chord built on IV (Example 199) will fall easily into a chord built on II
(Examples 200 and 201).

Example 199

IV

Example 200

II

Example 201

These progressions sound smooth and natural to the ear because of the intervallic progression of their root tones. In general, any one triad will seem to "progress" naturally to another when their separate roots move by certain intervals. These root progressions in order of frequency of use are:

1. Triad roots up or down a fourth or fifth.
2. Triad roots down a third.
3. Triad roots up a second.

The interval between roots of the triads in Example 198 is that of the fifth. And other triads connected by this interval, such as IV-I, VI-III, II-V, VI-II, will match well. A similar strength applies to triads falling within categories 2 and 3, shown above.

But though the above root progressions are overwhelmingly present in standard tonal music, the principles they follow are only loosely binding. For purposes of color, change of pace, and attaining the unexpected, composers have often juxtaposed triads that normally do not follow each other well.

Beethoven, in Example 202, follows a strongly driving V triad with

Example 202 Symphony No. 6, Opus 68 ("Pastorale"), Movement I, Beethoven

a sudden drop into a IV chord. The root movement here is down a second, sometimes called a ***regression***. What normally is expected at this point is the V chord "progressing" to a I chord or possibly to a VI chord—both showing strong root progressions. But the dramatic effect attained by the sudden wrench into an unexpected chord is exactly what the composer desired here. And, besides, the normal resolution of the V triad into the I triad is only delayed for four measures.

CADENCES

Triads, besides their roles as supportive agents for melody, generators of musical movement through progression, and providers of color and depth, also can be powerful agents in dividing a composition into meaningful, cohesive, inner segments. Just as the eye would find it difficult to isolate meaningful phrases, sentences, and paragraphs if no punctuation were present, so would the ear find it difficult to identify intelligible musical statements without ***cadences***. A cadence is a short, trenchant progression of chords that either holds back or terminates completely the flow of music in a composition. Cadences are found at the joints of form, at the end of formal segments such as the phrase, period, part, section, or movement (see Chapter 7). They signal the ear that a musical statement has either just finished or been interrupted before going on.

This feeling of closure or delayed closure is produced by a minimum of two chords connected by strong root progressions. These elemental progressions function as definitely and clearly in a composition as do periods, commas, and colons in a paragraph. Perhaps the most obvious to the ear is the ***authentic cadence***, consisting of a V chord proceeding to a I chord (Example 203) in an emphatic and definite

Example 203   Sonata No. 8, Opus 13, Beethoven

manner. In tonal music this is the strongest way of punctuating and finalizing a musical statement. A statement such as that in Example 203, because of its strong closing cadence, impresses the ear as solidly as a clear, complete sentence terminated by a period. And, just as the other various punctuation marks such as commas, question marks, and semi-colons condition a verbal sentence or phrase, making it lead to other statements and concepts, so do the less final harmonic cadences. For example, a statement pausing on a V chord (Example 204) is said

Example 204   Trois Fantasies ou Caprices, Opus 16, Mendelssohn

to end with a *half cadence*. The harmonic feeling is that of growing tension, culminating in the half cadence, followed by the relaxation inherent in the tonic chord. When the musical sentence is purposely taut and dramatic as in Example 205, the feeling is not unlike that of a

Example 205   Sonata No. 8, Opus 13, Movement 1, Beethoven

rubber band stretched to its breaking point and then allowed to snap back.

When the statement ends with a I chord preceded by a IV chord, the cadence is termed *plagal* (Example 206). Tension-relaxation also

Example 206   Winterreise, Opus 89, No. 16, "Last Hope," Schubert

occurs here as in the V-I cadence. But the plagal cadence is not as dynamic because the most dynamic note of the scale, the seventh (leading tone), is not found in the IV chord.

A statement punctuated by a V chord that is answered immediately by a VI chord (or other unexpected chord) displays what is called a *deceptive* or *evasive cadence* (Example 207).

Example 207

Other cadences are possible in triadic harmony and, indeed, cadence occurs within any harmonic system. For any music to be meaningful to the ear, harmonic pauses and harmonic arrivals achieved through the many possible cadence formulas must occur. Otherwise, musical pattern and definition cannot be.

MODULATION

The process of bridging from one key to another is called *modulation*. Any key, major or minor, may go to another. The modulating passage may be short, long, simple, or complex, the whole depending on the style, the historical period of the composer, and the work at hand. In general, the longer and more complex the composition, the more sophisticated will be the key scheme and the modulation techniques.

The Haydn rondo in the Score Profile at the end of this chapter offers an excellent opportunity for aural and visual recognition of effective use of key and modulation. All key changes and modulations are indicated below the staves.

Before moving on to the Score Profile, remember that the harmonic system discussed in this chapter, called tertian, is not all-inclusive. Other systems, based on other intervallic relationships, are possible and indeed exist. These will be discussed in Chapter 15.

Symphony No. 88, Movement 4, Haydn

This symphony was written around 1787, one of the "London" symphonies. It was much admired by Beethoven, who especially was influenced by Movement 2, Largo. Movement 1 is in the "hunt" style because of the emphasis of theme 1 on the interval pattern, third-fifth-sixth.

Orchestra:

> 1 Flute (FL)
> 2 Oboes (OB)
> 2 Bassoons (BN)
>
> 2 French Horns (HN)
> 2 Trumpets (TR)
>
> Timpani (TIMP)
>
> Violins (VL 1, 2)
> Violas (VA)
> Violoncellos (VC)
> Contrabasses (CB)

Form: Rondo-Sonata.

SCORE PROFILE

Score Detail: m. 22–24

Note the strong half cadence, ending with a V chord. The key here is temporarily G minor, the tonic minor. The sudden darkening of the tonality adds immeasurable zest to the sunny character of the music.

G minor: V6   I   +6   V

Melody also heard octave higher.

Modulation passage leading to _ _ _ _ _ _ _ _ _

VL 1,OB

𝑝 dolce

key of _ _ _ D major

𝑝𝑝   D minor until measure 66

𝑓 D major

Timpani plays note "d" (V) in preparation for the tonic (I), soon to arrive.

Score Detail: m. 61–65
This progression is probably the most colorful in the movement. Note the many chromatics.

Inv.   Inv.   Inv.   Inv.   I   Inv.   Inv.   Inv.   V

B minor

Unstable

key feeling

E minor

TUTTI

Note how the repeated "b", measures 140-143, is pivotal
for modulation.   It begins as the 5th of E minor and

then suddenly becomes the 3rd $\boldsymbol{p}$ V⁷ of G major
tone of G major, the home key.   (9th chord)

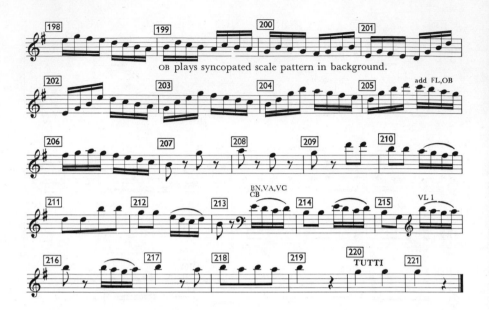

OB plays syncopated scale pattern in background.

Listening notes

Haydn's music is highly representative of traditional harmony. His life (1732–1809) spans the salient years of the classical period. The profile given here is particularly rewarding for assimilating the essential characteristics of chord structure, progression, and modulation.

First, to verify visually how important the triad is in all music displaying tonality, glance at the many outlined triads within the melody itself. Here are a few: **SP m. 4** G major triad, starting on third of chord; **SP m. 16** D major triad, starting on fifth of chord; **SP m. 92–93** E minor triad starting on fifth of chord.

Also note the use of extended chords beginning at **SP m. 146**. The minor ninth chord at **SP m. 148** is typical of Haydn and also of Beethoven who was to use it later as a powerful agent for musical drama. (See the Score Profile in Chapter 3 **SP m. 610**.)

The keys used in the scheme of modulation are expected and fairly routine. They are:

1. G major (tonic) several times
2. D major (dominant)
3. B minor
4. E minor

Haydn also touches briefly on G minor, the tonic minor **SP m. 20–23**, and D minor, the dominant minor **SP m. 57–65**. These last provide a darkening element, setting off the sunny, zesty music to fine advantage.

Inversion of chords is delicately handled by the fastidious Haydn. Note the score detail of **SP m. 61–65**, where no fewer than seven of the nine chords are heard in inverted position. Cadences are sturdy and clear throughout, and are primarily authentic cadences and half cadences. Examine **SP m. 30–32** for one that is typically Haydnesque.

For reference and review

New terms in the order presented:

harmony
chord progression
chords
horizontal
linear
vertical
tertian
triad
root
extended chords
fundamental, close position
bass
inverted
spacing

tessitura
block chords
open position
arpeggios
broken chords
progression
changes
regression
cadence
authentic cadence
half cadence
plagal cadence
deceptive or evasive cadence
modulation

6

More than one melody: polyphony

THE TERM POLYPHONY, as derived from the Greek, means *many voices*. Its usage, in musical terminology, denotes the combining and blending of two or more melodic lines. These lines may or may not be imitative. Voices or parts are distinguishable as separate melodies in direct proportion to the extent to which:

1. The "rhythmic diagrams" differ: this refers to both the lengths of notes and their moments of articulation.
2. The melodic contours differ.

As explained in Chapter 5, melody is linear and harmony is vertical. Therefore, polyphony—as a combination of melodies—is a multiple exposure of linear facets plus the concurrent tension and release inherent in simultaneous relationships. Polyphony is the most sophisticated of all musical procedures.

Homophony refers to the homogeneity of texture that results from the rhythmic simultaneity of the voices. The Greek word, *homo*, used as a prefix, means "the same." In homophony the notes of the various parts are articulated at the same time, and therefore sound like a harmonization of the melody and have no rhythmic independence of their own.

It may be shown that when any chords are played in succession, the ear seeks to find the melody in the highest pitched tones, regarding any of the notes lower in pitch as only a reinforcement or thickening of the notes on top. A simple experiment at the keyboard will illustrate. Play several chords on the piano at random, as in Example 208. The ear hears the notes in Example 209 as the melody. The har-

Example 208

Example 209

monizations found in songbooks or hymnals are usually homophonic. "America the Beautiful" may serve as an example (Example 210). This

Example 210   America the Beautiful, Ward

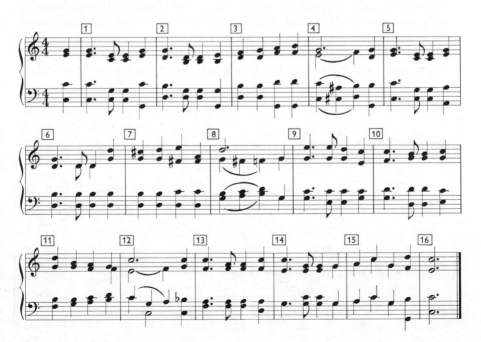

is almost pure homophony. The articulations are not in opposition, except briefly in measures 4, 8, and 12.

Even in homophony there is usually an attempt to keep each voice part somewhat interesting by making its melodic contour different from that of the others. These differences in melodic contour may be seen in "America the Beautiful" by inspection of the parts. Note particularly the bass part, beginning with the upbeat to measure 9. Beginning here, and continuing through measures 9, 10, and 11, this part assumes a greater degree of individuality through its imitation of the soprano part in measures 1, 2, and 3. But whatever differences of melodic contour there may be among the four voices, they are of minimal importance in any attempt to achieve a polyphonic style if the rhythmic articulations are simultaneous.

This vertical aspect of homophony refers to the chordal sound of the moment. What is this sound I hear, this piling up of tone upon tone to produce this as-of-the-moment effect? This became the composer's unstated question in the late nineteenth century. The search was on for the "magic moment." In the most banal sense, this "magic moment" is at the heart of Sullivan's "The Lost Chord." And, as well, it became the question at the heart of many a motion picture seeking in pseudo-seriousness the source of the mystery of a composer's talent.

Music has its magic moments, many of them, but they are not isolated sounds. They are sounds related both vertically and horizontally within a total concept. So, actually, the terms *polyphony* and *homophony* are exaggerations because all music that is more than one melodic line usually contains elements of both polyphony and homophony. The terms are only convenient labels to show the preponderance of either.

Example 211   Chorale, "Wir Christenleut," J. S. Bach

Thus, a Bach chorale is called homophonic that looks like Example
211. And a Bach fugue is called polyphonic that looks like Example
212. Inspection will show that there are some elements of polyphony
and homophony in both.

Example 212   Well Tempered Clavier, Book 1, Fugue 16, J. S. Bach

Applied polyphony

COUNTERPOINT

Polyphony refers to music of any age in which the linear aspect is
predominant. **Counterpoint** is a more specific term that refers to the
planned setting of one melodic line against another.

The term counterpoint is derived from the Latin **punctus contra
punctum**, point against point, i.e., note against note. The common
practice of counterpoint in its early stages was to set another melody, at
first note-to-note, against a melody already in existence, the **cantus
firmus**, the "established tune." Later, more florid melodies were set
against a cantus firmus. The florid melody set above was known as the
descant. Composers throughout the centuries have been intrigued with
the idea of using a theme or melody from sacred or secular literature
as a cantus firmus against which to write counterpoint (Example 213).

The basic idea of counterpoint is that one melody that has certain
note values and a certain melodic contour may be pitted against another melody that differs from it just enough in note values and contour so that the melodies, while being played together, may be heard

Example 213   Missa L'Homme armé, Kyrie I, Dufay

Reprinted with permission of the publishers from Archibald T. Davison and Willi
Apel, *Historical Anthology of Music: Oriental, Medieval and Renaissance Music* (Vol. I).
Cambridge, Mass.: Harvard University Press. Copyright 1946, 1949 by the President and Fellows of Harvard College.

separately as independent entities. *Independent* is not actually the right
term; *interdependent* is better because the pitting of two melodies against
each other admits of a relationship between the two.

The simplest and most concise definition of the term *counterpoint* is
countermelody, a melody written against another. Thus, we may speak
of writing a counterpoint to a melody. The result is one kind of polyphony. The term, in a broader sense, may refer to both melodies in
two-part writing, the expression being that "the voices are in counterpoint," or in "contrapuntal style".

Counterpoint, although de-emphasized during various periods of
music history, has continued to the present day, achieving a new propulsion in the music of some twentieth-century composers. The styles
of counterpoint have changed as the styles of music have changed. Its
style is dependent on many factors, for example, the amount of dissonance and the way it is handled; the amount or kind of imitation
between the parts; the melodic style, which may be vocal or instrumental, and the attendant amount of conjunct or disjunct motion; the
rhythmic emphasis. Thus, we may speak of sixteenth-century counterpoint and eighteenth-century counterpoint as related but different
manifestations within the broad realm of polyphony. Although both
spring from the same seed, they are rather like second cousins.

SIMULTANEOUS MOTION OF VOICES

In the music of any period, there are four possible kinds of motion
between any two parts: parallel, similar, oblique, and contrary.

In *parallel motion*, as the voices move, the intervallic distance between the tones is maintained. Parallel motion may be diatonic (Example 214), or chromatic (Example 215), or a combination of both (Example 216).

Example 214 SP m. 67

Example 215 SP m. 81

Example 216 SP m. 97

In *similar motion*, both parts move in the same direction, but one part moves by a larger interval than the other (Example 217).

Example 217 SP m. 71

In *oblique motion*, One part sustains or repeats as the other part moves (Example 218).

Example 218　　　　　　　　　　　　　　　　　　　　　　　SP m. 56

In *contrary motion*, the parts move in opposite directions; the intervals may be any size (Example 219).

Example 219　　　　　　　　　　　　　　　　　　　　　　　SP m. 56

In any polyphonic texture, the variety of the four types of motion depends upon the purposes of the composer. The use of parallel and similar motions leads toward placidity; oblique and contrary motions impart more dynamism to the texture (Example 220). It sometimes has

Example 220　　　　　　　　　　　　　　　　　　　　　　SP m. 2–4

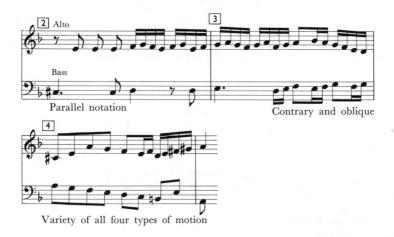

been said that contrary motion is the essence of counterpoint. This is not true. If it were, Example 221 would be exemplary counterpoint.

Example 221

The essence of counterpoint truly lies in the variety of all four types of motion combined with variegated, opposing rhythmic patterns. Example 222 will illustrate this. It shows two measures from the Score Pro-

Example 222   SP m. 88–89

file. Example 223 tabulates the use of the four types of motion between

Example 223   Tabulation of Kinds of Motion

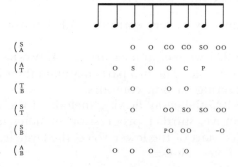

each voice and all other voices. We are leaving the second measure for the reader to analyze.

The four types of motion between each two parts are labeled, using the following abbreviations:

P = parallel motion
S = similar motion
O = oblique motion
C = contrary motion.

The designation of each type of motion is shown at the terminus of the simultaneous motion of each two voices.

The proportions and the variety of the four kinds of motion will vary not only in different periods and works, but also within the same work. You should analyze various works of different periods and compare the effects achieved by different contrapuntal textures.

NON-IMITATIVE POLYPHONY

Polyphony can be in two or more parts. Two-part music is the easiest to listen to, but in some ways the most difficult to write. Two-part writing by its very nature cannot have one voice rest for any considerable length of time. Thus, the unity and variety must be accomplished with a minimum of means.

Two-part writing also excludes any extensive use of parallel and similar motion, as this would tend to reduce the separate individuality of the two parts. The two parts may vary in their comparative importance. In simple two-part writing, one part may consist of basically long notes against which there is a more florid second part.

In three-or-more-part writing, it is possible to give one voice a rest for a short length of time. This accomplishes several things:

1. It changes and lightens the texture.
2. Re-entrance supplies another change of texture by thickening it.
3. Re-entrance by its very entrance adds interest.

In Example 224 we see, in measures 2 – 4, two-part writing that is mostly note against note. The two parts maintain their identities chiefly through their differing melodic contours.

In Example 225 the easily flowing melody of the right hand is set against the expansive, sturdier progression of notes in the left hand. Notice the delayed start of the lower voice, the large leap to the second note, the longer notes values.

Example 224   Piano Sonata, Opus 49, No. 2, Beethoven

Example 225   Microkosmos, Vol. IV, No. 100, "In the Style of a Folk Song,"
                                                          Bartok

Copyright 1940 by Hawkes & Son (London) Ltd. Renewed 1967. Reprinted by
permission of Boosey & Hawkes, Inc.

Example 226 from the opening bars of Ravel's String Quartet, is

Example 226   String Quartet, Ravel

only somewhat polyphonic. The strongest contrast in melodic lines is
found between the violin 1 part and the cello, in both the melodic
contour and the differing rhythmic values. Play these two lines alone on
the piano. However, the overall ascension of both parts somewhat
minimizes the polyphonic effect. Add to this the violin 2 part, which is
paired with the cello part in ascending diatonic parallel tenths. The
effect of the paired parts is one melodic voice rather than two, and the
steady quarter note successions cast a blandness across the whole

texture. This is an excellent example of writing that lies in the middle ground between homophonic and polyphonic styles.

In the Berg Violin Concerto (Example 227), we find the solo violin

Example 227   Violin Concerto, Berg

Used by permission of the Theodore Presser Company and Universal Edition A. G. Vienna.

part at first contrasting mildly with the viola part. During the first two measures, these two parts are playing different portions of the Bach chorale, "Es Ist Genug." The imitation of the viola in measure 1 may be seen in the solo violin in measure 3. Against these two parts the bassoons are playing the twelve-tone row that opens the work.

QUODLIBET

Quodlibet, which means "as you please," is the name given to the process by which two or more melodies, often popular tunes that originally had separate existence, are made to go together. This practice goes back to early music, and has been a part of popular culture until the present day. The first example of quodlibet that comes to mind is the mating of two tunes of American origin. They may be put together with some slight adjustments of the original melodies (Example 228).

Example 228

Dixie, Emmett
Old Folks at Home, Foster

Because they are not only fun, but require some ingenuity, quodlibets are not only found in the popular culture but have been explored by the master musicians as well. The more incongruous the borrowings in either tune or text, the more challenging they are. Quodlibets were one of the favorite pastimes of the Bach family through several generations of family get-togethers. Sacred and secular would be put together, or songs with texts in different languages. Sometimes they were written out; often they were improvised. Quodlibets have found their way into more serious areas as well. Johann Sebastian Bach included a quodlibet at the end of the Goldberg Variations. The bass line shown in Example 229 is the basis of Variation 30. Superimposed on this is a

Example 229   Variation Theme

popular song of Bach's time, "Ich bin so lang," shown in the second measure in the upper part (Example 230), and this is joined by another

Example 230

Ich   bin   so   lang nicht bei dir g'west
I've been so   long a - way from you

popular melody, "Kraut and Rüben" (Example 231). These two melo-

Example 231

Kraut   und   Rü - ben   hab - en   mich ver - trie - ben
Kale   and   beets have driv- en   me   a - way

dies constantly reappear in different voices throughout the variation (Example 232).

Mozart's letters show his facile mind playing with words. He would invent nonsense rhyming words, or he might write part of his letter backwards, or he might write in a mixture of Italian, French, and German. His facility in writing music and his facility with words sprang from the same well. What would be more natural for Mozart, or more

Example 232   Goldberg Variations, Variation 30: Quodlibet, J. S. Bach

characteristic of his personality, than a quodlibet-like structure? He writes one, combining three tunes in different rhythms, at the end of Act I of *Don Giovanni*. (Also see Chapter 3.)

Wagner has utilized the idea of quodlibet in his overture to *Die Meistersinger*. Three themes are introduced separately and then continued later. The very first notes of the opening theme sound with full orchestra (Example 233). In measure 40, the familiar flourish of the

Example 233   Overture, *Die Meistersinger*, Wagner

brass introduces this theme of martial character (Example 234). The

Example 234

mood changes, and at measure 97 the violins present the lyric theme (Example 235) from Walther's "Prize Song." Having established the identities of the themes separately, Wagner combines them (Example 236).

Example 235

Example 236

CANON

The strictest kind of polyphonic writing is the **canon**. The term *canon* (meaning *rule*) originally was not a title specifying a certain style as does *waltz*, or a certain form as does *rondo*, but was rather an *instruction* by which one voice was to be imitated by another in some specific way. This was the *canon* for that particular piece of music. Therefore, it was necessary to write out one melody only; the other was to be supplied by the performer according to the instruction. It was later that *canon* became a generic term referring to any composition in which the basic principle is *strict imitation throughout*.

Two things must be known about how the second voice should combine with the first:

1. What note it should start on.
2. When it should start.

One of the simplest two-part canons has intrigued many composers. This is the "Alphabet Song," also known as "Twinkle, Twinkle, Little Star."

Example 237   "The Alphabet Song"

If the melody only (Example 237) is given, with the instructions "at the unison," and "with a time-lapse of one measure" the realization will sound as shown in Example 238.

Example 238   Canon: "The Alphabet Song"

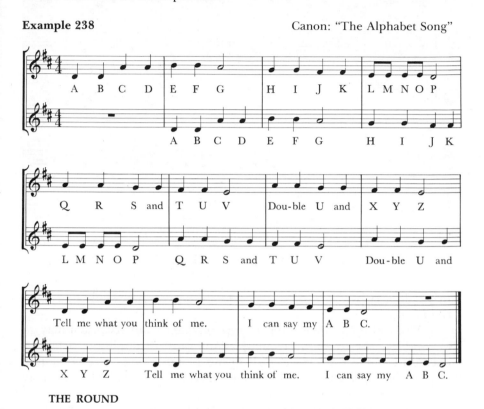

THE ROUND

The simplest kind of canon is the **_round_**, in the performance of which each voice continually returns to the beginning immediately upon the completion of the tune. The round consists of one melody only, but beginning the melody again in other voices sets the melody against itself, creating counterpoint. A round may be in two, three, or four parts, or sometimes more. Most readers of this text have sung *Three Blind Mice*, or *Row, Row, Row Your Boat*. *Frère Jacques* (Example 239) is another of the best known rounds. Since this is a simple round, each voice entrance is on the same note, middle *C*. The entrances in this case are spoken of as being "at the unison." After the initial start of the tune, the other entrances are successively two measures later. Thus, the entrances are spoken of as being "at a distance of two measures." So, in speaking of this particular round, we say in sum that the entrances are "at the unison at a distance of two measures." The second entry of a round could also begin upon a different tone, such as a fifth above the

Example 239   "Frère Jacques," French Round

original entry of the subject. This entry would then be spoken of as "at the fifth."

A round is an *infinite canon* (or *perpetual canon*) because it may go on and on, its terminus coming about only through the arbitrary decision to allow each voice to drop out in succession, or to come to a stop at some predetermined point wherever the individual voices may be.

A *finite canon* does not return to the beginning but continues on until it is desired to close, in which case the imitation must be broken, the voices concluding in free counterpoint. These last measures of free counterpoint are spoken of as the *codetta*.

Example 240 shows a perpetual canon by Bach on a far different scale. Note the different clefs. The numbers indicate the entrances at different pitches in succession, and the "holds" show the termination point in each voice after the round has been repeated one or more times. A realization of the first three measures (Example 241) shows the successive entrances of each part a perfect fifth higher.

CONTRAPUNTAL TECHNIQUES

Canon is such a strict procedure that various devices were employed to loosen the strictness of direct imitation. One of the simplest

Example 240   Perpetual Canon: Pleni Sunt, J. S. Bach

Example 241   Partial Realization: Pleni Sunt, J. S. Bach

of these was *inversion.* This device maintains rhythmic unity while changing the melodic contour so that it is exactly opposite. Another common practice in contrapuntal textures, especially canon, is to put the melody in reverse. This is *retrograde* motion. When the melody in the counterpoint is in retrograde, the term ***crab canon*** is used, because of the appearance a crab gives of walking backwards. The ultimate that can be done to a melody, still within the limits of imitation, is to write it both backwards and upside down simultaneously. This is *retrograde inversion.* A further testing of technique is to be found in the ***puzzle***

Example 242   Canon, per Augmentationem, contrario moto, The Art of Fugue,
J. S. Bach

canon. The single melody was written out in full, but no instructions were given as to the pitch or time lapse of the other voices.

However, the listener does not have to perceive all of the techniques of the composer, as in a play he does not need to know the techniques of building suspense, in order to enjoy the effect and to feel the cohesiveness of the whole. The devices or techniques are there for the composer to use to the extent that he sees fit. And they are only devices or techniques. The musical result, the quality of the work, as in any work of art, rests upon a broader base and is far more than the sum of the parts. It cannot be defined or explained. Analysis can only point the way.

There is no question that these devices and techniques at times become, for some composers, a snare in that they become entrapped in the technique, losing sight of the total concept. As well as being a trap for a lesser composer, these technical devices became a source of enjoyment for the greater composer and served him well as a subordinate device within his total concept.

Augmentation, diminution, and varied forms of these have been common in canonic writing because the principle of unity with variety is at the heart of these "altered imitations." An example of inversion and augmentation combined — "inverse augmentation" — may be seen in the canon following Contrapunctus No. 13 in Bach's *Art of Fugue* (Example 242). Each melodic tone has been numbered for easy reference in comparing the voices.

Motivic variation techniques are fully discussed in Chapter 7.

INVERTIBLE COUNTERPOINT

Invertible counterpoint refers to any two voices that are so written that later the parts can be inverted with felicitous results. The parts are inverted as intervals are inverted: the upper and the lower parts exchange their positions.

The question to be posed is, do the two parts in this inverted position still maintain the quality of "good" counterpoint within the style? This qualitative judgment of good counterpoint may be determined by ear and by analysis. Does the inverted counterpoint have a reasonably similar proportion of consonance and dissonance at strong and weak points to the original?

It is common to transpose either or both parts by the interval of an octave, but any interval of transposition may be used for either part, so long as their positions are interchanged.

In Example 243, from Mendelssohn, the tenors begin the ascend-

Example 243   Elijah, "He watching over Israel," Mendelssohn

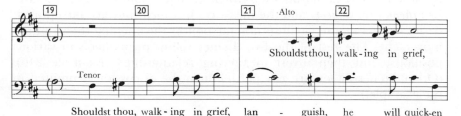

Shouldst thou, walk - ing in grief, lan - guish, he will quick-en

ing subject in measure 19 and are joined by the altos in measure 21 to produce two-part counterpoint. In measure 23 (Example 244) the

Example 244

Shouldst thou, walk-ing in grief

subject of measure 19 is transposed up an octave, and is sung by the sopranos. The subject previously presented by the altos in measure 21 is now transposed down an octave and is sung by the basses, beginning in measure 25. The tenor and alto parts continue in free counterpoint in measure 23 and following, but are not shown. As was done with the example from Hindemith, check consonance and dissonance by tabulation or listening.

Composers use imitation and inversion in all kinds of writing, from the strictest canon to writing in a basically free style. These devices are one of the means of unifying the material, and may be introduced at length or just briefly.

Invertible counterpoint for two voices is called **double counterpoint.** Double counterpoint may also occur in a three-voice or four-voice texture, where two of the voices are invertible. When it is possible for each of three voices to be above or below each of the other two voices, we have **triple counterpoint.** In similar fashion, we may have **quadruple** or **quintuple counterpoint.** The last is quite rare, as you may well imagine. However, Mozart, in the coda of the fourth movement of the "Jupiter" Symphony, combines five themes, presented earlier, so that they may be interchanged in all combinations. It is so artfully done that the listener may be hardly aware of it at first. Example 245 shows the five **themes** or **subjects** and the measures in which they are introduced. At measure 369, the violin section introduces the opening theme of the movement. The rest of the five themes follow on its heels in various positions, and then invert in varying relationships (Example 246). (Other orchestra texture not pertinent to the discussion is omitted in the example.)

Example 245   Symphony No. 41 ("Jupiter"), K. 551, Movement 4, Mozart

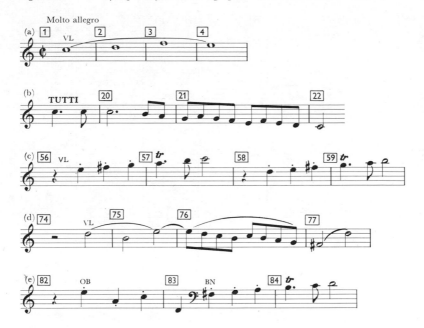

Example 246   Symphony No. 41 ("Jupiter"), K. 551, Movement 4, Mozart

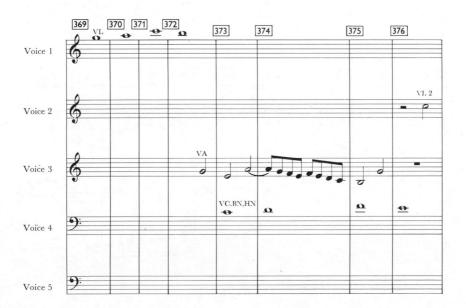

Example 246, cont.

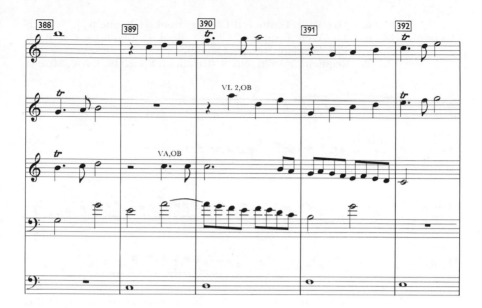

The process of fugue

The Latin term *fuga*, meaning *flight*, was in use in the sixteenth century in connection with canonic writing. The idea of one voice fleeing from the other is more aptly stated as one voice being the leader and the imitating voice being the follower.

The *fugue* when spoken of today refers to the development that reached its peak in the writings of Johann Sebastian Bach. The fugue differs from the canon in certain important aspects. It is not confined to strict imitation, but rather uses imitation as a "springboard" into areas in which there is a freer "transliteration" of the melodic materials than strict imitation would allow.

THE SUBJECT

The chief characteristic of the fugue is that it "grows" out of one theme called the **subject**, which is of moderate length (Example 247). The subject may be somewhat shorter or longer than those in Example 247, but there are two length requirements.

1. It must be long enough to be distinctive as a theme.
2. It must not be so long as to be diffuse.

This single theme becomes the "material" for the entire fugue.

Example 247
- **a.** The Well Tempered Clavier, Book II Fugue 6, J. S. Bach
- **b.** The Well Tempered Clavier, Book II Fugue 18, J. S. Bach
- **c.** The Messiah, No. 28, Handel
- **d.** Requiem, K. 626, No. 1 (Requiem) **Sp m. 49**, Kyrie, Mozart

The fugue retains one of the basic characteristics of contrapuntal writing: the "overlapping of melodies." A melodic cadence in a single voice does not result in a "cadential feeling," since the melody in another voice is already on its way. Thus, a fugue may not be sectionalized.

The fugue, like the canon, is a style of writing, or a "procedure." It is not a form, but it does have some formal aspects, which the canon does not. In a fugue there are three important areas of interest: *fugue exposition, working-out area*, and *closure*.

FUGUE PROCEDURE

Fugue Exposition.   In the exposition, the subject is presented at least once in all voices. There is tonic-dominant emphasis.

Working-out Area.   The second important area consists of the working out of melodic materials, using various contrapuntal techniques, and exploration of other keys. The working-out area may be any length.

Closure.   In the closure, one voice returns to the subject in the home key; others may follow. There may be homophonic emphasis near the close, and there are one or more cadences in the home key.

FUGUE EXPOSITION

Since the *fugue exposition* consists of the presentation of the *subject* in succession in each voice, the subject would naturally make its entry four times in a four-voiced fugue. Sometimes, however, the composer wishes to maké a fifth statement of the subject for emphasis before moving into the working-out area. This will be discussed shortly.

Example 248 shows the subject presented first in the tenor voice.

Example 248   Well Tempered Clavier, Book 1, Fugue 5, J. S. Bach

One measure and a half later the subject is presented in the alto. But there is an important difference in these two presentations. The first

entry begins on 1. The second entry begins on 5; this is a translocation of the subject. Tovey speaks of this shift in the location of the subject in this way: "The term answer is usually reserved for those entries of the subject that are placed in what may be called the 'complementary' position of the scale, whether they are tonal or not." This translocation we will refer to as the **subject transfer**, or simply **transfer**. Most textbooks use the term **answer**, but we do not feel that this describes the procedure, which is patently to *expose the subject* in each voice in succession. For convenience in labeling, the following abbreviations will be used:

S/1.   Subject begins on first degree of the scale
S/5.   Subject begins on fifth degree of the scale

There is a **brief extension** (often called **codetta**) of musical materials during the duet between the tenor and the alto before the third entry of the subject. This brief extension is usually **free counterpoint**, that is, non-imitative. The third entry in the Bach example is in the soprano, and the subject is again on "one," but now an octave higher than the first entry. The fourth entry is in the bass; the subject is on "five" and is an octave lower than the second entry. Thus, the subject has been presented four times in the order of *subject, subject transfer, subject, subject transfer.*

This is the most usual method of introducing the subject; but there are exceptions, one of which is Fugue 1 from Book I of the *Well Tempered Clavier*. In this case, the subject is presented in this manner: *subject, subject transfer, subject transfer, subject.* The voices chosen for the various presentations of the subject in the fugue exposition may be in any order.

In certain fugues, after the subject is introduced by each voice, there is an additional statement of the subject in the tonic. This is called an **extra entry**. Its purpose may be to emphasize the tonality, or to have the subject stated in tonic with all of the other voices involved, which heretofore was not possible.

A further point should be made with regard to the exposition of the subject. When the second entry of the subject conforms exactly in shape to the first entry, it may be spoken of as a **real transfer**. This is true in the fugue we have been discussing. The intervals need conform generically only, and this conformity is quickly apparent visually. However, in the second entry in many fugues there is often a small intervallic adjustment for purposes of maintaining the tonic-dominant relationship. This may be spoken of as a **tonal transfer**, and can be seen in the Score Profile, beginning at measure 52.

Note that the interval between the second and third notes of the first entry of the subject **SP m. 49** is a *third*. In the second entry of the subject, **SP m. 52–53** shows the interval of a *second* between the second and third notes. A *real transfer* of the subject, instead of this *tonal transfer* would have thrown the second entry outside of the tonic-dominant relationship that Mozart is establishing.

During the second entry of the subject (the *subject transfer*), the subject continues in counterpoint against this second entry. This will be referred to as the **continuation of the subject** and may be labeled "C/S." It lasts only as long as the subject transfer lasts. If, in addition, this continuation of the subject maintains its identity melodically and is presented in combination with each new entry of the subject, it is then specifically a **countersubject**, labeled "CS," and will often appear throughout the fugue combining with the subject. Subject and countersubject are usually written in double counterpoint.

EXTENSION

After all of the entries in the fugue exposition have been made there is usually some material in free counterpoint. This material does not contain any complete statements of the subject. It may be a spinning out of the previous materials or it may be considered as an interim passage before the subject is presented again. Since this material is a relaxation from the successive entrances of the subject in different voices it is more informal in character. For this reason we believe that the term *episode*, usually used to designate this material, is misleading. We shall use the term *extension*, which we think more correctly describes the activity. The extension leads from the end of the exposition to the beginning of the working-out area.

WORKING-OUT AREA

The extension concludes and the working-out area is entered at the next presentation of the subject. It is in the working-out area that the composer has room for the freest play in the presentation of the subject.

The tonic key is generally avoided, as is the formality of subject entrances found in the exposition. The entrances of the subject may now be at quicker or longer time intervals. The subject may be shortened or otherwise transformed. The various devices of contrapuntal writing may be employed. And it is in this area also that stretto is often used.

At the end of the working-out area there may be another digression away from the presentation of the subject in the form of an extension.

CLOSURE

Closure begins, as a rule, when the subject is presented much as it was at the beginning. It may be somewhat changed by different note values or a slight change in its contour, or it may be a shortened version. This entrance may even be part of a stretto section. But the key emphasis will be tonic. And various entrances of the subject, although not as formal as in the exposition, will ultimately serve to confirm the tonality of the home key. This affirmation, often combined with a texture that is more homophonic, brings the fugue to a close.

Composers, on occasion, use two *combining subjects* on which to construct a fugue. This is a *double fugue*, and the Mozart fugue in the Score Profile is an example of it (Example 249). For purposes of analysis, the following labels are convenient: S = Subject, SS = Subsidiary Subject.

Example 249   **SP m. 49**, Mozart

STRETTO

Our English word *strait* has the same origin as the Italian term *stretto*, meaning *narrow* or *tight*. Stretto refers to various entries of the subject in such a short space of time that one statement of the subject is not complete before the next entry is begun. (The subject may appear intact or it may be shortened or changed.) Stretto creates excitement and tension and thickens the texture. The composer may use stretto anywhere in a work, but because of its inherent dynamism it often occurs in the last half of the fugue. This may be seen in **SP m. 82 – 85**. Note, however, Bach's use of stretto in the exposition of Fugue 5 of Book I, shown above in Example 248.

Requiem Mass K. 626, "Kyrie" from Section I, Mozart

The Requiem was commissioned anonymously by Count Walsegg to be presented as his own composition in memory of his wife. It was Mozart's last work, written in Vienna in December, 1791. Although he did not live to complete it, it is a part of his crowning achievement. The entire Section I was Mozart's, and Süssmayer, a disciple of Mozart, who completed the work after Mozart's death, saw fit to conclude the Requiem in the hand of Mozart rather than his own. So the Kyrie fugue may be heard again as the concluding section of the "Agnus Dei."

Orchestra:

2 Basset Horns
2 Bassoons (BN)
2 Trumpets (TR)
3 Trombones (TB)

2 Timpani (TIMP)

Violins (VL 1, 2)
Violas (VA)
Violoncellos (VC)
Contrabasses (CB)

Organ

Voices:

Soprano
Alto
Tenor
Bass

Process: Fugue.

SCORE PROFILE

FUGUE EXPOSITION

Listening notes

The opening measures of the Requiem in *fugato* style prepare
the way for the Kyrie fugue, which forms the second part of Section I
SP m. 49.

The *Kyrie* is a double fugue. Since, in the fugue exposition, the
subject and subsidiary subject are *always* combined, in these Listening
Notes it will be convenient to speak of the subject only. The three-
and-a-half-measure subject is first stated by the basses (and accompanying instruments not shown). The subject begins on 5 and the
harmony is tonic-centered **SP m. 49—52.**

Since the emphasis must be tonal, there are two factors involved in
the second entry. First, the transfer must begin on 1. Second, the
harmony must be dominant-centered. To meet both of these obliga-
tions, there is a small adjustment in the contour of the second entry.
This results in a *tonal transfer* **SP m. 52—55**. Note the third entry of the
subject on 5, now in the alto **SP m. 56**, and the fourth entry on 1 in the
tenor **SP m. 59**.

Having stated the subject in each of the four voices, the fugue
exposition is complete. Beginning at **SP m. 63** there is a short extension
in free counterpoint for one and one half measures.

As the extension is concluding, the working-out area is entered
with a statement of the subject in the soprano. Beginning with this
statement, note the various entrances of the subject and the avoidance
of the tonic key: the subject is presented successively in F major **SP m.
64**, in G minor **SP m. 68**, in C minor **SP m. 71**, in B ♭ major twice, **SP m.
75** and **SP m. 77**, and in F minor in a shortened version **SP m. 80**, with
the subsidiary subject always accompanying the subject. This shortened
version of the subject prepares the way for a second extension, which
begins in the second half of **SP m. 81**. Here the bass entrance, which at
first appears to be the subsidiary subject in its normal relation to the
subject, turns out to be a shortened transformation of the subsidiary
subject. Note the chromatic character of this transformation as compared to the diatonic character of the actual subsidiary subject.

Mozart now proceeds with the transformed subsidiary subject,
without the subject, in stretto during five measures **SP m. 82—86**. This
produces a constant increase in rhythmic and dramatic tension that
explodes on the downbeat of **SP m. 87**. In this measure the tonic key is
definitely re-established and the closure begins.

The subject and subsidiary subject resume their normal roles. The
subject is presented in the bass in the tonic key **SP m. 87**, but note that
it now begins with a syncopation. The subject is stated again in the
tonic key with a syncopation in the alto voice in the second half of **SP**

m. 91. This turns out to be the shortened version, however. Does this suggest the transformed subsidiary subject? Yes. Mozart again goes into stretto, but this time tonic-centered. The stretto continues through three measures, leading us to the final four measures, which bring the fugue to an end in a powerful homophonic close.

For reference and review

New terms in the order presented:

polyphony
homophony
counterpoint
punctus contra punctum
cantus firmus
descant
countermelody
parallel motion
similar motion
oblique motion
contrary motion
quodlibet
canon
round
infinite canon
perpetual canon
finite canon
inversion
retrograde
crab canon
retrograde inversion
puzzle canon
augmentation
diminution
invertible counterpoint
double counterpoint

triple counterpoint
quadruple counterpoint
quintuple counterpoint
theme
subject
fugue
fugue exposition
working-out area
closure
subject transfer
transfer
answer
brief extension
codetta
free counterpoint
extra entry
real transfer
tonal transfer
continuation of the subject
countersubject
episode
extension
double fugue
stretto
fugato

7

Unity
with variety:
musical form

MUSIC IS THE most abstract of the arts.
　　Each tone glows, sometimes flames, then perishes to make
room for those yet to come. Where has it gone? Time must elapse
for music to be. The ear must not only assimilate several tones
sounded together, but also remember the ones that came before
and anticipate those coming. Otherwise the music is not intelligible. A work may only fill out a few seconds or it may span several
hours, but whatever its length, the listener must remember and
relate. He *must* abstract.

　　And beyond this, music, unlike painting or sculpture, must be
recreated each time it is heard. Thus, the musical thoughts of the
past masters are not directly available to an audience, but must
first be filtered through the personality of a conductor, a soloist,
or an ensemble. These recreations, or interpretations, necessarily
will vary with each performance and with each individual performer or performers. In other words, performers will not play a
piece twice in the same way, nor will different performers play it
the same. The listener, then, besides remembering and relating
tones that flit by and then vanish, is faced with trying to assimilate
and understand the whole composition, which is never heard the
same way twice in live performance.

　　But despite this and without getting into a discussion of
musical aesthetics, we will assume that it is patently evident to

everyone that there is "meaning" in music: music does make sense. Despite its ephemeral, abstract nature, individual compositions are the vehicles for vivid communication from composer to listener. This communication can never be completely understood or analyzed, but nevertheless it is unquestionably felt to exist. The pervading force that makes this communication possible is *musical form*.

We then will define musical form as the organization of tones progressing in time into patterns and shapes that the listener may relate and assimilate into a meaningful whole. The myriad formal structural patterns that exist and continue to be developed simply articulate the communication—emotional, aesthetic, intellectual—that the composer wishes to express.

Unity with variety

Slowly and painstakingly forms have evolved such as sonata, opera, rondo, theme and variations, etc. These are not only treated differently by different composers, but varied enormously by the individual composers themselves. Beethoven, for example, in his nine symphonies used sonata-allegro form for separate movements over and over again, but never in precisely the same way. There is great freedom and transformation in his use of this formal structure from symphony to symphony.

However, underlying the great diversity in his formal structures are a certain few principles that operate constantly. Of these, the most important are *unity with variety*. These are present also in all music. How this is handled is one test of the composer.

UNITY

Unity is provided primarily by repetition. It occurs constantly and on many levels. *Themes, motives*, rhythmic figures, chordal patterns and textures, *sections* of movements, etc.—all tend to be heard more than once in a composition. Example 250 clearly shows repetition as a basic structural principle bonding all of the notes into a cohesive whole. First, you will note the accompaniment patterns played by the pianist's left hand. The first one, measures 1–7, consists of a broken chord pattern (Example 251), played legato, and repeated almost on every beat. The next accompaniment pattern, measures 8–11, also consists of a chord outline (Example 252), but more active in feeling through the use of repeated notes played staccato. This pattern covers two beats. The pattern in measures 13–16 repeats exactly that heard before in measures 4–7.

Example 250

Rondo, Opus 51, No. 1, Beethoven

Example 251

Example 252

The uniformity and repetition of these figures provide homogeneity of background material, allowing the ear to concentrate on the melody above. Further note that the first 10 tones of the melody (Example 253) form a musical idea that is heard three times in exactly the

Example 253

same way through the short 16 measures of the excerpt. Another idea is heard beginning in measure 8 (Example 254), and is repeated imme-

Example 254

diately in the following measure with a slight alteration of the melodic contour. These melodic repetitions provide unity by allowing the ear to remember, compare, and relate.

Beyond all of this, overall unity is assured by the use of a simple structural plan: Statement A, + Statement B, + second half of Statement A. Measures 1–8 form a homogeneous statement labeled "A." Measures 9–13 form a contrasted Statement B. Measures 14–17 repeat exactly the last part of Statement A. Repetition in chord structure is particularly evident. The tonic triad, C-E-G, is heard 16 times; the dominant (triad or dominant seventh chord) is heard 14 times.

Thus, we see a homogeneous accompaniment consisting of many

repetitions of simple chord patterns, buttressing a melody that primarily revolves around two short musical ideas. And beyond this there is a superstructure, a simple overall circular design, symbolized by the letters A B A. The music flows and expands while repetitions on several levels provide for definition and cohesion.

VARIETY

Contrast.   Variety occurs through contrast. The ear needs to hear musical elements again, but it wants to hear them fresh. It also wants to experience the unexpected, the sharply different. A highly unified composition — for example, one built upon a single motive, a single rhythmic pattern, a single chordal texture — will be stale and uninteresting to the ear unless it is permeated with strong contrasts or variation.

Contrast comes in a great many ways. To name but a few of the most important, it may occur through change of chord, key, texture, articulation, melodic contour, range, rhythm, instrumentation, tempo, or form.

If we refer back to Example 250, we can see in Statement B considerable contrast relative to what came before and comes after. While A is *legato*, B is more nervous in sound, using much *staccato*. Motive 2 in B contrasts with motive 1 in A. Intervallically, it is disjunct, while motive 1 is conjunct. Note also the extension of melodic range in B as the thinning texture carries the musical thought into the high soprano register, and then down again. This also supplies contrast to A. B, markedly contrasted to A, provides diversion and fresh sound to the ear. The listener then relishes all the more the partial return of A.

Variation.   Contrast also comes with variation, the very essence of which lies in identity with change. The substance of this chapter, in fact, deals with this primary musical function. (See *transformation, variation techniques*, and *development* below.) All of the variation techniques described show the manifold ways that have been developed to satisfy the ear's need for identity with change. Variation techniques indeed point up the essential polarity of unity and contrast that exists in all of music.

A composition cannot be successful without both unity and variety operating in some kind of balance. We have said that music that emphasizes homogeneity at the expense of variety will be uninteresting. We now can state that it will be not only dull, but also unsuccessful.

The reverse is true as well. A piece that emphasizes variety at the expense of unity will be unintelligible and meaningless. All effective music, even the most simple, mixes unifying and contrasted elements.

The greatest masterpieces possess both in perfect balance. This can be seen and felt by studying and analyzing in detail any of the Score Profiles in this book.

Melodic elements

THE MOTIVE

A motive is a short, seminal, melodic idea. It usually spans two to several tones. It can be aphoristic, perhaps standing by itself at the head of a composition heralding the approach of important things to come (Example 255), or it can mesh with other motives to form a larger statement (Example 256).

Example 255   Symphony No. 4, Opus 36, Movement 1, Tchaikovsky

Example 256   Rondo in D, Mozart

Motives are usually striking and graphic: easily recognized and remembered (Examples 257 and 258). Often they outline triadic shapes

Example 257   Symphony No. 3, Opus 55 ("Eroica"), Movement 1, Beethoven

Example 258   *Egmont* Overture, Opus 84, Beethoven

(Example 259). Sometimes they are very brief (Example 260), other

Example 259   Symphony No. 8, Opus 88, Dvorak

Example 260   *La Tosca*, Scarpia's Motive, Act I, Puccini

times rather extended (Example 261). But the important thing to see about motives is that though they usually spearhead the musical thought, they are only building blocks, vital musical components within a larger design.

Example 261   *Madama Butterfly*, Love Motive, Act I, Puccini

It is sometimes possible to dissect the motive into a smaller melodic structure called a *figure*. The figure is also seen to be at the basis of many non-thematic passages, which then are said to be figurative in character.

THE THEME

A theme has more extension than a motive. It can be a complete musical statement (Example 262). It can be neatly tailored and clipped

Example 262   Variations in C Minor, Beethoven

in a symmetrical sixteen-measure frame (Example 263), or it can ramble on (Example 264).

Example 263   Waltz, Opus 34, No. 2, Chopin

Example 264   Rhapsody on a Theme of Paganini, Opus 43, Rachmaninoff

Used by permission of Charles Foley, Inc. Copyright 1934, copyright renewed. International copyright secured.

The term *theme* itself is rather loosely used by composers. When the form is labeled "theme and variations," the theme itself, whether written by the composer himself or taken from another source, is often extensive enough to display one of several simple forms to be discussed below, such as binary or ternary.

In general, a theme is a melodically striking component of a composition as distinguished from the more figurative, less melodic elements. The motive, usually shorter, will often itself be a component in the structure of the theme. **Subject**, as previously seen, is the specific term for the theme of a **fugue** and of related contrapuntal forms. It sometimes is used interchangeably for theme in other forms.

A **tune** is a simple melody easily played, sung, and remembered. Intervals in its construction are largely diatonic, with limited range, and the whole will be more complete in feeling than either a motive or a theme.

MOTIVE TRANSFORMATION

We have already touched on the primary importance of variation to achieve variety and extension in musical composition. We now will discuss basic techniques used. A simple motive (Example 265) here will be treated in various techniques.

Example 265   "Clementine"

1. A Motive may be repeated immediately (Example 266).

Example 266   Silent Night, Gruber

2. A most common transformation technique is called *sequence*. The motive is repeated immediately, but on different scale steps (Example 267). The pattern of each

Example 267

sequence in Example 267 is down a third—up a fourth —but others are possible (Example 268).

Example 268   Well Tempered Clavier, Book I, Prelude 12, J. S. Bach

3. *Rhythmic variation* is heard when one or more of the motive's durational values are altered while the pitches remain the same. What results is a change of rhythmic pattern. And rhythmic pattern being one of the dominant elements in music, it can be easily seen that minor alterations in note values will result in major variation effects. (Examples 269 and 270).

Example 269

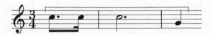

Example 270   Symphonie Fantastique, Movements 1, 5, Berlioz

4. *Augmentation*, a form of rhythmic variation, occurs when the durational value of each tone of the motive is lengthened, usually by the same durational value. The duration is often doubled for each tone (Examples 271 and 272).

Example 271

Example 272   Well Tempered Clavier, Book I, Fugue 8, J. S. Bach

Augmentation, of course, cannot be confused with change of tempo. It occurs only when the augmented motive is heard in the same tempo as is the original motive. Thus, the ear will compare and distinguish motive and its augmentation only if there is a common tempo for both. The net effect produced by augmentation is that of slackening of melodic motion despite the constant overall pace of the beat.

5. *Diminution* is the inverse of augmentation: the durational

values are shortened rather than lengthened (Examples 273 and 274).

Example 273

Example 274   Symphonie Fantastique, Movement 5, Berlioz

Example 275

6. **Intervallic variation** occurs when one or more of the intervals of the motive are altered. Intervals are either expanded or contracted (Examples 275 and 276).

Example 276

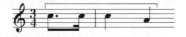

Often certain intervals are altered slightly so that the motive is heard in a different mode.

The change is often from the major to the minor, as in Example 277, but changes from minor to major, or from any mode to any other, are also possible.

7. A type of intervallic variation frequently seen is termed **inversion** (Example 278). Inversion may go in either direction, up or down (Example 279).

8. **Retrograde** occurs when the notes and durational values of the motive are heard in reverse order (Example 280).

Example 277   Symphony No. 88, Movement 4, Haydn

(a) Motive in D major

(b) Motive in D minor

Example 278

Example 279   Art of the Fugue, Contrapunctus I, III, J. S. Bach

(a) Subject, contrapunctus I

(b) Inversion, contrapunctus III

Example 280

9. One variation technique frequently seen is called ***orna-mentation***. Extra notes are added to the motive, resulting in considerable change in its contour (Examples 281 and 282).

Example 281

Example 282   Sonata K. 331, Movement 1, Mozart

(a) Motive

(b) Ornamentation, variation I

OTHER CHANGES

A motive may give the effect of being altered without actually being so. For example, supporting harmonies may change drastically, or counterpoints may be altered, added, or removed. Though pitches and durational values may remain unchanged, the motive will sound different because its environment will be different.

Changes of tempo, key, or timbre of the instrument or voice involved can also alter the motive's effect considerably without there being changes within the tones themselves.

COMBINED VARIATION TECHNIQUES

Often a motive is treated by several variation techniques simultaneously. For example, a motive is sometimes heard in retrograde inversion (see Chapter 6). Or it can undergo simultaneous intervallic and rhythmic variation. When enough of these techniques are applied at once, the ear is hard put to recognize the original at all. Indeed, late Romantics such as Wagner, Richard Strauss, and Liszt (Example 283)

Example 283   Sonata in B minor, Liszt

(a) Motive
Allegro vivace

(b) Transformation
Cantando espressivo

used simultaneous variation techniques — termed ***thematic transformation*** — as the cornerstone for many of their most important works.

Units of form

Thus far we have dealt with materials—motive and theme—that in themselves do not provide cohesion and definition to musical forms; they are not easily measured. They may be compared to ideas that permeate accepted literary forms. For example, the idea suggested by the title of Emerson's essay, "Self Reliance," does not by itself result in meaningful literary communication. This communication only happens when this and other ideas are developed and made articulate through the author's use of clear language and logic of statement conditioned by the structural principles of the literary form itself.

In the same way, motives and themes—the melodic "ideas" of a musical work—are made articulate in a total work only by the use of certain units of form. For purposes of analysis, these formal units may be measured according to the number of measures they span and named according to function. From smallest to largest, these units are: phrase, period, part, section, movement.

THE PHRASE

The *phrase* is the smallest formal unit in music. It can be compared in sentence structure to a phrase which, though clear in meaning, yet is incomplete. The phrase varies considerably in measure length according to the style of the music. Asymmetric measure groupings such as 3, 5, 7, etc., are often encountered, especially in folk music and in contemporary works. But very often the phrase's structure will fall into the close-cropped framework of a four-measure unit, as in Examples 284 and 285. This square, four-measure phrase often leads

Example 284   Auld Lang Syne

Example 285   The Chase, Burgmüller

to another answering phrase, the whole then suggesting a larger formal unit called a *period*.

When the first questioning phrase ends on a half cadence as in Example 286, it is termed the *antecedent*. Its answer, punctuated by an authentic cadence, then becomes the *consequent*.

Example 286

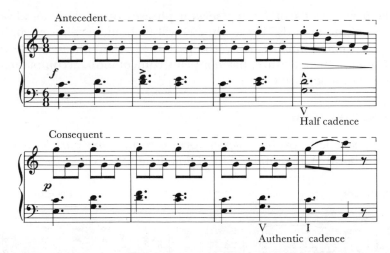

Symmetrical groups such as the above are particularly prevalent in the elegant, poised music of the classical period. However, as we have stated above, phrases and periods both vary considerably in size and function. The Burgmüller period above can easily be restructured into a different measure frame as in Example 287. Note that the phrases are

Example 287

now five measures long but still balance each other within the span of the period. In addition, the period itself does not close neatly as before on a solid tonic chord but stretches upward to the dominant where it urges the ear on. The whole period then becomes antecedent and requires another formal unit for completion.

In sum, phrases easily shape themselves into neatly parceled, eight-measure periods. But they also may be irregularly grouped, and further, may be part of periods that are not complete themselves.

Small complete structures: part forms

When we consider small, *complete* forms, we encounter units more extensive than phrase and period. These are **parts**; and the forms themselves, **part-forms**.

WHAT IS A PART IN FORM?

A part consists of few or several phrases often, but not always, organized into periods. These phrases will be homogeneous enough so that they unquestionably stamp the part as *one*. The phrases will often be alike in motive, texture, harmony, instrumentation, accompaniment pattern, key scheme, etc.

ONE-PART FORM

The smallest possible *complete* form is termed **one-part form** and is simply labeled A (Example 288). Though minute, these forms in the

Example 288   Prelude, Chopin

hands of masters such as Bartok, Chopin, or Schoenberg can be as vivid and satisfying as a Haiku poem.

BINARY FORM

Encountered much more often are the **binary** and **ternary** part-forms. A binary part-form, AB, consists simply of two parts usually separated by a double bar. Part A is frequently repeated as is the following section, B. The pattern can be symbolized thus: A :‖: B :‖ . The parts may be brief, as in Example 289, or rather extensive as in the

Example 289   Sonata No. 6, Movement 2, Haydn

keyboard *suites* of J. S. Bach. In the more extensive AB forms, the second section will tend to be the larger of the two. Often it will contain at least a portion of the A section. When this happens, though the music may appear visually to be binary, it is at least partly ternary (ABA).

TERNARY FORMS

The true ternary form consists of three sections, the third being a repetition, either exact or varied, of the first. The returning A section usually spans approximately the same number of measures as the first A. Indeed, in *da capo* ternary forms, the returning A is not written out at all. The sign D.C. indicates to the player that he should simply repeat exactly as before the opening section. However, one of the pleasures in tracing aurally small ternary forms, other than da capo, lies in the recognition of the returning A section despite its being subtly transformed through variation techniques. We now can compare and distinguish between five complete small forms.

One-part form:	A
Binary form:	A, B
Ternary da capo:	A, B, A
Ternary with varied return:	A, B, A^1
Hybrid binary-ternary:	A, B + $\frac{1}{2}$ A

Any of the parts within these forms may be repeated *before* the arrival of the following parts without changing the basic formal identity of the music. Forms where successive *different* parts are generated beyond the B part are called *additive*: ABC, or A, B, C, D, etc.

The complete part-forms discussed thus far are sometimes called *song* or *dance forms*. Though it is true that simple songs and dances easily fall into these patterns, music for other media and purposes also uses them. For example, simple binary or ternary forms underlie a great many of the *character pieces* for piano by Schumann, Schubert, Chopin, Brahms, and Mendelssohn.

Before going on to specifics about structure in the large forms, we will briefly pause to consider a striking facet of form in general. Small formal units are the basis for larger ones. Phrases group easily into periods that themselves are the basis for complete part-forms. Further, all of these small units can be present and integral to larger units, soon to be discussed. Within the large pattern, smaller, often quite different, patterns operate. All are interdependent, and they reinforce and complement each other.

Larger single member forms

We are now prepared to discuss the larger *single member forms* of music, remembering always that underlying all of them will be smaller, cohesive formal units. These larger forms can be complete in themselves as in a *concert overture*, or they may represent one member of an aggregate work.

The inner divisions of substantial forms such as sonata-allegro, rondo, theme and variations are termed *sections*. In this text they will be named according to their role in the form, not labeled with letters as are parts. Therefore, part-forms will be labeled with capital letters, while words such as *refrain, exposition*, etc., will describe sections.

THE SECTION

Sections are distinguished from parts in several ways. Usually they are larger. Also, the section allows for greater inner diversity than the part. For example, a development section (see below) may be very extensive and be informed by the greatest musical contrasts possible. Within the section one or more part-forms may operate, while the part will itself only divide into phrases and periods. The minuet, when found in the symphony or other large forms, frequently shows each section divided into binary and/or ternary part-forms.

Two types of sections may appear in any larger single member form. They are: *introduction* and *coda.*

Introduction. The introduction often immediately precedes larger instrumental forms, which are in fast tempo. They sometimes are fragmentary, like the introduction to the first movement of the Piano Sonata in B-flat minor by Chopin (four measures), or they may be lengthy as in the finale of the Symphony No. 1 by Brahms (61 measures). The tempo of the introduction is usually slow.

Coda. The coda occurs at the end of the larger forms. Like the introduction, it may or may not be present, and can be of any length. Unlike the introduction to allegro movements, often it is in fast tempo, either continuing in the tempo of the main movement or going much faster, resulting in a brilliant finish.

Thus, the roles of introduction and coda are similar. Each is optional, and their shape and size is indeterminate. The slow, serious introduction sets the stage; the coda punctuates and rounds out the form.

TRANSITION

In contrast to the introduction and coda, the transition is almost always present, but its position in the form varies with the work. Its role is to link relatively stable melodic elements. Its effect is that of considerable musical motion: of "going somewhere." Modulation is likely to be present, especially in the more extensive transitions. So is sequence. Often, in earlier styles, the music is highly figurative, featuring brilliant scales and arpeggios.

While introduction, coda, and transition occur in any of the larger forms, other divisions are integral to specific forms and will therefore be discussed with them.

SONATA-ALLEGRO FORM: EXPOSITION, DEVELOPMENT, RECAPITULATION

Sonata-allegro is a rather imprecise term used in formal analysis to describe a sophisticated movement prominently featuring development. Originally the term was used to label opening allegros of multimovement sonatas of the classical period. Because these opening allegros normally employed the formal plan—exposition, development, recapitulation—any form using this plan is now called sonata-allegro. Thus, any movement using the above divisions, regardless of tempo or placement within the total work, is labeled *sonata-allegro*. Because the plan exposition-development-recapitulation actually can occur in any movement and in any tempo, the term *sonata-allegro* will be considered here as a structural pattern, not solely as the description of opening allegros in sonatas.

Sonata-allegro is a most felicitous form, combining the psychological satisfactions derived from ternary principles with the energy and excitement generated by development. The form is ternary because the recapitulation is a restatement of the exposition, but with important modifications. The development bridges the two. The term *ternary* used here is not to be confused with **ternary part-form**.

Exposition. The role of the exposition is to present melodic and rhythmic materials in an orderly but vital manner. In standard works this is realized by themes—contrasted in character and indeterminate in number—appearing in succession, but often separated by transitions.

In the exposition of many works, two keys will prevail—the tonic for the opening theme, and either the dominant or mediant for later themes. Themes are numbered according to **entry**.

Development Section.   The development section is as free in shape as it is exciting in effect. As the term suggests, its role is to present in a new light the motivic materials already heard in the exposition. These materials are "treated" with an enormous array of compositional techniques, resulting in fascinating new musical shapes. A glance back at the section in this chapter on motive transformation will show some of the techniques used in development. Modulation occurs very frequently, the total effect in more dramatic works being one of growing intensity and excitement until the arrival of the recapitulation section.

Recapitulation.   As we said before, the recapitulation closely follows the pattern of the exposition with but one major change. Whereas the exposition is polarized by the presence of two contrasted keys, the recapitulation is harmonically homogeneous. It generally stays in one key, the tonic. A typical sonata-allegro form would then follow in this order:

Slow introduction (optional).

Exposition	Presentation of themes with transitions and modulation to dominant or mediant key.
Development	Exploration of motives and themes and treatment by various compositional techniques. End of this section built on dominant chord, which leads to recapitulation.
Recapitulation	Return of exposition with all themes in tonic key, and with other minor changes.
Coda (optional)	Usually in same tempo as exposition, development, recapitulation, but sometimes faster.

It should be remembered that the above outline of sonata-allegro applies only to typical patterns. In the hands of the masters, details of structure can and do deviate from the norm while sonata-allegro principles remain constant. This is indeed true of all forms.

Suggested Listening: Score Profile, Chapter 3, Beethoven, Leonora Overture No. 3.

RONDO FORM: REFRAIN AND EPISODE

The *rondo* is often located as the finale in a multi-movement sonata. Its structural pattern is more variable than that of sonata-allegro. There are two basic sections, the refrain and the episode, but these may be repeated often, and varied considerably. The one constant of the form is that the refrain returns no fewer than two times. Two very commonly seen arrangements of refrain and episode are *small rondo* and *large rondo*. Typical rondo patterns are:

Small, five-section rondo: Refrain, Episode I, Refrain, Episode II, Refrain.

Large, seven-section rondo: Refrain, Episode I, Refrain, Episode II, Refrain, Episode I, Refrain.

As we have seen, the distinguishing characteristic in sonata-allegro is the development section with its propulsive, eruptive power. But whereas sonata-allegro animates, the rondo charms. Its principal attraction lies in the refrain, which keeps coming back. Contrasted episodes separate these returns, and the ear delights during the latter portions of these in the anticipation of the refrain's return. In the simpler rondo, the refrain is likely to be repeated exactly as in its first entry. But in more extensive ones it often will appear in delightful mutations, including change of key and considerable variation. Sometimes Episode II itself takes on the character of development as it deals with thematic materials from the refrain. When this happens, the form becomes *sonata-rondo*, a hybrid. Codas regularly appear in rondos, but introductions only occasionally.

> *Suggested Listening:*   Small rondo: Brahms, Symphony No. 1, Movement 3; Large rondo: Beethoven, "Pathetique" Sonata, Opus 13, Movement 3; Rondo-sonata: Haydn, Symphony No. 88, Movement 4.

THEME AND VARIATIONS

Theme and variations as a structural pattern is rather ubiquitous. It can occur as a member of multi-member works, but just as often it will be seen as a complete composition, for any instrument or combination of instruments.

As in the rondo, the number of sections in the form is indeterminate. For example, Beethoven gives only three variations in the second movement of his Piano Sonata Opus 14, No. 2, but 33 in the Diabelli Variations, Opus 120. In that sense it is an open-end form.

The theme itself, as we said earlier, often consists of a complete part-form. It may be borrowed from outside sources or from another composition by the composer, or be especially written by the composer for the work at hand. Whatever its source, it tends to be of a simple and unadorned nature; thus will it lend itself more easily to full expansion and metamorphosis.

Variations are of two types: ornamental and characteristic. The ***ornamental variation***, occurring primarily in earlier music, is unpretentious. Interest lies in a graceful embellishment (Example 290) of the

Example 290   "Clementine" in Ornamental Variation

theme without major alteration of its basic length and shape. Indeed, it is sometimes possible to play or to sing the original theme simultaneously with any of the variations. The ***characteristic variation*** uses the theme as a touchstone. From within the theme itself, individual elements such as motive, rhythmic pattern, and harmony, are isolated and used as the basis for variations of a "character" often wholly different from that of the theme (Example 291). The connection between theme and ornamental variation is physiological; that between theme and characteristic variation is psychological.

> *Suggested Listening:* Ornamental variations: Mozart Variations on "Ah, Vous Dirai-je, Maman," K. 265, for keyboard; Characteristic variations: Elgar, "Enigma Variations," Opus 36, for orchestra.

MINUET (OR SCHERZO) WITH TRIO

Standard terminology here is confusing, although the actual formal pattern used is very simple. The listener is presented with a form (frequently the third movement of a large structure) called

Example 291   "Clementine" in Characteristic Variation

Andante

rall.

minuet. However, its inner sections are labeled *minuet* and *trio.* The contradiction is obvious. How could the first section of the form be a minuet when the whole thing is a minuet?

The pattern used is ternary. Section I takes its name, *minuet,* from the whole form, MINUET. Section II is the Trio. The final section is the repetition of the first. Section I and Section II are frequently quite contrasted. Section II is often in a different key with its clearer texture differing vividly from that in Section I.

The *scherzo* follows the same formal pattern as the minuet, differing in effect because of its considerably faster tempo.

The Minuet is also seen with two trios. The plan then becomes similar to that of a small rondo: Minuet-Trio I-Minuet-Trio II-Minuet.

> *Suggested Listening:* Mozart: Minuet with Trio, Movement 3, Symphony No. 41 ("Jupiter"); Beethoven: Scherzo with Trio, Movement 3, Symphony No. 2, Opus 36.

THE FUGUE

The fugue cannot be considered as a form in the same way that we have considered the structures above. It and many other strictly contrapuntal works are better considered procedures. Such works do not lend themselves easily to analysis in parts or sections. In true formal structures, identification and structural definition come through the horizontal juxtaposition and balance of parts and sections. For example, a recapitulation section has meaning only in relation to the antecedent exposition that came before. And again, a refrain cannot be a refrain with its own peculiar emotional impact without its antecedent episode or episodes.

A study of form in the purest sense then involves various *horizontal* arrangements of segments, large or small, which make sense only through their relationships with one another.

Contrapuntal structures are animated mostly through *vertical* relationships of two or more melodic lines and through motivic transformation. In the listing of forms at the end of this chapter these contrapuntal structures will be described in a general way, but for a more complete understanding of their principles of organization, reference should be made to Chapter 6.

Aggregate structures

Just as there need be pattern and logic within part forms and within larger single member forms, so there need be some kind of organic unity and balance when two or more of these forms are joined in **aggregate structures**. Some of these are: symphony, concerto, quartet, solo sonata, suite, song cycle, oratorio, opera, etc.

In instrumental music aggregate forms unite their members through certain techniques. The standard classical symphony, for example, will often show the same key for three of its four **movements**. The content in each movement will be such that there is follow-through as the work progresses. There will be a four-movement plan with a general tempo scheme of I fast, II slow, III moderate or fast, IV fast. The initial movement is almost always sonata-allegro; the third usually minuet or scherzo, and the last frequently rondo.

Occasionally two or more movements will be linked physically by a **bridge passage**. Sometimes a kind of formal superstructure, termed **cyclic form**, will firmly relate the movements. This consists of one or more themes recurring in two or more movements, often in addition to the regular themes of the movement.

In aggregate vocal forms, such as opera, song cycle, masses, and oratorio, unity is largely provided by the text. In ballet, the plot itself cements the various scenes and dances.

Whether it be the briefest tune or a gargantuan two-hour symphony, unity, organization, logic, balance, and organic development are part of all intelligible music. And all of this is tempered and leavened by the yeast of variety and contrast.

Selected listing of musical forms

The instrumental and vocal forms that follow should not be considered mutually exclusive. Vocal music, more often than not, will include instrumental forces. And instrumental music, such as the symphony, occasionally will include vocal forces.

FORMS FOLLOWING THE SONATA PATTERN

A *sonata* is an aggregate form ordinarily consisting of three or four loosely linked movements, contrasted in tempo and style.

The Solo Sonata. The *solo sonata* is written either for a single instrument with complete range such as the piano, organ, or harpsichord, or for instruments such as oboe, violin, or cello with a keyboard instrument. Properly these last should be termed *duo sonatas*.

> *Suggested Listening:* Beethoven, Sonata, Opus 81a, "Les Adieux," for piano; Hindemith, Sonata for Bassoon and Piano (1939).

The Symphony. A *symphony* is a sonata for full orchestra. Symphonies are often more extensive than sonatas for solo or chamber ensemble. The term *symphony* (*sinfonia*) is also used in baroque music to define instrumental forms prefacing choral or instrumental works.

> *Suggested Listening:* Bizet, Symphony in C, for orchestra.

Trio, Quartet, Quintet, etc. Chamber music media such as the *trio*, the *quartet*, and the *quintet* ordinarily follow standard sonata patterns. Their charm comes from an intimate character, not unlike that of the solo sonata, combined with the subtlety of musical dialogue found in all ensemble.

> *Suggested Listening:* Schubert, "Trout Quintet," for violin, viola, cello, contrabass, piano; Debussy, Quartet in G minor, Opus 10, for two violins, viola, cello.

The Concerto. A *concerto* is a sonata for one or more soloists with orchestra. They are almost always in three movements. There is no scherzo or minuet. *Cadenzas*, brilliant sections for soloist alone, are featured. The *concerto grosso*, originating in baroque music, features a small body of soloists, the *concertino*, set in opposition to a larger instrumental group, the *tutti* (*ripieni*). A concerto for orchestra does not allow for any set type or number of soloists. Rather, any or all instruments in the orchestra may lead momentarily without being considered *the* soloist or soloists. The writing for the orchestra here is usually virtuosic.

> *Suggested Listening:* Mozart, Concerto for Clarinet, K. 622; Brahms, Concerto for Violin and Cello, Opus 102; Beethoven, Concerto for Violin, Cello, and Piano, Opus 56; Bloch, Concerto Grosso No. 2 (1952); Bartok, Concerto for Orchestra (1943).

The Sonatine. A *sonatine* (sometimes sonatina) is a sonata of reduced dimensions. **Sonatina form** means sonata-allegro with absent or truncated development section.

> *Suggested Listening:* Ravel, Sonatine for Piano (1905).

VARIATION FORMS

Variation technique occurs in all forms. Whenever any musical element is repeated, with however slight change, it is varied. Variation forms may be complete in one movement, or part of aggregate structures.

Theme and Variations. The theme and variation form is an additive structure consisting of a theme repeated an indeterminate number of times, each time varied. The last variation is often climactic and dazzling, following one of slow, meditative character.

> *Suggested Listening:* Rachmaninoff, Rhapsody on a Theme of Paganini, Opus 43, for piano with orchestra; Score Profile, this chapter.

Passacaglia and Chaconne. The *passacaglia* and *chaconne* have an additive structure with a theme considerably shorter than that in theme and variations. These forms are often only a few bars in length. The passacaglia features an opening theme in the bass. Both tend to be more contrapuntal than theme and variations. **Ground** and **ostinato** are structures nearly identical with passacaglia, both suggesting a short figure in the bass overlaid with variations for each repetition. The notes of the ostinato usually do not change, and it may be heard in registers other than the bass.

> *Suggested Listening:* Brahms, Symphony No. 4, Opus 98, Movement 4 (Chaconne); Copland, Passacaglia (1922), for piano.

Chorale Prelude. The **chorale prelude** is an instrumental form, usually for organ and based on the *chorale*, a vocal form (see below). In one common version, individual phrases from the chorale are separated by transitions. These transitions continue as polyphonic commentary to the chorale phrases themselves. It is primarily a contrapuntal form.

> *Suggested Listening:* J. S. Bach, "Wachet auf ruft uns die stimme," for organ (see analysis of this in Chapter 11).

FREE FORMS

Many forms, both single and aggregate, have specific functions but are quite diverse in their use of structural pattern. For example, a rhapsody may be in the style of a rambling free improvisation, or it may follow strong classical structural patterns. The Rhapsody in G minor, Opus 79, for piano, by Brahms, for example, is cast in a powerful sonata-allegro form; and the Rhapsody on a Theme of Paganini by Rachmaninoff is set as a theme with 24 variations.

Prelude. The *prelude* can be either functional, as a preface to another piece, or independent. Many structural patterns are possible.

> *Suggested Listening:* Shostakovich, 24 Preludes and Fugues, Op. 84, for piano (functional); Puccini, Prelude to Act II of *Tosca* (functional); Chopin, 24 Preludes, Opus 28, for piano (independent); Debussy, Prélude à l'Après-midi d'un Faune, (1892–94), for orchestra (independent) (see Score Profile, Chapter 2).

Overture. The *overture* is similar to the prelude, but usually for full orchestra and substantial in dimensions. It is often cast in sonata-allegro form.

> *Suggested Listening:* Functional Overture: Beethoven, *Leonora* Overture No. 3, Opus 72b, for orchestra (see Score Profile, Chapter 3); Concert Overture: Brahms, Academic Festival Overture, Opus 80, for orchestra (see Score Profile, Chapter 4).

Fantasie. A *fantasie* is a work in free form, resembling an improvisation. In baroque and pre-baroque music it is sometimes prefatory to a fugue.

> *Suggested Listening:* Vaughn Williams, "Fantasie on a Theme by Tallis" (1910), for orchestra; J. S. Bach, Fantasia and Fugue in G minor, for organ.

Rhapsody.   A *rhapsody* is a work cast in any of many forms, usually quite imposing and substantial.

> *Suggested Listening:*   Liszt, Hungarian Rhapsodies, for piano.

Character Piece.   A character piece is a work displaying one mood, emotion, or idea. Such pieces are often programmatic. Typical titles are *Impromptu, Intermezzo, Song Without Words, Album Leaves*, and *Ballad.* The form is often ternary.

> *Suggested Listening:*   Bernstein, Four Anniversaries (1948), for piano.

Tone Poem.   A *tone poem* is a substantial composition, usually orchestral, of programmatic content. The sonata-allegro form is much used, but others are common.

> *Suggested Listening:*   Richard Strauss, *Death and Transfiguration,* Opus 24, for orchestra.

Suite.   A suite is any aggregation of pieces loosely bound together and contrasted to one another in style. Typical is the *dance suite.* This last, in the baroque, consists primarily of dances such as the minuet, *gavotte, gigue,* and is variously called *French suite, English suite, partita,* or simply suite.

> *Suggested Listening:*   J. S. Bach, Suite No. 2, for flute with strings; Bartok, Dance Suite (1923), for orchestra; Vaughn Williams, Folk Song Suite, for military band.

Opera and Ballet Suite.   The *opera* or *ballet suite* is a selection of characteristic music from opera or ballet, arranged in effective sequence.

> *Suggested Listening:*   Kodály, Háry János Suite (1926), from the opera *Hary Janos*; Stravinsky, *Firebird* Suite (1910), for orchestra, from the ballet *The Firebird.*

Incidental Music.   *Incidental music* is music written to accompany a play.

> *Suggested Listening:*   Schubert, *Rosamunde,* Opus 26, for orchestra.

Divertimento.   A *divertimento* is a suite of light, entertaining character. Other titles are *Serenade* and *Cassation.*

> *Suggested Listening:*   Ibert, Divertissement (1930), for orchestra.

Ballet. A ballet is an extended theater-piece for dance, often divided into acts or scenes. Ballet is similar to opera, with the text danced rather than sung. *Choreography* is the specific arrangement of steps and postures to the music.

> *Suggested Listening:* Milhaud, *La Création du Monde,* with chamber orchestra.

CONTRAPUNTAL STRUCTURES

As we have said above, *contrapuntal structures* do not segmentize easily and therefore are to be described according to contrapuntal technique rather than according to parts or sections.

Fugue. Fugue is the combination of two or more melodic parts, using techniques of imitation and motivic transformation.

> *Suggested Listening:* J. S. Bach, Well Tempered Clavier, Books I, II, for keyboard.

Invention. An *invention* is a less extensive contrapuntal composition in two or three melodic parts (voices). A prominent feature is inversion of the parts. Inventions are often canonic.

> *Suggested Listening:* J. S. Bach, 2- and 3-part Inventions, for keyboard.

Canon. The *canon* is a contrapuntal form based solely on imitation.

> *Suggested Listening:* Franck, Sonata for Violin and Piano, Movement 4.

Toccata. A *Toccata* is a primarily contrapuntal work originally for keyboard, but also for orchestra, featuring brilliant display work. In baroque music a toccata is sometimes appended to a fugue and occasionally itself divided into several movements.

> *Suggested Listening:* J. S. Bach, Toccata and Fugue in F, for organ.

VOCAL MUSIC

While all intelligible music must possess form, form is less apparent and freer in vocal music. The sonata-allegro pattern is diffuse and ineffective without motivic transformation and a sturdy overall superstructure including exposition, development, and recapitulation. But a song or an aria may very well ramble on, its inner segments only loosely connected, and still be intelligible. What makes this possible, of course, is the text, which largely dictates what the structure will be. Unmetered prose set to music tends to produce loose structures, while poetry suggests closer-knit forms.

Each stanza of a poem is frequently set to the same music, as in a church hymn. This form is called *strophic*. When each stanza is set to different music, it is termed *through composed*.

Single Member Forms. *Recitative* is a rhythmically free and melodically somewhat static setting of a narration or dialogue. The shape of the melodic line follows very closely the inflection of the voice. If the accompaniment (often played by harpsichord or organ) is minimal, it is called *secco*; if dramatic and elaborate (usually orchestral), it becomes *accompagnato*. It is seen mostly in opera, oratorio, *cantata*. Instrumental recitative, as in the first section of Movement 4 in Beethoven's Ninth Symphony, is a simulation of the vocal recitative.

> *Suggested Listening:* Mozart, Recitatives for *Don Giovanni;* Schoenberg, Variations on a Recitative, Opus 40 (1943), for organ.

Plain song, sometimes called *plain chant*, is a form used for settings of the liturgy. *Gregorian chant* is the setting of early Roman Catholic Church texts. Only gentle accents occur, with an undulating, gentle pulse. The melodic intervals are small, with conjunct motion primary.

> *Suggested Listening:* "Dies Irǎe" from the Requiem Mass of the Roman Catholic Church. (Also listen to utilization of this chant in: Saint-Saëns, Dance Macabre, Opus 40, for orchestra; Berlioz, Symphonie Fantastique, Opus 14, for orchestra; Rachmaninoff, Rhapsody on a Theme of Paganini; Liszt, Totentanz, for piano and orchestra.

A *song* is a setting of a poetic text for solo voice. A *part song* is for several voices. Songs are often ternary in structure.

The true *folk song* is anonymously composed, and undergoes considerable modification as it is transmitted from singer to singer. Also, songs and airs, such as "Au Clair de la Lune," written by Lully in the seventeenth century, and the simple songs of Stephen Foster have become folk songs with the passing of the years and through their immense popularity.

> *Suggested Listening:* Copland, Old American Songs (1950–54), for voice with orchestra or piano.

The ***art song***, termed ***lied*** in German, and ***chanson*** in French, is a setting by a master composer of a fine poem. Because both text and music are often of the highest caliber, the form is one of the richest in the literature for the voice. Art songs are usually performed by a single voice with piano, but orchestra is sometimes used.

> *Suggested Listening:* Schubert, song cycle *Winterreise*. (See Score Profile, Chapter 8, for last song of cycle, "Der Lier-mann.")

An ***aria*** is a song occurring usually in a large aggregate work such as an opera, oratorio, cantata, or passion. Accompaniment is orchestral and the aria amplifies and comments on emotions suggested in preceding recitatives. ***Aria da capo***, in early aggregate forms, is ternary with the final part not written out the second time. A loose ternary pattern is common for many other arias. A ***concert aria*** is not written as part of an aggregate work but otherwise follows the dimensions and structure of the above. An ***arioso*** is a hybrid between a recitative and an aria, showing considerable lyricism but tending to the rhetorical.

> *Suggested Listening:* Verdi, "Addio del Passato" from *La Traviata*. (See Score Profile, Chapter 8.)

A ***hymn*** is a simple setting of a religious or patriotic poem, suitable to be sung by untrained voices. Hymns are usually strophic in structure.

> *Suggested Listening:* Billings, Chester.

A ***chorale*** is an early hymn originating in the German Lutheran Church, and often seen in SATB arrangement as part of larger works such as the cantata and ***passion***. The chorale consists of short musical phrases punctuated by cadences, each with a fermata. The chorale as used by J. S. Bach is a compendium of harmonic devices of his time and forms the cornerstone of traditional harmony until its dissolution in the twentieth century.

> *Suggested Listening:* J. S. Bach, chorales in the *St. Matthew Passion*.

An ***anthem*** is a choral setting in English, usually of a religious text, accompanied often by church organ, but sometimes done a cappella or with other instruments.

> *Suggested Listening:* S. S. Wesley, "Blessed Be the God and Father."

A ***motet*** is a contrapuntal, choral setting of a sacred text, often in Latin, and frequently a cappella.

Suggested Listening: Byrd, "Ego sum Panis vivum," a cappella.

A *madrigal* is a setting of a secular text for mixed vocal ensemble. It contains a mixture of chordal and contrapuntal textures.

Suggested Listening: Bennet, "Thyrsis, Sleepest Thou," a cappella.

Aggregate Vocal Forms.   A *song cycle* is a group of art songs loosely related musically, frequently on poems by a single author.

Suggested Listening: Moussorgsky, Songs and Dances of Death, for voice with piano.

An *opera* is a play set completely to music, with all the words of the text (called *libretto*) sung. It includes many sections, any of which may follow diverse structural patterns: overtures (or preludes), recitatives, arias, duets, ensembles, choruses, ballets, incidental music, etc.

Number opera features the above-mentioned individual forms. In *continuous opera*, the demarcation between and identification of these is not pertinent. There is a continuous flow of music closely following the dramatic development of the play.

Some opera, especially that in a lighter vein, contains considerable spoken dialogue. Some of these are: English *ballad opera, singspiel, opera comique*, and *operetta*.

Suggested Listening: Menotti, *The Telephone*, number opera; J. Strauss, Jr., *Die Fledermaus*, operetta with spoken dialogue; Richard Strauss, *Elektra*, continuous opera.

An *oratorio* is a setting of a religious text with a similar structure and with forms as in opera. There are no costumes, scenery, or ballet. The soloists are often in fours, SATB. A narrator singing recitatives is commonly seen.

Suggested Listening: Mendelssohn, *St. Paul*, with soloists, chorus, orchestra.

A *cantata* is similar to an oratorio. However, cantatas are not always on a sacred text and are often shorter. Two kinds are the solo cantata and the choral cantata. A *passion* is an extensive cantata (or oratorio) on one of the Gospel accounts of the Passion of Christ.

Suggested Listening: J. S. Bach, Cantata No. 211 ("Coffee Cantata"), for STB, flute, strings.

A *mass* is a setting in Latin of certain portions of the liturgy of the Roman Catholic Church. Five of these portions are, the Kyrie, the

Gloria, the Credo, the Sanctus, and the Agnus Dei. A mass for the dead is called a *requiem* and includes a slighty different arrangement, including the dramatic portion, the Dies Irae. A mass that is more suitable for performance in the concert hall than in church is called a *concert mass*.

> *Suggested Listening:* Schubert, Mass No. 2 in G major, for soprano and orchestra.

Schubert, "The Trout," Opus 32

This lied (1817) is a delightful example of Schubert's lyricism. The part for keyboard shows the composer's gift for musical imagery and is highly suggestive of the babbling of a stream.

Voice Part: high

Form: strophic lied

Poet: Christian Schubart

Synopsis of poem: There darts a happy swift trout in a sparkling brook. A fisherman arrives. As long as the brook is clear the trout will not be caught. But the fisherman roils the brook and soon his fishing rod is bent. The trout is caught.

SCORE PROFILE

* Measure 6 is occasionally omitted in performance.
  The singer then begins in measure 5.

Fisch - lein zap - pelt' dran, und ich mit re - gem

Blu - te sah die Be - trog - ne an, und ich_ mit re - gem_

Blu - te sah die Be - trog - ne an.

Listening notes

The song, "The Trout," is interesting on several counts. Not only does its use by the composer in a later chamber work shed light on his predilection for song-like lyricism in general, but it is a masterpiece of its kind. The keyboard part, consisting of a fanciful broken-chord figure in the right hand with a springing bass in the left, is a charming bit of tone painting. To some it will represent the fisherman casting out his line; to others it may simply represent the rippling of the water as it tumbles over pebbles and stones. Whatever it is meant to represent, it serves as an admirable foil to the sprightly, folk-song-like melody in the voice. Note how the keyboard part at **SP m. 55** is tightened up considerably, reflecting the drama of the text in that stanza. It soon is changed entirely to exciting, repeated chords lasting until the climax of the song at **SP m. 66 – 67**.

The form of the song is simple but not uninteresting. It can be symbolized with the letters AAB. The first A spans **SP m. 1 – 26**, the second A, **SP m. 27 – 51**, and B, **SP m. 51 – 81**. The music for the first two stanzas is identical (AA); thus, that portion is strophic. The third stanza (B) is set to new music until **SP m. 68**, where a portion of the music of A comes back. Thus, the song is basically strophic with some modification.

The overall pattern then becomes:

	TEXT	MUSIC
First stanza:	(In einen Bächlein helle . . .)	A
Second stanza:	(Ein Fischer . . .)	A
Third stanza:	(Doch endlich . . .)	B with elements of A toward close.

Movement 4 of the "Trout" Quintet consists of five variations and a coda on the melody of the song discussed above. The first three variations are ornamental, with the shape of the theme always evident. Variation IV, of the characteristic type, is highly suggestive of Beethoven's music at its stormiest. Note the change of mode from the bright, sunny D major of the theme to a fulminating, trenchant D minor in this variation.

Variation V is captivating because of its harmonic ambivalence, consisting of several shifts from major to minor and modulation to unrelated keys. The transition to the coda (Allegretto) is most effective.

A comparison between the song itself and the theme and variations derived from it is most rewarding. First, note the changes in the theme of the variations. Schubert scores it for the four strings, with the piano part conspicuously absent. He also tightens up its form considerably, probably feeling that a succinct, simple structural pattern would be best for the extremely figurative variations that follow. The theme becomes a classically proportioned binary form, AB:A, **SP m. 1−8**; B, **SP m. 9−20**. Both sections are repeated.

Further note how the rhythmic pattern of the theme is transformed into a jogging pattern by the addition of dotted notes.

And although Schubert leaves out the keyboard figuration from the song here, he does not fail to introduce it later. The coda finds the theme tossed back and forth between violin and cello while in the background the original keyboard material is heard exactly as it was in the song, played mostly by the piano.

For reference and review

New terms in the order presented:

musical form	section
unity with variety	legato
theme	staccato
motive	subject

fugue
tune
sequence
rhythmic variation
augmentation
diminution
intervallic variation
inversion
retrograde
ornamentation
thematic transformation
phrase
period
antecedent
consequent
part
part-form
one-part form
binary
ternary
suite
da capo
additive
song, dance form
character piece
single member form
concert overture
section
refrain
exposition
transition
introduction
coda
sonata-allegro
ternary part-form
entry
rondo
small rondo
large rondo
sonata-rondo
theme and variations
ornamental variation
characteristic variation
minuet
scherzo
aggregate structure

movement
bridge passage
cyclic form
sonata
solo sonata
duo sonata
symphony
trio
quartet
quintet
concerto
cadenza
concerto grosso
sonatine
sonatina form
passacaglia
chaconne
ground
ostinato
chorale prelude
chorale
prelude
overture
fantasie
rhapsody
impromptu
intermezzo
song without words
album leaf
ballade
tone poem
dance suite
gavotte
gigue
French suite
English suite
partita
opera or ballet suite
incidental music
divertimento
serenade
cassation
choreography
contrapuntal structure
extension
invention

canon
toccata
strophic
through composed
recitative
secco
accompagnato
plain song
plain chant
Gregorian chant
song
part song
folk song
art song
lied
chanson
aria
aria da capo
concert aria
arioso

hymn
chorale
anthem
motet
madrigal
song cycle
opera
libretto
number opera
continuous opera
ballad opera
singspiel
opera comique
operetta
oratorio
cantata
passion
mass
requiem
concert mass

Performance media

THE FASCINATION with sound itself has beguiled the child in all of us throughout the ages. The wooden whistle made from the tree branch may have been our first introduction to the delight in sound itself—initially without melody, without form. The tinkle of a bell, even the sound of a locomotive in the otherwise quiet night, evokes a memory, dimly felt but enchanting in its resurgence.

By the use of instruments and voices the composer draws upon these sounds in their simplicity and in their sophistication to create in us a new awareness of things as they are or might be—to awaken us to new experiences. Even the electronic composer has not totally abandoned sounds which are imitative of the more natural sounds with which we are acquainted.

How do we designate the various instruments that have served for so long? How do we speak of the differences of tone quality between one singer and the next? How do we fathom the limitless blending of these instruments and voices?

8

Voices

SINGING IS a natural and pleasant experience to almost everybody. When music suddenly rises to the surface of our consciousness, nudged there perhaps by a beautiful spring day, we want to sing. Undoubtedly if we carried a flute at that moment and could play it, we would. But because most of us carry the possibility of song always with us, singing is the most natural and accessible way of making music, and by association, understanding it.

The sixteenth-century French philosopher, Michel De Montaigne, as a boy was awakened each morning by the sound of a musical instrument. These early impressions, carefully implanted in the child by a solicitous father, were undoubtedly beneficial. But we would venture to say that Montaigne's first childhood impressions, the tender songs perhaps imbibed from a peasant nurse at the cradle, were equally important. Indeed, vocal music is often with us from the very beginning of our lives and constantly surrounds us.

As soon as we can, we repeat nursery songs. At school, one of our first musical experiences is with song. Later on we sing at school gatherings, at rallies, at church, or with a community chorus. We can enjoy singing—on an unsophisticated level, to be sure—without the slightest technical training.

Even at a very sophisticated level of instrumental performance, the concept of song is not far away. The critics speak of a pianist's "singing tone," or we hear of "the eloquent voice" of the cello. And for the very reason that words are usually present, vocal music is easily assimilated. Indeed, we often think of a song in terms of its text, or its textual meaning, rather than its melody or harmony. In short, we easily relate to vocal music because of the words with specific or symbolic meaning. Singing is a natural, familiar way for us to express ourselves. In it are combined the directness and universality of the spoken word and the sensuous appeal of tones produced by the human voice. Thus, the voice rightly has been chosen by the masters as the appropriate medium for some of their most important musical creations.

Voice types

Men's voices differ from those of women primarily in pitch range. The female's overall range is one octave higher than that of the male. When a mixed group sings a melody together at a public gathering, the melody is not at the same pitch level, but at the distance of one octave.

Beyond this basic division, men's and women's voices are divided further into voice types corresponding to high, middle, and low *pitch ranges*. Thus, for the basic female voices we have, from high to low: *soprano, mezzo soprano*, and *contralto* (*alto*); for the basic male voices: *tenor, baritone*, and *bass* (Example 292).

Example 292

In mixed *choral music*—most often scored in four parts, soprano, alto, tenor, and bass (SATB)—parts are not often written for middle-range voices—mezzo soprano, and baritone. Thus, if a baritone possesses an exceptionally high range, he may join the tenor section as a second tenor or the bass section as a first bass. In exactly the same way, the mezzo soprano must fit her voice where she can, either with the altos or sopranos, depending on her range.

In certain other vocal forms, revolving around several *solo* parts, middle-range voices are often fully represented with parts written especially for them. For example, Verdi, in his last opera, *Falstaff*, assigned the leading solo parts to vocal types exactly corresponding to the six mentioned before. The parts are:

Sir John Falstaff, a rotund knight	baritone
Bardolph ⎱ retainers of	tenor
Pistol ⎰ Falstaff	bass
Ford, a wealthy burgher	baritone
Alice Ford, his wife	soprano
Ann Ford, their daughter	soprano
Fenton, Ann's suitor	tenor
Dr. Caius, another suitor	tenor
Mistress Page, a neighbor of the Fords	mezzo soprano
Dame Quickly, servant of Dr. Caius	contralto

THE SOPRANO VOICE

Coloratura Soprano. This is the highest and most agile of the soprano voices. A fine coloratura will negotiate precarious leaps, dizzying high notes, and cascading scales with ease.

Example 293

Though the music for this voice can be dramatic as in the "Queen of the Night" aria from Mozart's opera, *The Magic Flute,* it most often is light as in Example 294, from Gounod's opera, *Romeo and Juliet.*

Example 294   Romeo and Juliet, Act I, Gounod

It should be remembered that though music for coloratura soprano often emphasizes ***virtuosity*** and vocal gymnastics, it also can be very melodic and lyric. Also, the term ***coloratura*** is applied to any voice type when it engages in highly figurative, cadenza-like music.

Suggested Listening: Lucy's "Hello Aria" from Menotti's comic opera, *The Telephone*.

Lyric Soprano.   The **lyric soprano**, as the name suggests, is assigned song-like, sustained melodies. Most of the female leading parts in French and Italian romantic opera are sung by lyric sopranos: Marguerite in Gounod's *Faust*; Violetta in Verdi's *La Traviata*; Mimi in Puccini's *La Bohème*. Just as the coloratura soprano has its lyric moments, so the lyric soprano is called upon often to perform scintillating **runs** and **trills**, and to reach dazzling high notes.

One of the finest lyric soprano parts in opera is that of Violetta in Verdi's *La Traviata*.

Example 295

Dramatic Soprano.   A **dramatic soprano**, as can be seen in Example 296, sings in approximately the same range as does the lyric soprano. Like the lyric, she must often sing in an intimate, sustained manner as can be heard in the love song from Act I of Puccini's opera, *Tosca*. But for the most part, and especially in German romantic opera, she must sing with great **volume** of tone and dramatic intensity for long periods of time. Operas using dramatic voices ordinarily feature very large orchestras. Over these mammoth bands, sometimes totalling over 100 players, the dramatic soprano must project all the resonance at her command. Beyond the enormous vocal challanges occurring on almost every page of the score, a full, rich orchestra swells with throbbing sound under, over, and around the vocal part.

Example 296

Suggested Listening: The part of Isolde in the opera *Tristan und Isolde* by Richard Wagner.

Boy Soprano.   Though the **boy soprano** can attain most of the pitches in the female lyric soprano range, the quality of this voice is quite different. It lacks the voluptuous quality often heard in the female soprano. When well trained, it is remarkable for its purity of sound and has little of the **vibrato** often heard in the lyric soprano.

Suggested Listening: The part of the boy in Menotti's *Amahl and the Night Visitors.*

The ***castrato***, or male soprano voice, was very popular in seventeenth- and eighteenth-century opera. It was used in church choirs as well as on the operatic stage. Castrati were adult eunuchs who combined the range of the boy soprano voice with the power of the tenor. For obvious reasons, they are not used in our time.

Operatic roles originally done by castrati, such as Idamantes in Mozart's *Idomeneo* and Orpheus in the opera *Orpheus and Eurydice*, are done by a mezzo soprano in modern productions.

Example 297

The Mezzo Soprano. As mentioned before, parts for this middle-range voice are seldom found in music for chorus. But solo mezzo soprano parts in opera abound. As is the case with the baritone voice, however, *leading roles* do not often come its way. Well known exceptions are the flaming roles of Carmen in the opera by Bizet (Example 298), and Delilah in Saint-Saëns's opera, *Samson and Delilah.*

Example 298   Carmen, Act I, Bizet

Suggested Listening: The part of Octavian in Richard Strauss' opera, *Der Rosenkavalier.*

Verdi, "Addio del passato," Act III, La Traviata

Verdi's great drawing-room opera was written in 1853 and was first performed the same year in Venice. The libretto, by Piave, was based on a novel by Alexandre Dumas, fils, son of the celebrated author of *The Count of Monte Cristo* and *The Three Musketeers*. Perhaps because the opera utilized a text reflecting the manners and morals of urban life (the original story was based on fact), it failed at first; only later did it become a standard fixture in the repertory.

Soloist: Lyric soprano (Violetta).

Form: Aria with introductory recitative (recitative not included in Score Profile).

SCORE PROFILE

Listening notes

This, the first aria in Act III of Verdi's opera, *La Traviata (The Wayward One),* depicts Violetta's farewell to life and to her love for Alfredo. She has been abandoned by her lover and is now living with her maid, Annina, in a small flat in Paris. The doctor has just left, and Violetta knows without having been told that she is dying of consumption.

Note the poignant introduction in minor to the voice part **SP m. 1** as played by a solo oboe. Listen for the bittersweet quality it lends the music here and at **SP m. 19** and **SP m. 32**.

At **SP m. 12** Violetta sings of her love for Alfredo. Not only does the vocal line become more sensuous and passionate, but the voice is joined by the clarinet underlining the deep pathos of the situation.

Beginning with **SP m. 12**, when she asks God's forgiveness for her past life, the music changes to a major key and the melody soars to a touching climax.

Listen in this section for the throbbing, repeated chords in the orchestra.

FREE TRANSLATION

Farewell, happy dreams of yesteryear—already the color in my cheeks is fading.

Oh how I miss Alfredo, the love and comfort he gave me! Oh God, forgive me! Grant that I may see you!

THE CONTRALTO (ALTO) VOICE

Both *contralto* and *alto* apply the lowest-pitched female voice. The term *contralto* is ordinarily used when the singer is featured as soloist. When she is part of a section in a chorus or choir, the term *alto* is used.

Suggested Listening. The part of Cinderella in the opera by Rossini.

THE TENOR VOICE

Countertenor. The countertenor, or male alto, is the voice closest in technique to that of the female coloratura. By using a technique based on *falsetto*, a fine countertenor reaches a pitch range considerably higher than that of the lyric or dramatic tenor. His tone quality, while escalating through the notes of the scale usually sung by females,

" . . . especially in German romantic opera,
she must sing with great volume of tone and
dramatic intensity for long periods of time" (p. 264).

is transparent and considerably less virile than that of other male voices. His range is very close to that given in Example 299.

Example 299

Lyric Tenor.   The lyric tenor (Example 300), like the lyric so-

Example 300

prano, is assigned many of the loveliest melodies in opera and operetta, and often gets top billing. Operatic heroes and lovers are traditionally tenors, while baritones and basses are often cast as villains, fathers, and uncles.

> *Suggested Listening:*   The part of Romeo in the opera *Romeo and Juliet,* by Gounod.

Tenore Robusto or Heldentenor.   Both the terms **tenore robusto** and **heldentenor** refer to the dramatic tenor, whose role in opera is precisely like that of the dramatic soprano (Example 301).

Example 301

> *Suggested   Listening:*   The role of Florestan in the opera *Fidelio,* by Beethoven; The role of Radames in the opera *Aida,* by Verdi.

THE BARITONE VOICE

Though in opera and elsewhere the leading male role does not often come his way, the well trained **baritone** does have certain advantages. For one, his highest notes often have a brilliance and carrying power close to that of the tenor. On the other hand, the voice tends to have a rich, dark cast usually associated with basses.

Example 302

When the baritone voice has a pronounced dark cast and approaches in range that of the bass, it is then called **bass-baritone**.

> *Suggested Listening:* The part of John the Baptist in the opera *Salome*, by Richard Strauss.

THE BASS VOICE

Example 303

The **bass voice** in choral music anchors the total sound. Though it often sallies forth with a melody of its own, especially in contrapuntal music, much of the time it provides a tonal cushion upon which the upper voices depend.

The solo bass, however, is much used in vocal forms and is almost as diversified in tone quality and use as is its opposite member, the soprano. In addition to the quasi-bass, officially called *bass-baritone*, mentioned above, the **lyric bass** (**basso cantante**) and the **comic bass** (**basso buffo**) find ample representation in the operatic repertory. These last two voices differ not so much in tone color and in range but in style of performance. The *buffo* emphasizes acting and character portrayal, sometimes to the marked detriment of beauty of vocal sound, while the lyric bass cultivates a singing style where beauty of voice is as important as it is with the lyric soprano or lyric tenor. Example 304 shows a bass melody to be sung in *buffo* style. Example 305 shows a bass melody in the *cantante* style.

The **basso profundo** is a bass with an unusually low range. An occasional chorus exists where the true basso profundo will be heard underlying the already dark sound of the other basses. Russian choruses often boast many extremely low basses who will be able to plumb the depths and attain a pitch as low as Example 306 with ease, thus lending extraordinary solidity and majesty to the choral sound. This subterranean voice is called **contrabass**.

Example 304   The Barber of Seville, Act I, Rossini

(Dr. Bartolo)

Aun dot - tor del - la mia sor - te   Que - ste

scu - - se, Si - gno - ri - na!   Aun dot -

tor___ del - la mia sor - te Ques - te scu - se, O signo - ri - na!

Example 305   Don Giovanni, Act II, Mozart

(Don Giovanni)

Deh vie - ni_al - la fi - ne - stra, O mio___ te -

so - ro, deh vie - ni_a con - so - lar il pian- to mi - - o.

Example 306

Suggested Listening: Basso cantante: the part of Mephistoph-eles in the opera *Mefistofele,* by Boito; Basso buffo: the part of Baron Ochs in the opera *Der Rosenkavalier,* by Richard Strauss.

It should be remembered that all of the various voice ranges discussed above are normal-trained, or normal-untrained. Exceptions are often encountered. The tenor Caruso could sing strong low notes ranging down through the baritone range. An exceptionally low chorus alto will sometimes be found who is able to sing all the tenor pitches as well as the ones usual in her voice type. Also, range limits given for each voice type are to be considered as "working" ranges: pitches that are required of a certain voice type for concert performance. Professional singers are often capable of extending these limits but only do so in exceptional situations.

Vocal performance media

Before advancing to a description of the various physical combinations of voices with one another and with instruments, it is important to distinguish early and clearly between *vocal performance media* and vocal forms.

Vocal forms are the various structural patterns inherent in the music to be sung; they exemplify how the music is organized without regard to how many or what kind of voices are involved. (See Chapter 7.) Performance media are the various physical singing forces required to produce music written in these forms.

Thus, the *lied* as a form is a song sometimes cast in a strophic pattern but just as often through composed, using a German text usually of high poetical order. The performance medium used is the solo voice, of any pitch range, sustained by a piano accompaniment. But while the performance medium may change, as when Richard Strauss writes solo *lieder* with orchestra instead of piano, the basic formal structure of the music itself remains.

Vocal forms refer to musical ideas and patterns, vocal performance media to how many and what type voices are used. This distinction applies as well to the instrumental performance media discussed in Chapter 9.

THE CHORUS

The term *chorus* as understood in the broadest possible sense simply means a body of people singing together. These may be few or many — male, female, or both — divided into parts or singing in unison, accompanied by instruments or not, articulating a text or humming, and singing any kind of music in almost any setting.

In practice, however, choruses are classified and named according to their size, their social function, the kind of literature sung, and other characteristics. These important variations will be discussed after certain basic facts applying to them all are discussed.

Choral music is ordinarily divided into parts corresponding to voice types covering the highs, middles, and lows of music. The most common division is in four parts: soprano, alto, tenor, bass. A chorus thus constituted is called a *mixed chorus*, and the letter symbols used to describe it are SATB.

A men's chorus (usually TTBB) is necessarily more limited in pitch spectrum but achieves extremely rich sonorities. A women's chorus is usually divided thus: SSAA, or SSA.

When any voice type is itself divided as in the arrangement SSAA, the term *first* or *second* is used to distinguish between high and low parts. Thus, in the chorus division SSAA, there would be first and second sopranos and first and second altos, the first usually sounding as the higher voices. This division will allow for a full chordal or contrapuntal sound regardless of whether the chorus is high, as for women, or low, as for men.

Choral music often calls for more than the four parts. One arrangement often encountered, especially in older choral music, is that of SSATB; and several other divisions can occur.

Within the ordinary division, SATB, the composer will often call for a temporary further division of parts. Thus, a particular choral work may begin and end with the division SATB, but change to a combination of SSAATTB for a brilliant, climactic middle section.

Antiphony results when individual choruses, complete in themselves, answer one another. These are called double or triple choruses.

Though, as was mentioned earlier, any body of voices singing together can be considered a chorus, in practice the term is usually reserved for groups with a minimum of three to four singers to a part. An arrangement of SATB, two voices to a part, is rightly considered to be a *double quartet*, not a chorus.

A choral group numbering 12 to 50 singers is called a *chamber chorus*. Larger choruses may contain as many as 150 voices or more. A choral group performing without instruments is called an *a cappella* chorus or choir, and music sung by them is called a cappella.

VARIOUS CHORAL GROUPS

A *choir* is a chorus that is attached to a church or chapel. Though the normal church choir necessarily is of chamber chorus proportions, it is sometimes large. Also, though its repertoire will be primarily sacred choral music for performance at religious services, it will occasionally include secular music at special concerts or on tour. Church choirs ordinarily are peopled by non-professionals, but the largest churches, ordinarily found in large urban areas, will sometimes consist of professional singers.

Secular choruses vary greatly in type and function. They will run the gamut from the polished, disciplined, professional groups heard constantly on radio, on television, and in concert to the informal groups in colleges devoted to the cultivation of student songs.

The community chorus, depending on its locale, resources, and the ambition of its members, will vary in quality and number. Some will thrive on slight musical fare, while others each season will mount several magnificent performances of the greatest masterworks with full symphony orchestra.

The term **glee club** usually applies to a collegiate chorus, female, male, or mixed. But such is the interest in choral music at many colleges and universities that several choral groups may flourish simultaneously. There may be a large chorus, a chamber chorus, a men's chorale, a chapel choir, madrigal singers, and other groups. Some of these become so refined and competent that they sing and record with the finest symphony orchestras; tour periodically, sometimes on an international scale; and generally reach a high level of choral art.

Most of the kinds of choral groups mentioned above are rehearsed and directed by a conductor. Whether this person is a professor of music who leads the college glee club after teaching hours, the **chorus master** permanently attached to an opera house, or simply the best musician of the group who dares to stand up and lead, his role is vital—especially if the chorus is a good one. He must rehearse adequately for performances, choose repertoire, draw from the group good overall tone quality, monitor enunciation and pronunciation of words—often in foreign languages—and generally spark the group to produce effective and imaginative performances. Occasionally he will also need to direct a symphony orchestra or other instrumental group along with his chorus.

SMALL VOCAL ENSEMBLES

Ensembles, with but one to a part, are named according to the number of voices involved. Thus, the Brahms *Liebeslieder Waltzes,* for four solo voices (SATB) with piano duet, are written for what is called an accompanied **vocal quartet**. The medium here is chamber ensemble. But while the repertory for such chamber groups is fairly wide, vocal ensembles are more often encountered as a part of other massed vocal media.

Solo ensembles abound in opera, where the several principals join voices in every possible combination. Typical of this is the melodramatic **trio** (STB) heard in the last moments of Gounod's opera *Faust.*

Solo ensembles joining large choruses in the performance of oratorios, cantatas, and other vocal forms are rather conservatively constituted. The usual grouping is in **mixed quartet** (SATB) with the small ensemble sometimes set in dramatic opposition to the massed chorus, and at other times blending in with the whole.

THE SOLO VOICE

As a performance medium, the solo voice is universally used in combination with a great variety of instruments and in the realization of many musical forms. To name but a few, the solo voice is heard in opera and related forms, sacred and secular choral music, the symphony, with instrumental chamber music, and in the smaller song forms often accompanied by the piano, but also by other instruments and instrumental ensembles.

One of the most rewarding of these is the German art song, or *lied*, with piano. Contrary to the view of some, this is really a chamber ensemble and rightly can be considered a duet. As developed by the master German composers of *lieder*, Beethoven, Schubert, Mendelssohn, Schumann, Brahms, Wolf, Strauss, and Mahler, the *lied* as a medium allots as much importance to the materials in the piano part as to those in the voice part. The poems used are generally of a high order. Art songs as developed in several countries are ordinarily heard in solo *vocal recitals*, but may crop up elsewhere.

Schubert, "Der Leirmann," from
Winterreise, Opus 89, No. 24

Winterreise is a cycle of 24 *lieder* written in the last year of the composer's life. It is his crowning achievement, occupying a similar place in the development of Schubert's style to that of the *Art of Fugue* in J. S. Bach's, or the "Choral" Symphony in Beethoven's. The last song achieves universality through simplicity and great pathos.

Voice part: baritone.

Form: through-composed *lied.*

Poet: Wilhelm Müller.

SCORE PROFILE

dreht, und sei - ne Lei - er steht ihm nim -mer still.

Wun - der - li - cher Al - te,

soll ich mit dir gehn? Willst zu mei - nen Lie - dern

dei - ne Lei - er drehn?

Listening notes

The open, bare interval of the fifth that forms the bass throughout the piano part suggests to the listener the drone of a small portable organ. Through its cold, almost hypnotic repetition, it perfectly portrays the numb, defeated state of mind of the spurned lover as he listens to the organ.

The vocal line itself is repetitious, and does not change in basic contour until **SP m. 55**. Listen for the last few notes sung where the line ends on an agonized cry of remorse.

Listen for the many dissonances occurring in the piano part, **SP m. 4, SP m. 5**, etc., reinforcing the feeling of utter anguish and desolation heard throughout.

FREE TRANSLATION

Up near the village stands an organ grinder crank- ing with cold fingers as well as he can. He is barefoot on the cold ground without a coin in his cup. No one notices the little old man but the snarling dogs. He doesn't com- plain but keeps turning and turning.

Oh wonderful old man, shall I join you? Will you play for my songs?

For reference and review

New terms in the order presented:

soprano	tenore robusto
mezzo soprano	heldentenor
contralto	dramatic tenor
alto	baritone
tenor	bass-baritone
baritone	bass voice
bass	lyric bass
choral music	basso cantante
solo	comic bass
coloratura soprano	basso buffo
coloratura	basso profundo
lyric soprano	contrabass
run	vocal performance media
trill	chorus
dramatic soprano	mixed chorus
volume	antiphony
boy soprano	double quartet
vibrato	chamber chorus
castrato	a cappella
countertenor	choir
falsetto	glee club
chorus master	trio
vocal quartet	mixed quartet
lyric tenor	vocal recital

9

Instruments

THE COMPOSER, in addition to utilizing the structural elements of music—melody, harmony, and rhythm—is acutely aware of the unique sound of each instrument. Each sound, alone or in combination with other instruments, can be used to enhance, emphasize, or accent line or texture, or to add spice and variety.

Tone color, or **timbre**, is the quality of sound of an instrument that distinguishes it from any other. Tone color is initially dependent upon the number and strength of the overtones that are present in the tone being sounded. These are a result of the dimensions (*all* of the dimensions) of an instrument.

Most readers are familiar with the fact that a tuba, which is large, sounds lower than a trumpet, which is small. "Large" and "small," however, are general terms and more specifically include reference to two dimensions: the length and width of the bore. The tuba sounds lower than the trumpet only because its tubing is longer. Its bore is wider, but this affects quality of sound, not pitch.

Tone color is also dependent upon the materials from which the instrument is made, and upon the manner in which the sound is produced, whether by blowing, scraping, hitting, or plucking.

To take two instruments of the woodwind family—the clarinet and oboe—that are reasonably similar in certain aspects—range, register, materials of construction, and manner in which played—let us ask the question: Why do they sound different?

282

The clarinet, which is cylindrical and is a ***stopped pipe***, produces fewer overtones than the oboe. A stopped pipe suppresses the even-numbered overtones. Therefore the tone of the clarinet has a more "hollow" sound. The oboe has a conical bore and is an ***open pipe***. The open pipe allows the oboe to sound the overtones in succession, and its tone quality is therefore more vibrant. The materials of construction of the two instruments are the same, and they are both played by being blown. However, the clarinet uses a single reed fitted to the flat side of a wedge-shaped mouthpiece, whereas the oboe is equipped with a double reed. This very difference adds to this "hollow" sound of the clarinet, and the "reedy" sound of the oboe.

These differences between two instruments of the same family that play in the same general range may serve as an illustration of the reasons for the minute and the large differences in tone color between instruments of the same family and especially for the differences existing between instruments of different families.

It should not be necessary to do more than point out that the method of producing the tone results in further differences of tone color. Listen to the different quality of sound of the violin in instances in which the string is plucked as opposed to the more usual manner of drawing the bow across the string. Further, compare the tone color of the harpsichord, in which the strings are plucked, to the tone color of the piano, in which the strings are hit by felt hammers. For those interested, more complete information about the production of sound may be found in various texts on the subject of ***acoustics***.

The chief point for the listener is not so much to understand the reasons for the differences in tone color as to be able to recognize the differences with his ear, and to note in what manner the composer uses these differences—as well as the similarities—as an integral part of his composition.

Ranges

The ***range*** of an instrument refers to the total number of pitches capable of being produced on that instrument, from the lowest pitch to the highest. Thus, designation of the specific range for a particular instrument need show only the outside extremities.

In the following pages where the instruments are discussed separately, it should be particularly noted that:

1. On woodwind instruments, the bottom note given is an absolute. There are no tones possible lower than the tone

represented. Certain instruments of different manufacture sometimes have an extra key. In this case we are
not dealing with an exception, we are dealing with a different instrument.
2. On brass instruments, the lower note given represents the
lowest practicable tone. *Pedal tones* are possible but not
practical on most brass instruments. The only brass instrument to use pedal tones is the trombone.
3. On stringed instruments, the lower note given represents
the pitch of the lowest string vibrating its complete length.
4. The upper note given for all instruments represents only
a "comfortable" or "average" upper limit, and professionals play as much as an octave higher and beyond. The
upper range on all brass instruments is without limit acoustically, and each player has a different upper limit, dependent only upon his capabilities.

Four basic families of instruments

All musical instruments belong to one of four families: *strings, woodwinds, brass,* or *percussion.* Although there have been more scientific
descriptions of instruments, the professional musician — composer,
conductor, orchestrator, or instrumentalist — uses this terminology.

THE STRINGS

In the string family are the violin, viola, cello, and double bass.
The tone on each of these instruments is produced by a bow drawn
across a taut string. The body of the instrument acts as a resonator and
an amplifier. Stringed instruments on which the tone is produced in a
different manner — such as the piano, harpsichord, and harp — will be
treated separately.

The Violin.   Because of its extensive range in the soprano register
(Example 307), its facility, and its expressiveness, the *violin* may be

Example 307

"The violin is held under the chin with the left hand while the right hand holds the bow" (p. 286).

found in the hands of a Gypsy violinist pouring forth a sentimental melody in a dimly lit cafe, at a country dance playing a spirited jig, in the concert hall as the leading member of a string quartet or symphony orchestra, and, in the hands of a great violin soloist.

The violin is held under the chin with the left hand. The right hand holds the bow. The tone of the violin has been described as similar to the human voice. This is a poor comparison. The tone of the violin lacks the basic distinction of the human voice, which is that its sound is the result of a column of air that comes from the lungs of the performer and passes through the vocal cords, setting them in vibration. The oral cavity acts as a resonator. This method of producing tone is similar to the manner in which the wind player produces tone. The brass player's lips are the "vocal cords." The similarity of vocal tone to that of a wind instrument is well understood by the composer. Examples in the sections on brass and winds will demonstrate this.

It is better to describe the violin as the stringed instrument that it is. No stringed instrument by itself can have the power of the voice or a wind instrument. Instead of power, however, the violin has in its upper register a steely intensity, and in its middle register an insinuating lyricism; in its low register it can be dark, vibrant, and sensuous.

> *Suggested Listening:* Stravinsky, *Firebird Suite* (1919 ed.), beginning measure 7 of "L'oiseau de feu et sa dance."

The Viola.   The viola has all the appearances of the violin, and is also held under the chin, but it is a slightly larger instrument and it is pitched a fifth lower (Example 308). It is the alto to the violin's soprano,

Example 308

and indeed, ***alto*** is the French name for the instrument. It has a darker and slightly more full-bodied sound than the violin, and has just slightly less flexibility because the distances on the fingerboard from one tone to another are a fraction larger.

The composer not only uses the viola to fill out the middle register of the string section, but, aware of its expressivity and its uniquely introspective tone color, writes for it passages that portray a somber mood or a dark intensity. Sometimes the portrayal suggests a yearning, or possibly an introverted emotional turbulence.

Listen to the enchanting sound of the viola section in the opening bars of Tchaikovsky's Sixth Symphony (Example 309). The violas enter in the fourth measure.

Example 309   Symphony No. 6, Movement 1, Tchaikovsky

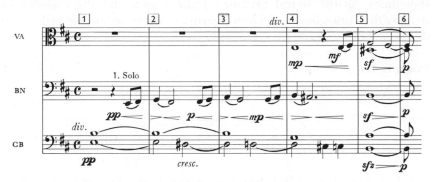

The viola is a regular member of the string quartet and plays a prominent part in much chamber music. Its solo repertoire is not extensive.

The Cello.   Violoncello is the full name of this instrument, but the shortened version, *cello*, is more often used. Because of its size it stands on the floor, using an extended end pin, and is held between the player's knees. This instrument has strings that are not only thicker than those of the viola, but twice as long. The cello is pitched an octave lower (Example 310) than the viola, and in its middle and upper register has a

Example 310

rich tenor sound that can be full and soaring. In its low register, it can be dark or warm as the composer requires. It can be quietly lyric, or it can give an effect of throbbing.

In addition to its use in the symphony orchestra, the cello is the bass member of the string quartet. The solo repertoire for this instrument is considerable.

Suggested Listening: Dvorak, Cello Concerto in B minor.

The contrabass. The **contrabass** is the largest instrument of the string family and the lowest-pitched. It is also called the **double bass** because it originally doubled with the cello on the bass line in the orchestras of the baroque and classical periods.

This instrument stands on the floor as does the cello, but, because of its size, the player stands or may sit on a high stool. With a deep, sometimes "gruff" sound because of the length and thickness of its strings, the contrabass is pitched nearly an octave below the cello, with its lowest note sounding E_3 (Example 311).

Example 311

The contrabass differs in certain aspects from the other instruments of the string section. Its strings are tuned upward in fourths, rather than fifths as the other stringed instruments are. On close inspection it will be noted that its shoulders are more sloping, and its back is flatter. These differing aspects are the result of its descent from the viol family. For this reason the contrabass is still called the ***bass viol***. But there are some contrabasses that have incorporated the features of the violin family, not retaining the differences we have mentioned. The contrabass of the symphony orchestra today has an additional fifth string that extends the range of the instrument down an additional major third to C_3.

The contrabass is a standard member of the jazz orchestra, having replaced the tuba in the earlier part of the century, and is more often referred to here as the ***bass fiddle***, the ***string bass***, or simply the ***bass***. Its function in jazz is chiefly that of a rhythm instrument, and the manner of playing is usually that of pizzicato, although the bow is used when the function of the instrument is to supply the foundation of the harmony in less rhythmic passages. In the jazz orchestra also, the double bass has had a fifth string added to the usual four, but it is a string pitched higher than the other four, rather than lower.

THE WOODWINDS

The term ***woodwinds,*** as a classifying name, was first used to differentiate wind instruments originally made of wood from those made of brass. This was not the only differentiating feature, but it did serve to classify, and it is still in use, in spite of the fact that some of the woodwinds are now made of metal.

Because of some basic differences in construction of woodwind instruments, this section of the orchestra has many more possibilities for variety of tone color than either the string section or the brass section. Note, for instance, that string instruments are basically the same in their proportions, materials, and manner of construction; they differ chiefly in size. The string section thus presents the most homogeneous sound of any section of the orchestra. The brass instruments, in spite of important differences in their bore measurements, are also reasonably similar in their proportions, materials, and manner of construction. The brass section sound is fairly homogeneous. By contrast, the instruments of the woodwind section are not "all of the same cloth," or even nearly so. There are three distinct types of woodwind instruments, differing from each other markedly in certain basic characteristics, and they may be grouped as follows:

flutes	piccolo
	flute
	alto flute
single reeds	E ♭ clarinet
	B ♭ clarinet
	alto clarinet
	bass clarinet
double reeds	oboe
	english horn
	bassoon
	contrabassoon

The tone on the flute is the most "open" of all the woodwinds. The tone is produced by the player's lips vibrating across an open hole. There is no reed. The flute does not blend well with the other instruments of the woodwind section. The manner of producing the tone on the flute is more similar to the manner in which a brass player produces tone, and, as a matter of fact, a flute coupled with a trumpet or trombone, surprising though it may seem, blends better than it would with a clarinet or, more especially, a double-reed instrument.

The instruments of the clarinet family use a single reed fitted against a wedge-shaped mouthpiece. The reed imparts a mild quality of reediness to the tone. The instruments of the double-reed grouping have no mouthpiece, using instead a double reed, which gives the tone an extremely reedy, penetrating sound. These double-reed instruments do not blend well with any of the instruments of the orchestra. When it is said that they do, what is actually meant is that they blend well if they do not predominate — in other words, if they are covered.

Example 312   Octet for Wind Instruments, Sinfonia, Stravinsky

It is not meant to be implied here that these differences are a hindrance. There are certain times, perhaps, when the composer, in a moment of fickleness, implies that he would like a woodwind section that would be "easier to get along with" — the differences mentioned make it difficult for the woodwinds as an isolated section to blend well, and intonation is a definite problem — but this fickleness is only momentary. The composer actually is glad for the sparkle, the color, the variety.

Example 313 shows woodwind writing in which the achievement

Example 313   Midsummer Night's Dream, Overture, Mendelssohn

of a good blend and good intonation is a problem. The problem is made even more difficult by the staggered entrances of the instruments.

The Flute.   Originally of wood, the *flute* often is made of silver, and occasionally of platinum or gold. The instrument is held horizontally to the player's right; the tone is produced by blowing across an open tone-hole in somewhat the same manner as one blows across the open top of a bottle to produce a tone.

Example 314

With the exception of the piccolo, the flute is the highest-pitched of the woodwinds and the most agile. The flutist can execute long lyrical passages, as well as ones of extreme technical complexity. The tone, acoustically, is the "purest" of the woodwinds because so few of the overtones are present in it. As it is the only instrument of the woodwind section that does not use a reed to set the air column in vibration, its tone has more of the quality of "wind" in it than the other woodwinds. Because it is not a reed instrument, its tone is the least insistent of all the woodwinds. In its middle register the flute's quality of tone may be suggestive of calmness or pensiveness. Through association with the shepherd's pipe, it sometimes suggests scenes of a pastoral nature. In its upper register the tone of the flute becomes brighter, and in staccato passages, more bell-like. Aware of the flute's similarity to the human soprano voice in its middle and high registers, composers have often used the flute in duet style with the coloratura in florid operatic writing.

> *Suggested Listening:* Donizetti, "Mad Scene," *Lucia di Lammermoor*," for soprano and flute.

In its low register its tone has a quiet breathiness that can suggest an air of intimacy.

In addition to its use in the symphony orchestra, the flute is also a regular member of the concert band. In recent years it has found its way into the hands of jazz performers. This has been made possible with the aid of the microphone, whereas formerly the flute could not compete with the instruments of greater volume.

The Piccolo.   *Piccolo* is but the short terminology for *flauto piccolo*. The term "piccolo" by itself only means "little." This *petite flute*, as the French speak of it, is pitched an octave higher than the flute and adds not only range but brilliance to the upper register of the woodwind section. Its tone is much brighter than that of the flute and also much

"In its low register its tone has a quiet breathiness which may suggest an air of intimacy" (p. 291).

Example 315

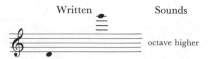

more penetrating. It is used in its middle and upper registers to add sparkle to the orchestration. The tone of its middle register is somewhat comparable to a person's whistle, which is indeed in the same register. In the upper register the tone may be described as shrill or even piercing. The composer uses this register with caution.

The piccolo sometimes doubles the flute part an octave higher. Ravel has used it in his "Bolero," placed a fourth above the first flute (Example 316). The orchestra piccolo is pitched in C, and is written an

Example 316   Bolero, Ravel

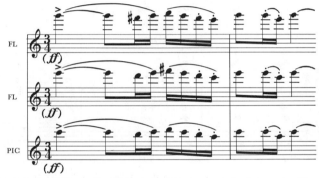

Special permission granted for reprint Durand and Cie, Paris, France; Copyright owners—Elkan-Vogel Co., Inc., Agents.

octave lower than it sounds in order to avoid the excessive use of leger lines. In the symphony orchestra, the third (or, in large orchestras, the fourth) flutist usually doubles on the piccolo.

In the final pages of his opera, *Salome*, Richard Strauss has made interesting use of the piccolo. As Salome carries the silver tray that holds the severed head of John the Baptist, she is about to sing, "I have kissed your lips, Jokanaan." Example 317 shows the piccolo in octaves with the oboe in a figure that is played seven more times at varying time intervals, over trills and tremolos and generally shimmering orchestration. The effect is one of the most eerie in music.

In the concert band the piccolo is used much more often than in the orchestra. In marches the piccolo often plays an obbligato high above the melody. Well known to many listeners is the piccolo obbligato in the trio section of Sousa's "Stars and Stripes Forever." In the interests

Example 317   Salome, Strauss

of showmanship it is now traditional for the members of the flute section to stand as they play this piccolo obbligato.

The piccolo used in the concert band is usually pitched in D-flat, sounding a semitone higher than the piccolo in C.

The Alto Flute.   The ***alto flute*** is sometimes spoken of as the bass flute, but the instrument we have in mind is that which is pitched a fourth lower than the flute. It is a transposing instrument pitched in G, somewhat longer than the flute, and with a larger bore. It is the alto to

Example 318

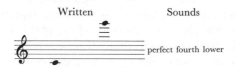

the flute's soprano, and has a larger, darker sound. Its use is rare. It has lately attained some wider use as an instrument in jazz orchestration, and as a solo instrument in jazz improvisation.

The Recorder. The *recorder* is a woodwind instrument that was in common use from the sixteenth century to the eighteenth. It was finally superseded by the flute for the same reason that certain other instruments lost favor: the flute had a more powerful tone. The recorder is end blown, and has a beaked wooden mouthpiece that fits between the lips in the manner of an ordinary wooden whistle. Its tone is unusually pure and is even more mellow and "hollow" than that of the flute.

To J. S. Bach "flute" meant recorder; when he wished to use the flute that we know today he wrote "flauto traverso." There were several sizes of recorder making up a family, or consort; the most usual sizes were the descant, treble, tenor, and bass. The recorder has been revived in recent years to play baroque music as it was written, and also as a beginning instrument for children or adults.

The Oboe. The double reed of the *oboe* imparts a tone quality to the instrument that is easily recognizable. Sometimes spoken of as nasal, its tone quality can perhaps be better described as reedy and quietly penetrating, as opposed to the clarinet tone, which is more bland. It often alternates with the clarinet in assuming the role of the soprano in the woodwind section (Example 319), especially in a lyric, cantabile

Example 319

melody. There are many examples of its use as a solo instrument. The well known use by Tchaikovsky shown in Example 320 shows the ability

Example 320 Swan Lake Ballet, Scene I, Tchaikovsky

of the oboe to sustain an expressive legato line of quiet intensity in its middle register.

Suggested Listening: Brahms, Symphony No. I, Movement 2.

The oboe tone becomes thinner as it proceeds into the high register and its singing quality becomes less, but composers use the high range for special effects.

The oboe has no tuning slide as does a brass instrument, nor has it a mouthpiece that may be adjusted to lengthen the instrument as do the clarinet and flute. Thus the pitch is somewhat fixed. The orchestra tunes to the oboe. This does present a problem in the symphony orchestra in a performance of a piano concerto. It is always hoped that the pitch of the oboe and the piano will coincide. There have been instances to the contrary.

The English Horn.   The *english horn* is a double-reed instrument pitched in F (Example 321), a perfect fifth below the oboe. Larger and

Example 321

longer than the oboe, it is an alto instrument. In addition to its extra length, it may be distinguished from the oboe by the slight curve at its upper end and the globe-shaped bell at the lower. Its sound is darker and fuller than that of the oboe and has a husky plaintiveness that is unique. At times it may sound melancholy, and on occasion, quietly raucous. Broad lyric lines become it. Rarely is it used in passages of a highly technical nature (as are the oboe and the bassoon), being favored by the composer for its interesting tone color.

Suggested Listening: Berlioz, Symphonie Fantastique, Movement 3 ("Scene in the Country").

The Clarinet.   Not only is the *clarinet* one of the most agile of instruments, but also, in its nearly four octaves, it has the greatest range of all the woodwinds (Example 322). It also has the largest dynamic range

Example 322

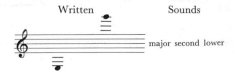

*"It can be wild as a shriek in
its upper register"* (p. 298).

of the woodwinds, varying from the lightest whisper to an impressive forte.

Brought into general use in the symphony orchestra by Mozart in his "Paris" Symphony, No. 31, the clarinet remained there as a favored instrument of many composers, chiefly because of the wide variety of tone color of which it is capable. It can be as wild as a shriek in its upper register. It can sound hollow or other-worldly in its lower, *chalumeau* register (Example 323). In its middle register, it can be lyrical and warm, or dry and light. And it can be bland as no other instrument can.

Example 323   Romeo and Juliet, Tchaikovsky

Suggested Listening: R. Strauss, *Till Eulenspiegel.*

The clarinet is most commonly pitched in B♭, but there is also the clarinet in A, pitched a semitone lower. Both instruments are standard equipment for the clarinetist in a symphony orchestra. Composers in the past often wrote for the A clarinet, not only to make it somewhat easier for the player to negotiate in sharp keys but also to take advantage of the slightly darker quality of the lower-pitched instrument. With the continual improvement in the manufacture of the instrument, however, and the simultaneous advance in the mastery of technique among clarinetists, the choice of instrument is now that of the clarinetist rather than the composer. That is to say, the clarinetist, regardless of the written part, chooses the instrument that will make it easier to achieve a better tone or better intonation, or will facilitate the fingering of a particular passage.

The clarinet has had wide use in the playing of folk music and dance music in many countries. It has been used in orchestras in the United

States ever since the Civil War, when it was borrowed from the marching bands of the day ultimately to become a standard instrument in the early jazz bands. Its use continues to the present day in dance orchestras and theater orchestras, where it is considered a "natural double" for the saxophonist. However, its use in the jazz orchestra has lately decreased.

The B♭ clarinet is a leading member of the concert band, the clarinet section equating in a general way with the violin section of the symphony orchestra.

The E♭ Clarinet. A shorter and higher-pitched instrument than the B♭ clarinet, the *E♭ clarinet* extends the range of the clarinet section up by a fourth (Example 324). This instrument has a tone that may be

Example 324

described as thinner and shriller then that of the B♭ clarinet. It is also somewhat more difficult to play in tune. At its worst it is strident; at its best, brilliant. Although it is a regular member of the symphony orchestra, it is used much more sparingly than the B♭ clarinet.

The Alto Clarinet (in E♭). This instrument, pitched a fifth lower than the B♭ clarinet (Example 325), is a longer instrument. If it had a

Example 325

fuller sound, it would be an adjunct to the clarinet section in filling out the middle register. However, its tone being somewhat weak or shallow, it is not often used in the symphony orchestra. It is a regular member of the concert band, however, where it is not used as a single instrument but stands in the position in the clarinet section that the viola holds in the string section. Its upper end is slightly curved because of the length of the instrument.

The Bass Clarinet.   The **bass clarinet** is a fairly recent addition to the woodwinds, not coming into general usage until the second half of the nineteenth century. Sounding an octave below the B ♭ clarinet (Example 326), it is curved both at the upper end and at the lower end, with

Example 326

the lower curve turning upward into a bell shape. In its middle and lower registers it has a tone color that perhaps is described by the phrase, "broad, but gentle."

Without the bite and the reediness of the bassoon, its volume is about the same. Therefore its tone can be easily covered by more sonorous instruments. The composer uses it often in exposed passages, in addition to having it supply the bass for quiet woodwind or string writing. In the upper part of the register, the tone of the bass clarinet "thins out." Its upper range is therefore used somewhat sparingly.

The Bassoon.   Music for the **bassoon** is written in the bass and tenor staves. In rare instances the treble staff is used (Example 327).

Example 327

It may be noted that its name in German, *Fagotte,* or Italian, *fagotto,* is equivalent to the English word "fagot," which means several sticks bound together. This is the "look" of the instrument. This was more true in the earlier stages of the instrument's development when the workmanship was less refined. Now, although it retains its original shape, it is a sleek instrument made of maple, with a dark cherry finish brought to a high luster.

The English name, *bassoon,* only refers to the fact that it is a bass instrument. With a range of three octaves or more and a surprising agility for a low-pitched instrument, the bassoon has many uses in the orchestra. In addition to providing the bass to the woodwind section, it is an excellent solo instrument with an expressive, individual sound. Its double reed gives its tone an edge, but it is a tone less penetrating than that of the oboe, its counterpart in the higher register.

In the orchestra of classical dimensions, it often doubles the cello or double-bass part, adding piquancy and verve to a fast-moving line. In its upper register it has a thinner, drier sound that has been used by Stravinsky with remarkable effect in the opening measures of *Le Sacre du Printemps* (Example 328).

Example 328   Le Sacre du Printemps, Stravinsky

Copyright 1921 by Edition Russe de Musique. Copyright and Renewal assigned to Boosey & Hawkes Inc. Revised version copyright 1952 by Boosey & Hawkes Inc.

The Contrabassoon.   Also known as the ***double bassoon***, the ***contrabassoon*** is pitched one octave lower than the bassoon (Example 329), and

Example 329

it is used by composers to achieve a depth not possible with any other instrument of the orchestra. Its lowest note is but a semitone above the lowest note on the piano, and when the instrument is played in its lowest range, the tone may almost be said to resemble a "rattle" because the vibrations are so few. Its use in the symphony orchestra is occasional, although it was used by Haydn in *The Creation* and by Beethoven in his Fifth and Ninth Symphonies.

The Saxophone.   The ***saxophone*** is one of the few instruments that was invented as a complete family covering the ranges from soprano to bass (Example 330), with the complete family still in use today. It is a

Example 330

B♭ Soprano	E♭ Alto	B♭ Tenor	E♭ Baritone	B♭ Bass
major 2nd	major 6th	major 9th	major 13th	major 16th

lower

hybrid instrument. Made of brass, it has a mouthpiece and a single reed like those of the clarinet.

Invented by Adolphe Sax and patented by him in France in 1846, the saxophone did not gain acceptance into the symphony orchestra until the late 1800's, and since then its use has been somewhat occasional. Richard Strauss introduced a quartet of saxophones into his "Domestic Symphony," and Ravel wrote for three in his "Bolero."

> *Suggested Listening:*   Debussy, Rhapsodie for Saxophone and Orchestra.

The chief use of the saxophone has been in American popular music and jazz. In the early 1900's it found its way into dance bands and jazz bands, and since then it has become the basic section of the large jazz orchestra, supplying the fundamental body of sound as the strings do for the symphonic orchestra. The alto saxophone, the tenor, and to a lesser extent, the baritone, have been the instruments of some of the finest jazz soloists.

> *Suggested Listening:*   Recordings by Coleman Hawkins, Charlie Parker, Gerry Mulligan, Stan Getz, and John Coltrane.

The soprano saxophone, pitched in B♭, has made sporadic appearances as a jazz solo instrument, and has recently been in the spotlight again. The bass saxophone is rarely seen.

The parts for all saxophones are written in treble, as shown in Example 330, regardless of their registers. They are the only instruments with fixed upper limits. The upper limit can be exceeded by performers who are able to play harmonics, but this is somewhat exceptional.

THE BRASS

The instruments of the brass section are the trumpet, the french horn, the trombone, and the tuba, representing respectively the ranges of soprano, alto, tenor, and bass. The symphony orchestra carries a minimum of three trumpets, four french horns, three trombones, and one tuba. This is the most sonorous section of the orchestra. Individually and as a section these instruments can produce the greatest volume of sustained sound. In sustained, tutti passages the brass dominate.

Listen to the opening measures of the overture to *Die Meistersinger* and look at the first page of the full orchestral score. Notice the predominance of the brass sound in spite of the fact that these instruments are, in number, only 11 out of the entire orchestra.

Also, because of their sonority, the brass are useful in adding to the texture to produce climaxes of sound.

The sound on all brass instruments is produced by a column of air set in motion. The air from the player's lungs causes the lips to vibrate. The lips control the pitch. The position of the player's lips on the mouthpiece is called *embouchure*. Special effects that can be obtained with different degrees of effectiveness on the various brass instruments include **double tonguing, triple tonguing**, and the **flutter tongue.**

Gunther Schuller has used double tonguing less as a special effect and more as a normal tool of the brass player in a very felicitous manner in his Symphony for Brass and Percussion. Directions for double tonguing are not given in the score. It is the metronome marking of $\downarrow$ = 144 that indicates the necessity for double tonguing the sixteenth-notes. (Example 331).

All of the brass instruments have a cup-shaped mouthpiece with the exception of the french horn, which has a mouthpiece that is funnel-shaped. The manner of producing the tone is the same on all brass instruments.

Many mutes have been invented for the brass instruments, but there is only one that has become standard in the symphony orchestra. Made of metal or fibre, it is cone-shaped and is known as a *straight mute.* When the part specifies mute, it is understood that the reference is to the straight mute. The mute is fitted into the bell of the instrument, and not only softens the tone but changes its color completely so that it no longer has the basic sound of a brass instrument. The tone changes to one with an edge to it, more similar to the tone of a double-reed instrument. For example, the tone of the trumpet is changed in volume and tone color to such an extent that it is not too unlike the tone of the oboe. The straight mute is used principally in the trumpet and trombone sections, but on occasion even the tuba is called upon to use the mute. This is a huge mute, since it has to fit the upright bell of the instrument, and the free-lance tuba player avoids carrying the mute with him if at all possible. The cup mute, so called because of its shape, is rarely used in the symphony orchestra. It also softens the tone, but it gives the brass instrument a mellow sound more similar to the tone of a flute. The

Example 331   Symphony for Brass and Percussion, Movement 4, Schuller

straight mute and the cup mute have long been standard equipment in the large jazz orchestras. The jazz musician has used many devices to change the natural sound of the brass instruments. In addition to the straight mute and the cup mute, there is the harmon mute. This was originally used to produce a "wow-wow" effect (with the aid of the left hand), but now is more often used without this effect and used instead to produce an intense, soft sound. Other mutes, such as the "solotone," which looks like a double cone and produces a somewhat hollow tone, have mostly gone out of use. Some orchestras, such as that of Duke Ellington, have long used a "plunger"—this is actually the rubber end of a bathroom plunger—to produce a deep hollow sound, and in the hands of an expert trombonist it sounds oddly imitative of the human speaking voice.

The Trumpet.   The *trumpet* is the soprano voice of the brass section (Example 332). With tubing that is narrow-bored and mainly cylindrical,

Example 332

the trumpet has a brilliant, commanding tone that can "carry" above the entire symphonic orchestra playing at full volume.

Before the advent of valves in the early nineteenth century, the trumpet was employed to reinforce the fundamental harmonies and certain rhythmic figures of an orchestral work, often in conjunction with the timpani. Without valves the trumpet was limited to the notes of the overtone series based upon the fundamental tone of the instrument. In this respect it was similar to the bugle of today. This very limitation was the spur that drove trumpet players in the baroque period to develop the extreme high register. Note that in the fourth octave of the harmonic series the notes are close enough together to enable the player to produce the notes of the major scale. To play in this octave is exceedingly demanding with regard to endurance and control. It is analogous to the performance of the coloratura soprano. However, a virtuoso school of trumpet playing developed—although these players were as scarce as coloraturas—and composers of the time wrote for them. The trumpet part in the Brandenburg Concerto No. 2 (Example 333) originally was written for a valveless trumpet, a larger and lower-pitched trumpet than the B♭ trumpet in use today. It was essentially an alto trumpet, pitched in F.

Example 333   Brandenburg Concerto No. 2, J. S. Bach

(actual sound)

   With the addition of valves to the trumpet, virtuoso high-register
playing died out, and today the baroque trumpet parts are usually
played on a trumpet that is much smaller than the B♭ trumpet. This is
the *piccolo trumpet*, sometimes referred to as the ***Bach trumpet***, pitched
an octave higher.

   Most trumpet players in symphony orchestras have G^2 within their
range on the B♭ trumpet, and a very few can perform the Brandenburg
Concerto on this instrument—producing a larger tone than is possible
on the piccolo trumpet, this larger tone being more similar to the original sound of the early baroque trumpet. Performances of the Brandenburg on the B♭ trumpet are few, however, because of the problem of
endurance. In a way, it may be compared to playing the children's
game, "King of the Mountain." It is not so much a matter of getting
there as staying there.

   The Cornet.   The *cornet* (Example 334) is occasionally called for in

Example 334

Written

Sounds

major second lower

a symphonic score, but its chief use is in the concert band.
   The tubing of the B♭ cornet and the B♭ trumpet is exactly the same
length, in spite of the fact that the cornet looks shorter. The cornet
appears to be shorter only because its tubing is coiled differently. In
addition to their length being the same, both instruments have the same
valve system, and are playable by both cornetists and trumpeters. The
tone of the cornet is mellower than that of the trumpet because its bore
is larger and more conical. The bore of the trumpet is basically cylindrical, which accounts for its more brilliant tone.
   It has sometimes been said that the cornet is easier to play than the
trumpet. This is true in a very limited way; the more conical bore allows
for a certain "easiness" in making the instrument speak and in the playing of a legato line. However, the chief reason that has always been ad-

vanced for its use as a leading member of the concert band is its mellow-
ness of tone, the trumpet tone being regarded as too brilliant.

The Fluegel Horn in B♭.   The *fluegel horn* in common use today is
the one pitched in B♭, a soprano instrument with the same register and
range as both the B♭ trumpet and the B♭ cornet (Example 335). It is

Example 335

the descendant of a whole family of fluegel horns that came in many
sizes and were pitched in all registers from the soprano fluegel horn
in E♭ (comparable to an E♭ trumpet) to the contrabass (comparable
to a BB♭ tuba).

This surviving instrument stands in relation to the cornet as the
cornet does to the trumpet. That is to say: as the bore of the cornet is
larger and more conical than that of the trumpet, and the sound is
mellower, so the bore and the sound of the fluegel horn are even more
so. Although its tubing is the same length as that of the B♭ trumpet and
the B♭ cornet, it appears shorter because of its coiling. The wider bore
is apparent as well as the more conical tubing, which flares into a larger
bell than that of the cornet. Its chief use has been in the concert band to
add a mellow, darker sound in the soprano register. Separate parts have
been written for it, but at times it has been used on the cornet parts,
along with the cornets, to darken the cornet section sound. This is no
longer common. The fluegel horn has lately found its way into the jazz
field, where a certain few trumpet players have become intrigued with
its less incisive, broader sound, using it chiefly in solo improvisation.

The French Horn.   The *french horn*, usually called simply the *horn*,
is the alto instrument of the brass section (Example 336). The only brass
instrument to use a funnel-shaped mouthpiece, it has a natural tone that
is somewhat mellower than that of the trombone. Its tone is further mel-

Example 336

lowed, or darkened, by a practice that is unique in the playing of brass instruments: the normal method of playing the horn is with the player's right hand inserted into the bell, with the hand "cupped" so as to somewhat muffle the tone.

The horn is also the only brass instrument in which the valves are played with the left hand. Before valves were invented, the horn was held with the left hand, the right hand being inserted into the bell in order to "manipulate" the tones. As the valveless horn was limited to only the tones of its overtone series, the player could produce some "in-between" tones by inserting the hand in the bell, changing the air column enough so as to affect the pitch. This practice is known as "stopping," and continues today as a special effect. When valves were invented, horn players were already accustomed to using the right hand in the bell.

The mellow tone of the horn enables it to blend with the woodwinds as well as the brass in the symphony orchestra. It is an excellent solo instrument, as Example 337 shows. The range of the horn is exception-

Example 337   Till Eulenspiegel, Richard Strauss

ally large, and the example from Strauss shows use of this large range. However, since horn players sometimes specialize in "high horn" and "low horn," on occasion the last two notes of the solo above have been played by another horn player in the section.

When the horn was valveless, the player carried a number of U-shaped crooks on his arm. These would be of varying lengths, and upon being inserted into the instrument would lengthen it by a given amount, changing the fundamental tone correspondingly. This gave the composer a larger number of available tones, and was especially valuable in modulations to new keys in the course of the composition. These U-shaped crooks were named for the fundamentals that they produced. Thus, when in the horn part there would be the instruction "in G," the horn player would exchange the current "crook" for the "G crook," the instrument now having *G* as its fundamental.

Today the horn player uses one instrument only, that pitched in F, and transposes the parts in the older scores. This is a formidable task, but it is a part of the training of all french horn players.

The french horn that is standard among symphonic players today is a double horn. That is, in addition to the basic horn pitched in F, there is. a separate set of tubing pitching the instrument in B ♭, a fourth above. By use of a valve that re-routes the air column, the player has a choice of either set of tubing, and uses this convenience to achieve better intonation or tone, or to facilitate fingering.

The horn has only occasionally been used in large dance orchestras, and only rarely has it been the instrument of the jazz soloist. It lacks the technical elasticity of the trumpet or the saxophone or other keyed instruments.

The Alto Horn (in E♭).   The **alto horn**, also called the *upright alto*, today exists almost exclusively in marching bands. It is a descendant of the E♭ alto saxhorn, but today has a tuning slide adjustment so that it may be pitched in F (Example 338). It and the baritone are the only

Example 338

instruments in use today that descend from the family of saxhorns introduced by Adolphe Sax in 1843. Its tone is neither mellow nor brilliant, but rather dry and hard, and in many older, unimaginative scores it was often relegated to the playing of the off-beats in a march. It thus became colloquially known as the "peck horn."

A new version of the alto horn came into existence for two reasons. The first was an attempt to make the sound somewhat less hard, and more mellow, so it was called the **mellophone**. Secondly, the french horn was becoming more and more common in public school musical organizations, so the shape of the alto horn was changed to correspond to that of the french horn. However, it was still an alto horn, and no matter which shape it came in, upright or circular, it could not do justice to the horn parts of the orchestral literature even of a high school group. Gradually it was supplanted by the french horn, first in the high school orchestra, and later and somewhat more gradually in the concert band. It no longer exists in professional symphonic bands.

The Trombone.   The **trombone** is a tenor instrument pitched an octave below the B♭ trumpet (Example 339). Because its bore is narrow and mostly cylindrical, it has a tone brighter than that of the horn, and more akin to the trumpet. Its name, which is Italian, actually means "large trumpet."

The trombone historically is the oldest type of brass instrument in

Example 339

wide usage that still exists in its original form. Because of its slide, which can elongate the instrument through seven positions, thus supplying seven different fundamental tones, it has always been able to play the chromatic scale. Playing a prominent part in early music, it did not come into use in symphonic writing until Beethoven introduced it in the last movement of his Fifth Symphony.

Although the trombone had not been accepted in symphonic circles in Mozart's time, Mozart made notable use of it in certain of his operas, often for the representation of the supernatural. In *Idomeneo* the trombones accompany the voice of the oracle speaking from the waterfall. This is their only use in the opera and the sounds come, not from the pit, but from backstage, accompanying the voice. In *Don Giovanni* Mozart again uses the trombone as part of a supernatural effect. He reserves their use throughout the entire opera until the appearance of the statue (or ghost) of the Commendatore whom Don Giovanni killed in a duel at the beginning of the opera. The trombones here also are backstage, and the other instruments are in the pit with the rest of the orchestra.

A unique piece of trombone writing is to be found in Mozart's Requiem in the "Tuba Mirum." This is a part written for the tenor trombone in duet with the bass soloist (Example 340). The first 13 meas-

Example 340   Requiem, K. 626, No. 3, "Tuba Mirum," Mozart

ures are considered to be by Mozart, with the following written by his amanuensis, Süssmayr. The solo is found in the second trombone part, because in that day there existed the true *alto*, tenor and *bass trombones*, and Mozart wanted the tone color and range of a tenor trombone.

All trombones used in this country today are really tenor trombones. The alto trombone has become obsolete, and parts written for it in the scores of Bach, Handel, Haydn, Mozart, and Beethoven are performed on the tenor trombone. However, an exception may be made to this statement. A few first trombonists have lately been having alto trombones custom made. The bass trombone of today, although called that, is really a tenor trombone with a wide bore and an extra length of tubing to carry it into the bass trombone range. The extra tubing is made available by the use of the F-valve, or "trigger," which adds a fourth to the lower range of the instrument. Many tenor trombones are now equipped with the F-valve and tubing as a utility feature, resulting in a tenor-bass trombone.

The trombone has had wide usage throughout all periods of jazz. In the early days of jazz it was borrowed from the marching bands to play the bass line in Dixieland, or "tailgate" from the back of a truck. It was one of the instruments of the blues, and went from there into the large dance bands and jazz orchestras. It received its lyric voice from Tommy Dorsey, and continues today in big bands, television studios, and in many jazz groups. The trombone has also been a constant in the band, from the front line of the marching band to its position in the concert band, which is basically similar to its position in the symphony orchestra.

Baritone or Euphonium.   The *baritone* (or *euphonium*) is one of the most mellifluous of the brass instruments. Its chief use has been in the concert band; and because of its facility, its flexibility in extreme ranges, and its mellow tone, its position in the band has often been likened to that of the cello in the orchestra. Although this is a facile analogy, it is reasonably true.

Although its extreme ranges cannot match the cello's, it can compete in a general way. It is really the only brass instrument in the band in the tenor-baritone-bass range (Example 341) with a full, singing

Example 341

sound, and the flexibility of the trumpet. The baritone can execute extremely technical passages as well as sing a bel canto line with the niceties of an opera singer. In fact, in transcriptions of operatic music for band, the baritone is often called upon to execute the tenor, baritone, or bass solo of the opera.

As to the difference between a baritone and a euphonium, it may be put this way: the euphonium is to the baritone as the cornet is to the trumpet. That is, the bore of the euphonium is larger than that of the baritone; it is also more conical. These two features result in a mellower sound, in the same manner in which a cornet has a mellower sound than the trumpet. The baritone is a descendant of the saxhorn family, whereas the euphonium is more similar to the tuba. Thus, the euphonium tone is broader and mellower than that of the baritone.

The matter of two bells has to be treated separately. The idea that a euphonium has two bells and a baritone one is incorrect. Either instrument may have one or two, although it has been more common for the euphonium to have the two bells. This is something of an oddity, since the baritone or the euphonium is the only instrument that exists today with two bells. The second bell, which is smaller, produces a sound similar to that of the trombone. The baritone or euphonium may also have a fourth valve which, similar to the F-attachment on the trombone, extends the range of the instrument down to C^2.

The baritone or euphonium is occasionally used in symphony orchestras to play the parts written for tenor tuba, chiefly found in the works of Wagner and Strauss.

Saxhorn.   Adolphe Sax, who invented the saxophone, also invented a family of upright brass instruments in ranges from soprano to bass. They are three-valved instruments, and were intended by Sax to add a new color to the tonal palette of the orchestra and band. These instruments belong to the *saxhorn* family.

There are no instruments in general use today that are spoken of as saxhorns, but the baritone in its bore and general dimensions corresponds to the tenor saxhorn. The euphonium, on the other hand, with its larger bore, has the general proportions of the tuba. Thus it corresponds to a tenor tuba, and plays the part so labeled in Strauss's *Don Quixote*.

The Tuba.   The *tuba* most commonly used is the BB♭ (the double B♭), pitched an octave below the B♭ trombone, and with tubing twice as long. With the aid of a fourth valve, which serves the same function as the F-attachment on the trombone, extra tubing is made available and the blacked-in notes shown in Example 342 are theoreti-

"The predecessors of the tuba were the ophicleide, which was the bass instrument of the keyed bugle family, and the serpent, so named because of its shape" (p. 315).

Example 342

cally possible. However, it is not usual to write below D_3. The tuba has an extremely wide bore—wider in proportion to the length of its tubing than that of any other brass instrument—and thus has a very broad, sonorous sound.

The tuba, with no history prior to the invention of valves, was the last of the brass instruments to become a member of the symphony orchestra. The predecessors of the tuba were the *ophicleide*, which was the bass instrument of the *keyed bugle* family, and the *serpent*, so named because of its shape.

> *Suggested Listening:* Mendelssohn, "A Midsummer Night's Dream," Overture

Symphonic tuba players also use a tuba in C, pitched one tone higher than the BB♭. This instrument provides a slight advantage in the upper register, and also "manipulates" just a bit more easily. Its tone is slightly less obtrusive. More rarely, smaller tubas pitched in E♭ and F are used in the symphony orchestra.

In the concert band, the BB♭ tuba is the standard instrument; but the tuba in E♭ is very common. The chief reason for the E♭ tuba in the band is its smaller size and lighter weight, which is more practicable for high school or college students who may not have the "heft" necessary to handle the large instrument. This is especially true when the instrument must be carried while marching. A further aid to the tuba player in marching is the use of the model known as the *sousaphone*. This is an instrument of the *helicon* type, in which the bell faces forward, and was the innovation, although not the invention, of John Philip Sousa. The instrument encircles the player and "sits" on his shoulder.

The tuba has been in and out of orchestras in the popular and jazz fields since the late 1800's. Before the turn of the century the most accessible and the least expensive instruments were those that had become "army surplus" after the Civil War. Thus it was only natural that the clarinet, trumpet, trombone, and "brass bass" (or tuba) were instruments of the early jazz orchestras. The tuba's position was gradually usurped by the bass fiddle, and by the mid-thirties it had become a rarity.

Wagner Tuba. The Wagner tuba family of brass instruments was the idea of Richard Wagner who introduced them into the orchestra to extend the tone palette of the horn section. They are not tubas in any modern usage of the term. The higher pitched Wagner tubas are actually modified french horns, in a helicon shape with a less conical bore, and are played by members of the horn section. The mouthpiece is funnel-shaped like that of the horn, and although originally the mouthpieces were larger, today french horn players use their regular mouthpieces.

The parts for the lower pitched Wagner tuba are now being taken over by the euphonium.

THE PERCUSSION

The basic instruments of the percussion section have a history that precedes that of the other families of instruments that have been discussed. The bass drum, the snare drum, and the timpani are but variants of the ancient drums of different sizes that were used in primitive cultures as an integral part of festivals or religious ceremonies, as signals in time of danger, or to set the rhythm for the dance. The ancient drums were made by stretching the dried and treated skin of an animal over one end of a hollowed-out tree trunk or gourd.

Timpani. The most refined of the membrane percussion instruments are the *timpani.* They are the only instruments of the membrane type that are tuned to specific pitches (Example 343). There are hand

Example 343

| Written | | | | Sounds |
| 30-inch | 28-inch | 25-inch | 23-inch | as written |

screws on the upper rim that control the tension of the head (the membrane). The tension of the head must be uniform around the upper rim. Adjusting the tension may be compared to tightening the nuts on the wheel of an automobile consecutively and uniformly — except that it is a far more delicate operation, and the adjustment depends entirely upon the ear of the timpanist.

The classical orchestra usually employed two timpani (performed by one player), one tuned to the tonic of the key and the other tuned to the dominant. As noted in the section on the trumpet, the timpani and the trumpets were often used in conjunction with each other.

The timpanist is the principal player of the percussion section. With the bass drum and the snare drum, the timpani are often employed in performing passages of a pronounced rhythmic nature, but in producing a definite pitch the timpani are often the foundation of the harmony. For these two attributes of the timpani, one conductor of long experience with major symphony orchestras has said, "If you don't have a good timpanist, you don't have an orchestra."

The Snare Drum. The *snare drum* (Example 344) differs from every other kind of a drum in that it has a set of coiled wires strung

Example 344

across the bottom head of the drum. These coiled wires are known as *snares.* When the top of the snare drum is struck, the snares add a crispness of sound that is useful in rhythmic passages requiring a dry, distinctive staccato effect.

A well known use of the snare drum in the symphonic orchestra is Example 345 from Ravel's "Bolero", which is repeated throughout the entire work in a constant crescendo to the end.

Example 345   Bolero, Ravel

Special permission granted for reprint Durand and Cie, Paris, France; Copyright owners—Elkan-Vogel Co., Inc., Agents.

The snare drum is familiar to all as the instrument that plays the "street beat" in the marching band when the band is not playing. The snare drum part may be written on the third space, or on a separate line. The snare drum is a basic part of the equipment of the jazz drummer.

The Tenor Drum. The *tenor drum* is larger than the snare drum, and is so-called because its pitch, although indeterminate, is lower than that of the snare drum. It does not have snares, and produces a somber tone.

The Bass Drum.   The **bass drum** hardly needs to be explained or described, but it may be said that it consists of two heads of stretched membrane, each stretched over opposite ends of a barrel-type wooden (or metal) structure. Although bass drums vary in size, they are always the largest drums in either the band or the orchestra.

Example 346

The bass drum has hand-screws on both rims that control the tension of the heads. Although of indefinite pitch, it has been said that it should be tuned to somewhere in the neighborhood of G_2. This may or may not be true, but the best *tone* for the purposes of the symphony orchestra or the concert band is that which is between the one extreme of a "boom"—which is too reverberating—and the other extreme of a "thud"—which has too little reverberation.

The importance of the bass drum cannot be overemphasized. As correct tempo is the first requisite in performance, the rhythmic function of the bass drum is vital.

Cymbals.   **Piatti**, which is the Italian term for **cymbals**, literally means *plates*. The term well describes the general shape of cymbals. Made of spun brass, they come in all sizes. The cymbals used in the symphonic orchestra and the concert band are eighteen inches or more in diameter, and are capable of a large dynamic range, from a whispered "z-z-z" to a resounding crash.

A pair of cymbals is played by one man. They are sounded by being struck against each other with a technique that might be described as "striking together obliquely."

There are also smaller cymbals, in various sizes, that may be played in different ways: the single cymbal may be struck with a felt-headed mallet, or a drumstick; or a roll may be played on a cymbal. In fact, the possibilities are many, and the twentieth-century composer often goes to great lengths to explain in the player's part just how he wants special effects produced. In the orchestra of the theater pit, the television studio, or the jazz orchestra, the suspended cymbal (or several of them in different sizes) is preferred to the larger "concert" cymbals.

The Tam-Tam.   The **tam-tam**, or **gong**, is of Chinese origin. A giant cymbal, sometimes as large as four feet in diameter, it is struck with ·a round, soft-headed mallet to produce a reverberating tone that spans a range in volume from the softest whisper to a thunderous roar.

The lowest sounding of all the cymbals, it has a lip at its outer edge, facing away from the player. Because of its immense size it is hung on a free-standing frame. The player on certain occasions starts the vibrations ahead of time by hitting it very lightly.

The Xylophone. The modern ***xylophone*** is of comparatively recent origin, and because of its hard, dry, staccato sound it is used in the symphony only in special passages. Its keyboard resembles a portion of the piano keyboard. The xylophone bars (keys) are made of wood.

Set horizontally on a stand, the xylophone is normally played with two mallets, but on occasion three or four mallets are used. The lower range may extend down to F_1 on larger models.

Example 347

Suggested Listening: Stravinsky, "Petrouchka"

The Marimba. The ***marimba***, which is a larger version of the xylophone, has the added feature of resonance, which the xylophone does not have. Rare in its appearance in the symphony orchestra, it is used when the composer desires a deeper sound than the xylophone, and a continuation of sound, which the xylophone cannot produce.

Also resembling the piano keyboard in its four-octave range, its bars are of wood. Set horizontally on a stand, it also is played with from two to four soft rubber mallets. Under each bar there is a resonating tube that gives it its unique deep, hollow sound. The player also has a foot-pedal, which may damp the tones or allow them to ring.

The marimba has occasionally been used in dance orchestras, but is more commonly associated with the performance of the solo night club entertainer who performs on all of the "mallet" instruments.

Orchestra Bells. The keyboard of the ***orchestra bells*** resembles that of the xylophone, but the instrument is smaller and its lowest *C* is pitched an octave higher (Example 348). The bars are made of metal, and when struck with a hard-headed mallet give off a sound similar to actual silver bells. Orchestra bells are also well known by their German name, **glockenspiel.** They are standard equipment in today's symphonic orchestra, although their use is only occasional.

Suggested Listening: Mozart, *The Magic Flute*

Example 348

The use of the orchestra bells is far more common in the band, as they are often given passages that accent a melody played in the brass or winds. They are also used as a solo instrument. Fast passages are not usually written because of the carry-over of the sound: one tone will blur into the next, as there is no damping system on the instrument.

The orchestra bells, or glockenspiel, when used with a marching band, are referred to as the **bell-lyra**, as the bells are then in a vertical position, contained within a lyre-shaped frame.

Chimes.   The **chimes** are long metal tubes, one and one quarter or one and one half inches in diameter, suspended vertically from a rack. They are struck at the top with a wooden hammer, and give out a sound that resembles that of church bells (Example 349).

Example 349

There is a foot pedal mechanism, which may damp the tone or allow it to ring.

The Triangle.   The **triangle** is a round metal tube, about one half inch in diameter, bent at two points to form the triangle shape, and open at the end. It is struck with a small metal bar, and gives off a sound, indeterminate in pitch, which may best be described by the onomatopoetic term, "ting."

The triangle was first used by Gluck. One of its more familiar uses is in Beethoven's "Turkish" variation of the choral theme in the Ninth Symphony. Here it is used simultaneously with the bass drum and cymbal to produce the "Turkish" effect.

It is a standard part of the percussionist's equipment in symphony, theater, and studio orchestra.

> *Suggested Listening:* Beethoven, Symphony No. 9, movement 4; Liszt, Triangle Concerto in E♭

The Tambourine.   The *tambourine* is also a standard part of the percussionist's equipment. In addition to the single membrane stretched over one side of a small hoop, it has pairs of small circular metal disks inserted in the hoop. When the head of the tambourine is struck with the hand, the pairs of circular disks produce a sound that can be described in only one way: they "jingle." There are various ways in which the tambourine may be played: with the knuckle, the fist, the moistened thumb drawn across the head to produce a roll, and others.

The Castanets.   The *castanets* are probably familiar to all—certainly to anyone who has seen a Spanish dancer, and to anyone who has attended a performance of Bizet's opera, *Carmen.* They are small, slightly hollowed-out pieces of wood or other material, and they always come in pairs. As they are struck together, the hollowed sections facing each other produce a "cluck" or a "clack."

There are other percussion instruments that are certainly important in providing the composer with a variety of sound effects, but they need only to be mentioned briefly.

The Wood Block.   The *wood block* is a small rectangular block of wood with a slit cut part way into it near the top, and another near the bottom on the opposite side. When tapped with a drumstick, a dry, hollow sound is produced. The two slits usually produce a slight difference of sound. The performer chooses the one more appropriate.

The Slapstick (or Whip).   The *slapstick* consists of two pieces of wood, which are somewhat longer than the usual wooden ruler, and are hinged together at one end. The contact of the two pieces of wood simulates the sound of a *whip.*

Temple Blocks.   Chinese in origin, the *temple blocks* were once a standard part of the drummer's equipment in dance orchestras. They are called for occasionally in arrangements for theater orchestra, and in compositions for symphony orchestra. They are five in number in graduated sizes. They are more or less oval blocks of wood, hollowed out, with a mouth that emits the most hollow sound of the percussion instruments that strive for this general effect. Each of the five temple blocks emits a pitch that is not pre-determined and is unique with that block. The largest gives the lowest sound.

Various other percussion instruments need only be mentioned. These include the *rachet*, the *sleigh bells*, and various kinds of whistles, such as the *bird whistle* and *train whistle*. There are others that are used on rare occasions, and of course composers will continue to search for ever newer ways to produce percussive sounds that will result in even more instruments being added to the array that the percussionist will be responsible for.

It should be of interest to note, in this connection, the percussion instruments that were called for in the score of a recent long running musical comedy:

timpani (A♭ and E♭)	steel mallets	tom tom
bells	slap stick	tambourine
bongos	wood block	steel chime
vibes	cow bell	bamboo sticks
bones	chinese cymbals	sarna anklet bells
xylophone	finger cymbals	siamese bell tree
cymbals	gong	triangle
bass drum	high hat	temple block
snare drum	3 stones	

Other instruments

THE PIANO

The *piano* is probably the most well-known of all musical instruments. According to the American Music Conference, 22,300,000 Americans play the piano. With the exception of the organ, it has the largest range. Its 88 keys arranged in semitones from A_4 to C^4 serve as reference chart in designating the ranges of all other instruments.

The piano is actually a percussion instrument. Each tone is produced by the hitting action of a felt hammer against the strings. And although the task of each pianist in playing a lyric or legato passage is to make the tone as sustained as possible, each tone begins to die away immediately after it is begun, in the same manner that the sound of a cymbal dies away after being struck. However, the piano has the advantage over the cymbal by virtue of two particular features, one tangible and the other intangible. The tangible feature is the sounding board under the strings, which amplifies and helps sustain the tone.

The intangible feature is the ear or mind of the listener. Whereas a cymbal produces an indeterminate sound, each tone produced by the piano is a specific pitch, and the listener "sustains" the sound in his mind to some degree because of its significance with relation to surrounding tones in the melodic or harmonic context.

The dynamic range of the piano is considerable, from crashing chords to a feathery wisp of sound. The piano has three foot-pedals that add certain features to the expressivity of the instrument. When the damper pedal, on the right, is depressed it releases the dampers from the strings. This allows the strings to sustain the sound. The pedal on the left, the soft pedal, moves the hammers so that one less string produces the tone. The pedal in the middle (not practicable on some upright pianos) is the sostenuto pedal. This sustains the sound of selected tones during the playing of others that are not to be sustained.

Almost every major composer has written important works for the piano as a solo instrument, or in combination with other instruments.

The name *piano* is in reality an abbreviation of its former full name, **pianoforte**, which was its original designation, signifying that it could play both softly and loudly from touch alone, in contradistinction to the harpsichord, which it superseded.

Invented in Italy in 1709, the piano was in general use by Mozart's time, but it had a much lighter sound than does our piano of today. It is interesting to note that Johann Christian Bach, an older contemporary of Mozart, wrote keyboard works in which he specified "harpsichord or forte-piano."

> *Suggested Listening:*   Schubert, Piano Quintet in A ("Trout"), Opus 114; Stravinsky, *Petrouchka.*

THE HARPSICHORD

The **harpsichord**, usually in a shape similar to the grand piano, has a smaller range. The tone of the harpsichord, softer than that of the piano, is produced by a plucking action. When a key is depressed, a plectrum is moved upward, plucking the string as it passes. A harpsichord often has two sets of manuals (keyboards), and these are often played in combination to achieve various nuances of sound. A system of foot pedals also permits coupling of the two keyboards in various ways, including octave doublings, which allows for a variety in expression that some find more interesting than that of the piano.

With the renewed interest in music of the baroque period in recent years, there has been a resurgence of interest in the harpsichord, and it now makes its appearance quite regularly on the concert stage.

> *Suggested Listening:*   J. S. Bach, Well Tempered Clavier.

THE VIRGINAL

The tone of the *virginal* is produced in the same manner as that of the harpsichord. Its shape is rectangular, and its much smaller size permitted it to be carried from room to room and set on a table. Indeed, it might be thought of as a "portable harpsichord." However it did not have the potential for expression that the harpsichord had, being limited to one keyboard and having a smaller range. It was a favorite instrument for the home in sixteenth-century England, and much harpsichord music was performed on it. The best known collection of music written specifically for the instrument is the Fitzwilliam Virginal Book.

THE CLAVICHORD

The *clavichord* is the earliest of the keyboard instruments with strings. In the baroque period the clavichord was a sister instrument of the harpsichord. Of earlier origin, its tone was softer but nevertheless more expressive. The manner of producing the tone differed from that of the harpsichord. The tone is produced by a brass wedge (called a tangent), which touches the string. The force of the tangent may be varied by the pressure on the key that sets it in action. Thus, the control of volume is similar to that on the piano, although on a smaller scale. Also, since the tangent maintains its contact with the string while the tone is sounding, an expressive vibrato may be produced by the action of the player's fingers on the keyboard.

Music written for the clavier (keyboard) in the baroque period was performed on either the harpsichord or the clavichord, the choice being dependent upon the music's character and style.

THE HARP

The name *harp* derives from the Italian term for the instrument, *arpa*, which suggests the natural aptitude that the instrument has for playing arpeggios, broken chords. This natural aptitude is likewise, to some degree, its limitation.

The strings are arranged, not in semitones, but in diatonic scale steps in the key of C♭ major. By a system of foot pedals the player can raise the pitch of each string by one semitone, or by one whole tone. There are seven foot pedals, each standing for one note of the scale in all octaves. There are three separate notches for each foot pedal. When all of the pedals are in the highest notch the instrument is then in C♭. Placing all of the pedals in the middle notch shortens each string so that the instrument is then pitched in C. Placing each pedal in the lowest notch pitches the instrument another semitone higher. Various combinations of the foot pedals allow for a limited amount of chromatic writing, but in anything but slow tempos, the harp is essentially a diatonic instrument.

The harp is one of the oldest instruments, but it did not make its way into the symphony orchestra until the nineteenth century. It is now a regular member of the symphony orchestra. In large orchestras there are two harps. The solo and chamber music literature for the harp is not large.

> *Suggested Listening:*   Ravel, Alborada del Gracioso, for orchestra (score includes two harps).

THE ORGAN

The *organ* is the most complete single instrument in its range of volume and by virtue of its possibilities of registration. Registration refers to the various combinations of tone colors that may be produced by the operation of organ stops. These stops, which may be adjusted by the player ahead of time or during the course of the music, change the quality of tone. The number of stops varies with each organ, and therefore the variety of tone color differs with each instrument. Some of the stops are designated by terms such as *trumpet* or *oboe*. But to the organist these stops are not so much an imitation as (with the other stops) they are a means of differentiating the array of colors available on the organ.

The organ is one of the most ancient of instruments, and was known as the *hydraulis* by the Greeks and Romans. Its golden age ended with the baroque period, but the nineteenth century French composers showed much interest in the instrument.

In recent years there has been a constant renewal of interest in reproducing the smaller instrument that was used in the baroque period. This baroque organ may be a single instrument, or it may form a part of the design of a large organ. The return to the sound of the baroque organ parallels the return to the use of the harpsichord, both the result of a constantly burgeoning interest in the authentic performance of baroque music.

The solo literature for the instrument is vast. It quite often makes its appearance (as well) with the symphony orchestra.

Most organs have at least two manuals and one pedal keyboard, allowing for possibilities of polyphony and contrast of color not possible on any other keyboard instrument. The registration of the manuals may be kept distinct or they may be combined by the use of couplers.

The sound of the organ is produced by wind, which is forced through pipes that are of a whistle type (such as a recorder) or a reed type (such as a clarinet). The wind was at one time pumped by hand, and this chore often was performed by choirboys. The wind is now usually provided by an electric blower.

THE CELESTE

The *celeste* (also called *celesta*) is a small keyboard instrument with a range of four octaves (Example 350). The tones of the instrument re-

Example 350

semble the sound of small silver bells. The sound is produced by a hammer action on small steel plates, similar to those of the orchestra bells, or glockenspiel, but the added feature of resonators enhances the sound.

Its first use in the symphony orchestra was by Tchaikovsky in the *Nutcracker Suite* (Example 351).

Example 351   Nutcracker Suite, Dance of the Sugar Plum Fairy, Tchaikovsky

Symphony orchestra

When the Pilgrims arrived in the New World in the year 1620, the piano had not yet been invented; the viol family of stringed instruments had not yet been superseded by the violin family; the brass instruments did

Figure 9

Possible Seating Plan of the Full Symphony Orchestra

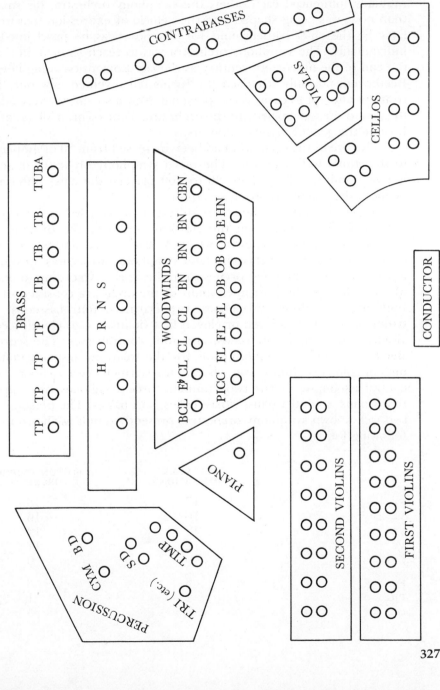

not have valves; there was no such instrument as a tuba; indeed, the beginnings of the symphony orchestra were over a hundred years away.

In the second half of the eighteenth century, as Haydn and Mozart mutually influenced each other, the symphony orchestra, far smaller than now, was being shaped into the vehicle of expression that would later be the chief battleground for Beethoven as he proclaimed his individuality. The symphony orchestra was to reach its peak in size at the end of the nineteenth century as the late Romantics, going beyond Beethoven, not only stretched the forms but invented new ones in a constant attempt to express the personal. New instruments were added to expand the tonal palette of the orchestra. Tone color in all its variety became the goal of many composers.

The size of the orchestra had been increased from 30 or 40 players to sometimes well over 100. The usual symphony orchestra of today is now standardized at about 80 to 100 players, the chief differences being in the size of the string sections.

A glance at the orchestra at different periods will point up the orchestra's expansion from the classical period to the present day.

The Mannheim orchestra, which Mozart visited and which influenced him to add clarinets to his later symphonic works, was considered at the time to be the finest orchestra in the world. According to one of Mozart's letters, the instrumentation of the orchestra consisted of the following: two flutes, two oboes, two clarinets, four bassoons, two trumpets, two timpani, ten or eleven first violins, ten or eleven second violins, four violas, four cellos, and four contrabasses. The score of Beethoven's Fifth Symphony calls for the following instrumentation: one piccolo, two flutes, two oboes, two clarinets, two bassoons, one contrabassoon, two horns, two trumpets, three trombones, two timpani, first violins, second violins, violas, cellos, and basses. The personnel of two well known symphony orchestras presently stands as shown in the following listing:

	NEW YORK PHILHARMONIC	BOSTON SYMPHONY ORCHESTRA
VL 1	17	18
VL 2	16	16
VA	12	12
VC	12	11
CB	9	9
FL	3	3
PIC	1	1
OB	3	3

	NEW YORK PHILHARMONIC	BOSTON SYMPHONY ORCHESTRA
EHN	1	1
CL	2 B♭, 1 E♭, 1 bass	2 B♭, 1 E♭, 1 bass
BN	3	3
CBN	1	1
HN	6	6
TR	4	4
TB	4	4
TU	1	1
TIMP	1	1
OTHER PERCUSSION	3	4
HARPS	1	2

Chamber orchestra

The term *chamber orchestra* most often means an orchestra small enough in size to play in a room for a more intimate gathering than would be found in a symphony hall. It is not possible to be precise about numbers. More to the point is the intent of the composer and the manner in which he handles the instruments. At the heart of the matter is the concept of treating the instruments more individually. Thus, there is often only one player on each type of instrument, for example, one clarinetist or one french horn player rather than a clarinet section or a french horn section. The strings are somewhat exceptional, and may or may not be reduced to one player per instrument. It will make the issue clearer if we speak of the music written for a chamber orchestra, or a chamber group, as it is often called.

The term *chamber music* may specify music written for a chamber orchestra, but actually it is a more encompassing term and generally refers to music written for perhaps six or more players up to the limits of a chamber orchestra. The term also may refer to music with parts for voices as well as instruments. Some examples of chamber music are: Richard Strauss, Serenade, for two flutes, two oboes, two clarinets, four horns, two bassoons, and contrabassoon or bass tuba; Stravinsky, *L'Histoire du Soldat*, for clarinet, bassoon, cornet, trombone, percussion, violin, and contrabass; Stravinsky, Octet, for flute, clarinet, two bassoons, two trumpets, and two trombones; Stravinsky, Cantata, for soprano, tenor, (small) female chorus, two flutes, two oboes (oboe II doubling on english horn), and violoncello.

Smaller chamber ensembles and solo performance

Also falling in the category of chamber music is music of a more soloistic character. Rather than being spoken of by the generic term, *chamber music,* however, music in this category is more often referred to by the specific traditional groupings of the instruments written for. These are the **woodwind quintet**: flute, oboe, clarinet, horn, bassoon; the **brass quintet**: usually two trumpets, horn, trombone and tuba; the **string quartet**: two violins, viola and cello; **string trio**: violin, viola, cello.

When the strings are joined by another instrument the group is specified by the distinguishing name of this instrument. Thus when a piano is added to a string quartet the ensemble is called a **piano quintet**. But the "Trout" Quintet of Schubert is an exception to this; the instruments are piano, violin, viola, cello and contrabass. A **piano quartet** is a string trio plus a piano: piano, violin, viola, and cello.

Works written for two players are not spoken of as duets. Because of the soloistic nature of such works the two instruments are mentioned specifically, for example, "Sonata for Violin and Piano." Within this category fall works written for two pianos.

There are many works for solo instruments, but the instrument with a superabundance of such literature is the piano. Compositions for other solo instruments are much more unique, as well as often being a considerable challenge. On opposite sides of the spectrum are J. S. Bach's Sonata in A minor for flute unaccompanied and Leonard Bernstein's *Elegy for Mippy II*, for trombone and foot.

> *Suggested Listening:* Francis Poulenc, Trio for Oboe, Bassoon, and Piano.

It may be worthwhile to mention in passing that the string quartet has often been referred to as the vehicle for "the purest expression" of a composer. This may have been said partly because of the fact that some composers have found their purest expression here. But others have not. Or it may be that the string quartet presents the greatest challenge to a composer. However, to reserve this "potential for expression" to the string quartet is to denigrate all other combinations of instruments as vehicles for expression.

The concert band

Although the **concert band** is often sneered at as a performance vehicle for serious music, it actually has the potential for the presentation of the highest expression of any composer. The reason for the supercilious attitude toward the concert band is usually based not on its potential, which is great, but on the quality or type of music that has been performed by it in the past, and in many cases as well, on the quality of the performance itself.

At the turn of the century the Sunday band concert in the park was a diversion for the average family, a light-hearted presentation of popular songs of the day, potpourri of well known operatic selections, and usually some very "flashy" solo work by a cornet or trombone soloist, often in the form of variations on a theme. The soloists were outstanding technicians, and the well known bands of Sousa and Pryor contained some of the best musicians of the day, but the musical fare was geared to the tastes of the average. In short, it was a commercial venture, rather than an artistic one. The concert band did not intend it to be otherwise, except perhaps in the presentations of transcriptions of symphonies. But this was only borrowed glory.

And here is the nub of the matter. In an attempt to play works of a more artistic nature, the band of necessity borrowed from works written for the symphonic orchestra, and although it might be said in some cases that the attempt was laudable, any attempt to perform a work originally intended for orchestra can only be a miscarriage if played by a musical organization that is distinguished by the fact that it contains no stringed instruments.

The era of the concert band first began to decline with the advent of radio. With so many forms of entertainment now available at the turn of a dial, the band today exists mostly as a social outlet for students in high school or college. These are obviously not intended to be professional organizations, and since professional levels of performance cannot be obtained here, the composer does not have the incentive to write music for concert or symphonic band. However, there are notable exceptions in certain colleges, and several professional symphonic bands do exist. For example, the symphonic band at the Massachusetts Institute of Technology now performs original works for band exclusively, and often commissions composers to write for it.

The concert band — or *symphonic wind ensemble*, as some prefer it — consists entirely of wind instruments, with the exception of the percussion section. As suggested above, there are no stringed instruments. The concert band evolved from the marching band, which of necessity used instruments that had the advantages of volume and portability. However, since the concert band has divorced itself from the marching band concept and moved into the concert hall, it has now made some exception to the concept of "wind instruments only" and has added string basses to the tuba section to attain a mellower sonority. It has added timpani, as well.

Figure 10   Concert Band Seating Arrangement

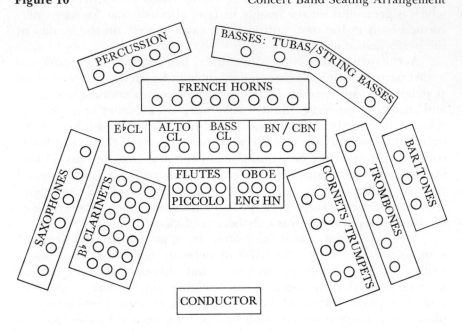

The basic sound of the symphony orchestra is that of the strings; the basic sound of the concert band is winds. The concert band lacks strings, but in its woodwind section it has a far greater potential for variety of tone color than that of the symphony orchestra because of its greater number and variety of woodwind instruments.

In this century composers have written for the concert band as a normal vehicle for serious artistic expression.

> *Suggested Listening:*   Milhaud, Suite Française; Hindemith, Symphony in B♭ for Band; Persichetti, Divertimento for Band; Psalm for Band; Holst, Suites Nos. 1 and 2 for Band; Vaughn-Williams, Folk Song Suite.

The Young Person's Guide to the Orchestra, Variations and Fugue on a Theme of Purcell, Opus 34, Britten

The *Young Person's Guide* was written in 1945 on a commission from the Ministry of Education in England for an educational film describing in picture and in sound the instruments of the large symphony orchestra. Britten chose the variation form as the most felicitous for presenting the instruments. Not only is this form apt for presenting the various instruments, but its sectional aspect allows the narration to intervene without interrupting. The fugue presents the instruments again in quicker succession as they make their fugal entrances.

Orchestra:

1 Piccolo (PIC)
2 Flutes (FL)
2 Oboes (OB)
2 Clarinets (CL)
2 Bassoons (BN)

4 Horns (HN)
2 Trumpets (TR)
3 Trombones (TB)
1 Tuba (TB)

Percussion (PERC):
  Timpani (TIMP)
  Bass Drum (BD)
  Cymbals (CYM)
  Tambourine

Percussion (cont.):
  Triangle (TRI)
  Side Drum (SD)
  Chinese Block
  Xylophone (XYL)
  Castanets
  Gong
  Whip

Harp (HP)

Violins (VL 1,2)
Violas (VA)
Violoncellos (VC)
Contrabasses (CB)

SCORE PROFILE

Score Detail: m. 141–144

The rhythmic background, in a quasi-Spanish style, lends an exhilarating effect.
(The background parts are condensed.)

VARIATION L

Score Detail: m. 399–400

This score detail shows what all of the percussion instruments are doing, but the timpanist is the soloist.

Score Detail: m. 459–462

The fugue subject has been introduced consecutively by the piccolo, the flutes, the oboes, the clarinets, each time with the starting note a fourth higher. With the entrance of the bassoons on *D*, we see the configuration of the five separate strands of the fugue.

Score Detail: m. 520–523

Note the built-in orchestral crescendo in the consecutive application of layers of sound. This is shown in the strings, but the technique is used in all sections.

Horns and other brass enter consecutively in stretto.

For reference and review

New terms in the order presented:

tone color
timbre
stopped pipe
open pipe
acoustics
range
pedal tones
strings
woodwinds
brass
percussion
violin
viola
alto
violoncello
cello
contrabass
double bass
bass viol
bass fiddle
string bass
bass
woodwinds
flute
piccolo
flauto piccolo
petite flute
alto flute
recorder
oboe
english horn
clarinet
E♭ clarinet
alto clarinet
bass clarinet
bassoon
fagotte
fagotto
double bassoon
contrabassoon
saxophone
embouchure

double tonguing
triple tonguing
flutter tongue
trumpet
piccolo trumpet
Bach trumpet
cornet
fluegel horn
french horn
horn
alto horn
mellophone
trombone
alto trombone
tenor trombone
bass trombone
baritone
euphonium
saxhorn
tuba
ophicleide
keyed bugle
sousaphone
helicon
Wagner tuben
timpani
snare drum
tenor drum
bass drum
piatti
cymbals
tam-tam
gong
xylophone
marimba
orchestra bells
glockenspiel
bell-lyra
chimes
triangle
tambourine
castanets

wood block
slapstick
whip
temple blocks
rachet
sleigh bells
bird whistle
train whistle
piano
pianoforte
harpsichord
virginal
clavichord
harp

organ
celeste
symphony orchestra
chamber orchestra
chamber music
woodwind quintet
brass quintet
string quartet
string trio
piano quintet
piano quartet
concert band
symphonic wind ensemble

PART THREE

History

EACH AGE in history is, in fact, an age of transition. But in retrospect it seems that certain periods more than others were periods of stabilization. Tendencies, although sprung from different sources, lead toward the same focal point and finally merge. Though these merged tendencies seem clear enough now, it is often doubtful that during these periods the figures who now loom large to us as leaders would have thought of their times in terms of stability. To the philosopher, to the statesman, to the artist who is in the middle of the stream of thought or action, it is always a time of transition, a time of trying to reach some landing point that cannot yet be seen.

From our vantage point now, however, the smaller details blur and the large outlines remain, showing us the more important trends and their culmination points. In hindsight we can check the truism that "every man is the product of his age." The age he lives in is the age he knows. "We sleep, but the loom of life never stops, and the pattern which was weaving when the sun went down is weaving when it comes up in the morning." And we are part of the texture. It is not more true of the artist than it is of the common man, but it is more important. It is more important because the artist leaves us an expression of his age.

In recognizing that each artist is a product of his age we should not attempt to equate the expression of one artist with that of another — to equate the output of the musician, for example, with the output of the architect. The inspiration of the painter and the musician, the author and the architect may all be triggered by the same environment, but their manners of expression will be individual. Similarities may be found in the ethos, but not necessarily in the expression of it. The uniqueness of the "comment" or expression of each artist will depend upon two things: the degree to which his expression is original, and the manner in which he handles his material.

Attempts to correlate the various expressions of artists have taken us to many a dead end. These attempts have resulted in describing baroque music as though it were baroque architecture; in characterizing impressionistic music in the terms of impressionistic painting; in equating the rhythms of jazz with the rhythms of certain twentieth-century paintings. Similarities and relationships are certainly apparent in these various pairings, but the similarities are in the original concept, not in the expression. Each one in the pair may complement the other, but they are not of the same kind. Comparisons have gone even farther, reaching the ultimate in vapidity in the phrase, "Architecture is frozen music." Neither music nor architecture can benefit by this. None of this is to say that it is not illuminating to compare the arts within a period. But the comparisons should not result in facile phrases.

No, each art form, each specific work must be considered as something unique. Instead of forcing superficial relationships upon the arts we should try to see how the same influences resulted in different expressions. Similarities will exist, but they will be of mood or style, not of design or form.

Each art will flower on its own branch. Thus we must look for the growth, the evolutionary progress, of music basically in its own history and its own expression of the happenings of each age.

10

Pre-baroque

Sing joyously of God our strength;
  Shout aloud of Jacob's God.
Raise the chant and beat the drum,
Both the pleasant harp and the lute.
Blow the trumpet at the new moon,
At the full moon on our festal day.
        *Psalm 81**

THESE LINES from the 81st Psalm are reminders that singing and the playing of instruments in religious ceremonies date back to early times. There are many other references in the Old Testament that testify to the Hebrews' long association with music. It was only natural that the early Christians were influenced by the music and the ritual of the synagogue.

During its first three centuries, Christianity was expanding, but its followers were constantly persecuted by the powers in Rome, and many meetings had to be held in secret. In the fourth century certain things happened, affecting both the church and its music. In the year 312, Constantine, Emperor of Rome, embraced Christianity and gave it legal sanction. The Christians could now

*Smith, J. M. P., ed & trans.: *The Complete Bible: An American Translation.* © 1939 by the University of Chicago. (The Apocrypha & the New Testament translation by Edgar J. Goodspeed.)

come above ground and conduct public services. Greek, the language of the New Testament and until this time the language of the church, was replaced by Latin. A vestige of Greek still exists in the language of the mass. In the latter part of the century, Ambrose, bishop of Milan, gathered together a large number of hymns and antiphonal psalms for use in the church service. It is conjectural whether Ambrose contributed as composer to this collection, but in any event this large body of work has come to be known as Ambrosian Chant.

Inspired by the writings of Augustine, and with the foundations of the Roman Empire beginning to crack, more and more of the people turned to the church and away from the state. When the Empire disintegrated in the fifth century, the church became the dominant authority for many. The church grew and the body of its music grew, borrowing from various sources. These sources included Eastern as well as Western culture, pagan as well as religious, secular as well as sacred.

In the sixth century Gregory, who was Pope of Rome from 590 until his death in 604, felt it was time to draw together the loose ends of the heterogeneous—or, perhaps better, miscellaneous—collection of church music: to make choices out of the large abundance of materials that were in existence, to "purify" in some cases, and to establish an ideal of what the main body of sacred music should be.

That he was successful is only too well established. Gregorian Chant, as this body of music came to be known, has served the church to the present.

Gregorian chant

The Gregorian chant may be sung by a solo voice or a chorus singing in unison; or it may be responsorial, alternating from solo to choral singing, or antiphonal, alternating from chorus to chorus. The range of the chant is not large, very often being contained within an octave.

In general the Gregorian chants were based upon the church modes. The scales for these are given in Chapter 2. Only the first four (Dorian, Phrygian, Lydian, and Mixolydian) in their authentic and plagal forms are used in Gregorian chant.

Gregorian chant, in the quiet undulating motion of its melody, sung by male voices only, conveys a feeling of purity and otherworldliness that lends itself well to the Catholic liturgy. The serene quality of this music is uniquely refreshing to ears accustomed to the more turbulent, emotional expression of later days.

The melodic style of the chant may be *syllabic*, one syllable to each tone; or **neumatic**, in which two, three, or four tones are sung to one syllable; or **melismatic**, in which more tones are sung to one syllable.

Gregorian chant degenerated from its purity of style in later centuries, until in the nineteenth century the monks of Solesmes, a Benedictine order in France, began a restoration of the chants to their original style. Some of the results of their work are now available on recordings.

Organum

The first deviation from the prevalent unison singing occurred sometime before the tenth century. There is only speculation as to how this started. It may have been in secular music, or in music of the church. At any rate, a second part was now added, which was sung in fourths or fifths along with the basic chant. This parallel motion, called **organum** (Example 352), in which the lower voice was a "shadow" of the upper,

Example 352   Organum

must indeed have sounded exciting after centuries of unison singing. The theory of organum was first described in *Musica Enchiriadis*, written in the ninth century.

In time the two voices of organum were doubled at the octave above. This is called **composite organum**. A further development, referred to as **free organum**, allowed more freedom of parts, especially at the beginning or end of the chant (Example 353). Out of this arose the first use of

Example 353   Free Organum

oblique motion, as the chant would now start or end on a unison, with the second part moving into and out of parallel fourths or fifths.

The next step shows the added part above rather than below the plain chant, and the intervals varied so that the two parts show differing melodic contours. Here are the seeds of polyphony. But one step more is needed to attain the true aspect of polyphony: to the differing contours of the separate melodies must be added rhythmic distinction. By the twelfth century this had been achieved. Against the plainsong the upper part is a weaving, florid line.

The setting of a florid part against the chant necessitates holding the tones of the chant longer. As the lower tones became stretched out, this lower part became known as the tenor (from the Latin, *tenere*, to hold).

Notre Dame

In Paris, in the twelfth and thirteenth centuries, the church of Notre Dame was the fountainhead of new developments in polyphony. Late in the twelfth century, Leonin, organist and composer, and his successor, Perotin, contributed many works. The thirteenth-century motet evolved out of their work, to become one of the most important forms of this period. To a melismatic portion of a plain chant, used as the tenor (and the basis) of the musical work, two upper parts (usually) would be added.

Unlike organum, which was mostly rhythmically free, the motet was organized into rhythmic patterns, but with the tenor part in longer note values. The melismatic portion taken from a plain chant as the basis for the motet would be changed into a fixed rhythmic pattern. This, in many cases, would be played by instruments. Above this would be added two or three parts with words of secular origin. The term **motet** arose out of the French *mot*, or word. In addition to the mixture of music derived from both sacred and secular sources, a polytextual element was also introduced. One part above the tenor might be in French, another in Latin.

A further development toward rhythmic regularity can be seen in Latin songs of this period. The **conductus**, for example, consisted of a tenor part not derived from the chant but composed; thus the complete work is now original. The parts are mostly homophonic.

Secular music

During the first 10 centuries the systematic preservation of church music resulted in a body of music that is available to the musicologist. But there is no equivalent with respect to the secular music of these centuries. The church took great pains to preserve its music, but the preservation of music outside of the church was mostly ignored. Only in the last 100 years have scholars realized that the music of a people is an important part of their culture, and therefore made intensive studies in these directions. There is little secular music extant that precedes

"The term jongleur originally meant jester or juggler, and to these talents the jongleur added singing, and often dancing or playing an instrument" (p. 360).

the tenth century; the largest body of secular music that has been preserved is from the eleventh and twelfth centuries. In southern France in the twelfth century we find the **troubadour**, usually of noble birth, singing songs of love and of chivalry. The troubadour songs were in a style meant to communicate easily and directly. The exact rhythmic basis of these songs is still not quite clear, but most transcriptions show it to be simple and repetitive.

Travelling about from town to town the troubadour (and later in Northern France, the *trouvère*) would often have in his company a *jongleur*, a man of many talents but not of noble birth. The term *jongleur* originally meant jester or juggler, and to these talents the jongleur added singing, and often dancing or playing an instrument.

In Germany the art of the troubadour was carried on by the *minnesinger* and the *meistersinger*. The meistersingers eventually formed guilds, and awarded prizes for composition within specified "rules and regulations." This was actually a surrender of the original freedom of improvised song. An excellent illustration of the guild movement may be seen in Wagner's opera, *Die Meistersinger*.

Sumer Is Icumen In

The oldest example of a six-part polyphonic style that has been preserved now resides in the British Museum. Termed a *rota*, "Sumer Is Icumen In" is an infinite canon (or round) for six men's voices (Example 354). It is written so that four voices form the canon, accompanied by two others that sing a bass line as a double ostinato. The canon is at the unison at a distance of four measures. "Sumer Is Icumen In" is believed to be from about the middle of the thirteenth century.

A free rendering is given of the old English, so that the round is practicable for singing. For the original text see the *Historical Anthology of Music*.

> Summer is a-coming in,
> Loudly sing cuckoo.
> Groweth seed and bloweth mead
> 　　and springeth woodland new.
> Sing cuckoo.
>
> Ewe now bleateth after lamb,
> Low'th after calf, the cow,
>
> Bullock starteth, buck he grazeth,
> Merry sing cuckoo.

Example 354   Sumer Is Icumen In, Rota

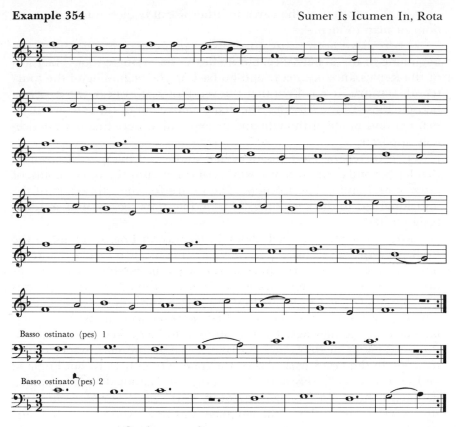

Cuckoo, cuckoo.
Well sing'st thou cuckoo,
Nor cease thou never, now.

Pre-renaissance

The flowering of an age is a fascinating display, and perhaps the most
fascinating age of all is the Renaissance. Before the Renaissance, common man, when not worshipping God, had his eyes on the ground. On
his shoulders were the burdens of tradition and superstition; feudalism
dominated his way of life. His moral choices seemed to be for the most
part between God and the devil; he was the victim of diseases of society
as well as of the body; he was circumscribed by important limitations
of the mind as well as those of his physical universe. He had yet to look
beyond the horizon, not only of the western ocean but of his limitations
of knowledge. Perspective was yet to be found not only in painting, not

only in the relation of the earth to other astral bodies, but in the relations of man to men.

There have been many attempts to pinpoint a single date as the beginning of the Renaissance, but no flower has a single root. The roots of the Renaissance are many and go back to the beginning of the fourteenth century. It was here that the sense of restlessness, the desire to become loose of the shackles, the itch to move out of the restrictions of manner and mode of thought and its expression were first most noticeably apparent.

The travels of the Crusaders had awakened many to the worlds that lay beyond their borders — worlds of other cultures and customs, of other moral and political beliefs. The desire for the expression of the individual led to the beginnings of a middle class society, and serfdom began to fade.

Roger Bacon, who died about 1294, was an English monk in the Franciscan order. In his experiments in chemistry, optics, and astronomy we find the modern concept: the scientific method of inquiry as opposed to belief based on tradition. Dante, although in other respects a medieval man, made the greatest impress toward the use of a modern language in his writings, and is the first representative figure of the new language of the new age. Latin continued to be spoken and written in the universities in Italy. In 1305 Dante writes, and encourages others to write, in the best vernacular of the time. Not only Italy, but England and France as well, were at the beginnings of a national language and a national culture. In Chaucer's greatest work, *The Canterbury Tales*, the stories were medieval, but the language was new. And late in the fourteenth century, we have Wycliffe's translation of the Bible into the common tongue.

In the century that followed, the voyages of Columbus opened the way for further explorations and also established avenues for international trade and commerce, which ultimately freed man not only from his physical insularity but from his insularity of thought, preparing him to acknowledge the existence of ideas and customs that could differ from his own.

More constantly questions were raised about the individual's position in society. Dante had written, "We must now determine what is the purpose of human society as a whole. . . . There is . . . some distinct function for which humanity as a whole is ordained, a function which neither an individual nor a family, neither a village nor a city, nor a particular kingdom has power to perform. . . . The specific characteristic of man is not simple existence, . . . it is rather the possible intellect, or capacity for intellectual growth."

The restlessness was apparent in the world of music as well. Early in the fourteenth century a treatise ascribed to Philippe de Vitry was titled "Ars Nova," to describe the new styles in music, as opposed to those of the earlier century. The music of the earlier century became then known as "Ars Antiqua." The treatise was essentially a discussion of notation and rhythm, and advanced an argument for the use of duple as well as triple meter. The prior concept that triple meter was the "pure" meter stemmed from the traditional concept of three as the perfect number, the trinity being at the center of Christian theology. The title of the treatise was felt to express the spirit of the times, and it was taken up and adopted as a label to symbolize the new freedom of expression that was arising in France, and — a little later — in Italy.

The "New Art" of the fourteenth century, as contrasted to the musical practices of the previous century, shows a greater use of thirds and sixths in part writing and a freer use of dissonance. The new interest in rhythm resulted in new means of expression. Regular rhythmic patterns had become a part of the final developments of organum and had been firmly established in Latin songs such as the *conductus*, which was mostly homophonic. Dance forms such as the *estampie* had carried this rhythmic regularity even further. The modal rhythms that had been in effect were now cast aside as being too restrictive. Now there was to be an interesting combination of a freer polyphony that nevertheless carried within its framework repetitions of rhythmic patterns.

Machaut

The leading composer of this period was Guillaume de Machaut. Born around 1300 in Champagne he was to dominate French music in both sacred and secular works. In addition to setting the music to his own poetry in *Remede de fortune*, he established an important body of repertoire in his ballades, rondeaux, and virelais as well as his polyphonic chansons. There are also motets and a complete mass. He was the first composer to singly set the ordinary of the mass.

In Machaut's mass as well as in most of his motets we see examples of the new rhythmic concept: **isorhythm**. This term refers to the repetition of *similar rhythmic patterns* within what is nevertheless a polyphonic flow.

A charting of the rhythmic patterns will make this clear. Example 355 is a rhythmic reduction of a portion of the Agnus Dei from the Machaut mass.

Also in the Machaut Agnus Dei there may be seen use of the **hocket** ("hiccup"), which had appeared in the thirteenth century but was much used in the fourteenth. The term refers to the interruption, by a short

Example 355   Machaut

rest, of the syllable being sung. During the rest the singer would take a quick breath and then return to singing the interrupted syllable. Often during the rest another voice would insert itself, creating an "in-and-out" effect that added rhythmic variety and accent to the texture.

Another development of the fourteenth century was the use of chromatics, not written in the music, but introduced by the performer. Termed *musica ficta*, these would often occur at the end of a phrase in a melodic cadence, 7 – 8; or they might occur during the piece to make a smoother melodic line.

Burgundian school

In the early fifteenth century the important developments in music sprang chiefly from a group of composers working for the court of Burgundy. We now see developments in polyphonic style taking place that will ultimately lead to the refined style of Lassus and Palestrina. The Burgundian school was influenced by the writings of John Dunstable in England whose use of imitation represented the beginnings of contrapuntal style. His interest in setting words in their "conversational" usage resulted in an expression the opposite of the melismatic. And the use of vertical structures emphasizing thirds and sixths was to lead to a later appreciation of the triad as a building unit.

In the music of Guillaume Dufay, leading composer of the Burgundian school, we see the use of imitation. In the tenor part we may still have the cantus firmus, but the other parts are beginning to "loosen" into a flowing, expressive style.

Finally, the restriction of the lowest part to a cantus firmus was done away with, at first by putting another part below the tenor. This lowest part became ultimately the *bass* part, and the part above the tenor became the *alto*. The voice above the alto, tenor, and bass (in the superior position) ultimately became the *soprano*. Thus, about the middle of the fifteenth century, the basic four voice parts were established that have remained as the norm for choral writing to the present day.

The use of instruments at this time not only on an instrumental part but also in the doubling of the vocal parts foreshadows the use of instruments and voices, although in a more refined way, in the baroque period. Whatever instruments were handy were called upon. These might include recorders, viols, an organ, and perhaps a brass instrument.

Josquin

The roots of the Renaissance were in the fourteenth century. The Renaissance itself is most conveniently designated as the period from 1450 to 1600.

The first outstanding musical figure of this period is Josquin des Prez. He has been spoken of by some writers as the "first genius of modern music." His music is the first that registers with us as being of the musical language that we know. His melodic lines have continuity and coherence as we understand it, his harmonies are colorful and expressive, and his phrases and cadences have the rise and fall that are familiar to us.

Born about 1450 in the Netherlands, his name was Josse. The diminutive, Jossekin, became Josquin. He traveled widely, spending much time in Italy, at one time in the service of the ducal court at the Sistine Chapel in Rome, and at other times serving as court composer in Milan and France.

From Ockeghem, and from the influence of Obrecht and Busnois, he learned not only the highly complex devices common to contrapuntal writing at the time, but the art of musical expressiveness that goes beyond the devices and uses them as a means rather than an end in themselves. Riddle canons had been the delight of composers of the time, but some of the composers had become lost in the presentation of the puzzle, losing sight of the musical end. The oft-quoted statement of Martin Luther bears repeating: "Josquin is a master of the notes; they have to do as he wills, other composers must do as the notes will." Naumann, in speaking of the Netherlands school in general, said,

"Henceforth counterpoint was but a means to an end, and art-music began to assume for the first time the characteristics of folk-music, i.e., the free pure and natural outflow of heart and mind, with invaluable addition, however, of intellectual manipulation." The way was opening for a musical expressiveness that was to find its culmination in the fugal style of Bach.

Lassus and Palestrina

Lassus and Palestrina, one Flemish and the other Italian, both died in the year 1594, and it is this date that is usually taken to denote the close of the "golden era" of polyphony.

Lassus was born Roland de Lattre, in Mons, and was the last of the great masters of the Netherlands school. He is known by the Italian form of his name, Orlando di Lasso, or the Latinized version, Orlandus Lassus. Like Josquin, he traveled widely, but his travels began under circumstances that are somewhat unusual. Because of the excellence of his voice as a boy, he was kidnapped three times. The first two times he was recovered by his parents, but the third time marks the beginning of his journeys, which took him first to Milan and Naples and then to Rome, where he became a chapel master. At various times he visited France and England, and ultimately he married and settled in Munich. The profound "Penitential Psalms" are of this period. Writing constantly, both sacred and secular music, he became famous throughout Europe. Contrary to the experience of many composers, he received the rewards of an adoring society, he was knighted, and he received the order of the Golden Spurs from the Pope. He was one of the most prolific composers of all time. For example, he left over 500 motets.

Giovanni Pierluigi was born in the town of Palestrina, not far from Rome. He has been called the greatest of the church composers, and his music is also considered to be the "purest expression" of the polyphonic school of the sixteenth century. Whereas Lassus traveled widely and wrote in all forms, both secular and sacred, Palestrina spent most of his life in the service of the church. As a result almost all of his large output is music for the church. The music of Lassus is highly expressive, but most of the music of Palestrina is purposely subservient to the sacred text.

Palestrina at once represents the close of the Flemish school and the beginning of the Roman school in music for the church. He is considered to be the greatest composer of the Catholic church, and in him we find a purity of expression that seeks not to let earthly passion obtrude in the service of worship but to express the serenity and the other-worldliness inherent in the hushed chapel. Versed in all of the compositional techniques of the Netherlands school, Palestrina, however, sought a purer expression. As the Lutheran chorale later would be the foundation for the music of Bach, so the Gregorian chant was the foundation on which Palestrina built.

Also in the interest of purity, he reduced in his music the amount of chromaticism and dissonance that was common in the works of other composers. His musical lines are more conjunct and less disjunct. When he does introduce leaps, they are often counteracted by a returning conjunct movement, which fills in the interval of the leap. Thus each voice is a constantly undulating line, intended to propel the listener on quiet waves of sound.

The words of Palestrina will show his earnestness in striving for the essence of purity in his music:

> Music exerts a great influence upon the minds of mankind, and is intended not only to cheer these, but also to guide and to control them, a statement which has not only been made by the ancients, but which is found equally true today. . . . anxiously have I avoided giving forth anything which could lead anyone to become more wicked or godless. All the more should I . . . place my thoughts on lofty, earnest things such as are worthy of a Christian.

11

The baroque

TO THE NEOPHYTE listener, the music of the Baroque (approximately 1600–1750) is frequently perplexing. He searches hard but scarcely catches a tune. Sometimes so many tunes assail his ears at once that he cannot distinguish between them. The tunes that he does isolate from the thick web of sound strike him as either jagged and spiky or rambling and diffuse. However, he does feel rhythm, indeed, sometimes a very insistent, steady beat. But he is likely to consider it to be monotonous, like the clacking of an old fashioned treadle sewing machine. And what bothers him more than anything else is a kind of formidable facade of dignity and reserve that seems to keep his emotional responses at arms length.

Thus, before musical enlightenment comes, he gives only part of himself to the fugues, concerti grossi, cantatas, and passions that he encounters from the period. This he does despite perhaps what we might call unconscious appreciation of the best known pieces from the period. He glories in singing the carol by the great baroque master, Handel, "Joy to the World," He is touched by the *Messiah*, and he dearly loves the romantic composer Gounod's "Ave Maria" without realizing that it is based entirely on a prelude from J. S. Bach's *Well Tempered Clavier*.

On the other hand, a certain kind of practiced listener will often revere the music of the seventeenth and eighteenth centuries to the exclusion of every other musical period and style. Once he has had his Beethoven fling, his Tchaikovsky mania, he will finally settle for and revel permanently in the partitas, inventions, and fugues of the Baroque. He might even purchase a recorder, or a harpsichord, or a lute, to find out first hand what makes his favorite kind of music tick.

Why do some listeners find the Baroque remote? The answer lies in many directions. But most pertinent is the truth that the Baroque was indeed a remote age. The next two periods, the Classical and the Romantic, produced a music that we readily identify with, that is more familiar.

Baroque music represents to many people a Europe dominated by grand monarchies and the pomp and splendor of a sumptuous, although eroding, court life. And it symbolizes an age of rationalism where the great philosopher-mathematician Pascal could say, "All the dignity of man consists in thought."

The contrast that exists on the purely musical level between the Baroque and following periods is very pronounced. The prevailing texture in musical composition in the Baroque is polyphonic, while that in the classical and romantic periods is primarily homophonic. We who have been weaned on homophony in our immediate social activities with hymns, folksongs, and patriotic songs, take very readily to the clearly marked leading melodies buttressed with the colorful

harmonies of Haydn, Mozart, Beethoven, and Tchaikovsky. But we are puzzled at the thick tangle of melody lines and rich luxuriant detail of the Baroque. Thus, to enter into the beauties of much of the music in the Baroque we must undergo a certain amount of aural reconditioning. We must learn how to perceive and truly experience simultaneous melodic lines.

Similarly, the forms of the seventeenth and eighteenth centuries are not those with which we feel most comfortable. For example, the many elegant dance forms of the Baroque and earlier periods are quite foreign to us as living dance vehicles. On the other hand, the waltz, which flowered in the nineteenth century, is still danced extensively today. The minuet, gavotte, and sarabande, are emblems of a munificent, luxuriant society only encountered now in films. The instruments of the period—the harpsichord, clavichord, tracker organ, recorder, viola da gamba—have only recently been the object of renewed interest.

General characteristics

MELODY

Looked at from the viewpoint of basic shape and type, baroque melody shows an interesting dichotomy. On the one hand, it is frequently highly expansive, personal, even romantic. At other times the "melody" is a mere fragment, a wisp of a tune that becomes important only through its elaboration and working out.

Example 356   Well Tempered Clavier, Book I, Fugue 4, J. S. Bach

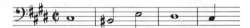

The few notes in Example 356, followed by their blossoming into great music, remind us of the rationalistic philosopher Descartes' raising enormous edifices of wisdom on his simple yet potent idea: "I think, therefore I am."

Baroque melody frequently has a spiky, rather jagged contour. Often it takes on life only through the poignant ornamentation dotting its surface.

RHYTHM

There is a certain expectedness to baroque rhythms that to some people is disconcerting. Especially in many of the allegros we hear repeated rhythmic patterns, propelled by an unflagging beat. And we do not hear a great variety of tempos, as we do in Beethoven, Chopin, or Tchaikovsky. All of this is apparent when we compare the dreamy, flexible chant from previous periods with the straight-gaited beat of a chorus in the late Baroque.

This rigidity, however, occurs only on the surface of baroque music. Underneath the rather plain rhythmic exterior exist perhaps the most subtle and sophisticated rhythmic structures of any period.

Among the many rhythmic riches, perhaps the most exciting is that of syncopation. A great many baroque compositions make astonishing use of syncopation. If played with a steady, motoric underlying pulse, and if the melodic line is accented according to its natural beat, the music of Example 357 is surprisingly close to jazz. Indeed, fine jazz artists of our day are increasingly admiring and playing baroque music.

Example 357   Invention No. 6, J. S. Bach

HARMONY

The Baroque is particularly interesting in the area of harmony. Of course, some impetus from the Golden Age of Polyphony remained: contrapuntal structures such as fugue, chaconne, and canon evolved and indeed tended to predominate. But, simultaneously, homophony came to the fore, with the musical center of gravity shifting to a single commanding melody. And although much of the music is either primarily polyphonic or homophonic, often there exists a masterful blend of the two. Thus, the Bach chorale not only is considered to be the fountainhead for all later tonal developments in vertical relationships, but also represents an ideal model for organizing four separate, but cooperating, melodic parts.

This development of massive polyphonic structures side by side with the homophonic, and the potent mixture of the two, could not have happened without the emergence of the two diatonic scales, major and the minor. These were the foundation of a powerful homogeneous tonality. In the pre-Baroque the major scale (formerly Ionian mode) and the minor scale (formerly Aeolian mode) were only two of several possible scales underlying the structures of the Renaissance and earlier. But the hardy, homogeneous system of major-minor tonality was so satisfactory to many baroque composers that it must have seemed as eternal and fixed to them as the basic mathematical principles established by Newton and Descartes were to contemporary philosophers.

As early as 1602, figured bass can be seen. Later it had become so universal that Rameau in his several treatises, including the *Treatise of Harmony*, incorporated the whole into a comprehensive harmonic system. The principles of figured bass are not difficult to understand. Accompanying a bass line are certain numbers, either one or several, which indicate notes to be added above each bass note. These notes always were "figured" up from the bass, and were meant to be played by the keyboard performer. He would often use the resulting chords for extensive extemporaneous elaborations, accompanying the principal melody or melodies. In effect, this was a shorthand system that saved the composer much time and also allowed for interesting personal contributions from the player involved (Example 358).

Figured bass served a purpose similar to that of the chord system used in the popular music of our day. The player "realizes" a lead line accompanied by a special system of chord letters and figures. And though baroque harmony did become extremely solid, rational, and self-contained, it should never be thought that it was dull and colorless. Operating within the limits of major-minor tonality and figured bass were vertical sounds and progressions that are as trenchant and voluptuous as the vibrant colors in a Rubens painting.

RANGE AND DYNAMICS

As might be expected, both range and dynamics in baroque music were limited in scope. Most of the music of the period fits comfortably within a range of four or five octaves.

Because so much of the music of the Baroque is polyphonic, it is obvious that every voice—bass, tenor, alto, soprano—will at times carry leading melodic parts. But the favored range is decidedly the high soprano. Instruments with the ability to climb very high, such as the clarin trumpet (*clarino*) and soprano recorder were much used. The Baroque organ is distinguished by the many "mixture" stops, which often highlight the brilliant upper soprano range. Many of the trio

Example 358   St. Matthew Passion, Recitative, J. S. Bach

sonatas by Corelli are written for two violins, which frequently criss-cross and hang high in the soprano. Beneath is the continuo part in the bass, realized by cello and keyboard. The rather bare middle range area was left to be "filled" by the keyboard player reading the figured bass.

Dynamics were most conservatively used. A modest forte or piano sufficed for most of the music. Significant crescendo and diminuendo was impossible on some keyboard instruments and sparingly used in general. It was not until the classical period, particularly with the orchestra at Mannheim, that colorful, graduated dynamics came into strong favor. Indeed, the mere fact that Rossini was called "Signor Crescendo" attests to the novelty of this effect.

Baroque masters were not unaware of the emotional impact derived from artfully utilized dynamics. But rather than rely on crescendo and diminuendo, or on extremes of dynamic levels, they preferred to use the sharp juxtaposition of forte with piano.

PERFORMANCE AND INSTRUMENTS

Performance standards were rather high in the Baroque, and the gulf that exists today between performer and composer was largely absent then. Many master composers were also brilliant performers. Daquin astonished all who heard him because of the brilliance of his passage work at the keyboard. Corelli, Torelli, Locatelli, and Vivaldi all were renowned violinists. Domenico Scarlatti astounded the courts of Italy, Spain, and Portugal with his digital gymnastics at the harpsichord. J. S. Bach was perhaps better known for his playing at the organ than for his compositions.

Of the 381 instruments owned by King Henry VIII in sixteenth century England, 272 were winds. Only 109 were strings, including keyboard instruments. Winds certainly predominated in the Renaissance; strings were emphasized in the Baroque. The seventeenth and early eighteenth centuries saw the flourishing of the master instrument builders at Cremona: Stradivari, Amati, Guarneri, and others. There is no question that the finest literature of the period is written for strings. The string family formed the backbone of many of the orchestras of the day.

Keyboard instruments—clavichord, harpsichord, organ—also were prominent. The piano, though existing in the late Baroque—J. S. Bach is known to have played on Frederick the Great's new Silbermann pianofortes—did not displace the harpsichord in the affections of musicians until the time of Mozart and Haydn.

FORMS

Opera, cantata, passion, the liturgical mass, the chorale, and many forms occupied a vital position in the musical thinking of Baroque masters. In both vocal and instrumental music, polyphonic structures predominated. Bach felt so challenged by the fugue that he wrote 24 preludes and fugues spanning all possible major and minor keys in a volume known as the *Well Tempered Clavier*. Then, 22 years later, he wrote 24 more. In this effort, however, he was anticipated by Johann Caspar Fischer who, in 1715, published 20 preludes and fugues covering 19 different keys.

There is no question that the enormous technical challenges found in polyphonic composition appealed to the rationalistic facet of the baroque composer's personality. The miracle of it all is that these ultra-sophisticated contrapuntal structures manage, in the hands of the masters, to achieve great emotional impact.

At the same time that traditional approaches to compositions were employed, many forms appeared that were destined to achieve dominance in later periods. Thus, we see early forms of the concerto, symphony, sonata, suite, aria, and overture. Each achieved ascendancy later in the classical and romantic periods. These early forms only anticipate in a general way the actual dramatic structures of the late eighteenth and nineteenth centuries. The baroque solo concerto, though it and the later Viennese concerto both follow the fast-slow-fast pattern, is vastly different from the structures developed by Mozart and Beethoven.

The composers

It was a long time from the days of Monteverdi, at the turn of the seventeenth century, to the ripe musical days of J. S. Bach. There is even more contrast between the works of the early Baroque masters and those of Bach and Handel than there is between early Haydn and late Beethoven. It will follow, then, that no single, overriding aesthetic outlook will permeate all of the figures in this period. There was tremendous variety of style during these many decades. For example, a comparison of Antonio Vivaldi and J. S. Bach, contemporaries writing in similar idioms, uncovers tremendous differences. Among these are the closely cropped textures and complexity of Bach's rhythms, as opposed to the near-folk-song simplicity of Vivaldi. Despite huge contrasts in their respective styles, Bach so admired Vivaldi that he transcribed, among other Vivaldi works, a concerto for four violins by the Italian into one for four claviers.

EARLY ITALIAN COMPOSERS

There are six major figures at the outset of the Baroque. Each had deep roots in the renaissance period, and wrote many works clearly in the sixteenth-century style. Yet each was an innovator, breaching reactionary defenses and catapulting music into a new age. All were Italian: Giovanni Gabrieli (1551 – 1612), Don Carlo Gesualdo, Prince of Verona (1560 –1613), Giulio Caccini (1546 – 1618), Jacopo Peri (1561 – 1633), Claudio Monteverdi (1567 – 1643), and Girolamo Frescobaldi (1583 – 1643).

Peri and Caccini collaborated on the first opera ever written, *Daphne,* but to Caccini alone goes the honor of writing the first opera published, *Euridice.* These men were in the artistic-intellectual group revolving around Count Giovanni Bardi, scholar and patron of music. This group, called the "Camerata," wished to bring back the simplicity and directness of expression that they associated with ancient Greek culture. This resulted in the monody of Peri and Caccini, which might seem rather bland and anti-lyric now. In fact, much of it consists of little but a recitative-like single line sustained by block chords. But to these men, accustomed to the thick, clustered web of ecclesiastical polyphony of the renaissance style, this new, direct mode of musical expression seemed the perfect tool for the humanism that they advocated.

Monteverdi.   Monteverdi in his operas such as *Orfeo,* through the immensity of his genius, outstripped by far his predecessors in the field. Though he did not write instrumental music as such, he greatly expanded the role of the orchestra in vocal music. Novel effects introduced by him, such as pizzicato and tremolo in the strings, startled the music world. In his unique way with harmony he anticipates much of modern usage. Unprepared dissonances and trenchant juxtaposition of chords usually not heard side by side can be heard in his madrigals, operas, and songs. If Peri and Caccini were the founders of monody and opera, Monteverdi must be considered the founder of modern harmony.

Other Early Masters.   Frescobaldi and Giovanni Gabrieli were both renowned organists. Both were vital in the development of instrumental forms. Frescobaldi in his ricercari anticipated one of the late Baroque's most important structures, the fugue. Gabrieli created pieces for grouped instruments such as the *Sonata pian e forte,* where the winds are juxtaposed to the strings in the antiphonal style. Gabrieli reveled in the color possibilities of antiphony, sometimes dividing his massed voices into four choirs singing back and forth.

Following closely on the heels of the composers discussed above came Giacomo Carissimi (1605 – 1674), who was instrumental in the creation of oratorio. That form at first was distinguished from early opera only by its sacred text. But with Carissimi's masterful balancing of choral and soloistic forces, and the addition of the narrator, the oratorio took on tremendous meaning for the future.

VIOLINIST-COMPOSERS

Shortly after the blooming of the new vocal forms of opera, oratorio, and others, there developed an extensive and long-lived school of composers whose primary interest lay in music for the violin. It was quite fitting that Italy, the mother of *bel canto,* should have produced this brilliant group of player-composers, and that the Italian city of Cremona should have produced the finest stringed instruments that the world has yet known. With many magnificent instruments by Nicolo

Amati (1596 – 1684), Antonio Stradivari (1644 – 1737), and Giuseppe Guarneri (1681 –1742) available, Italian composers set about composing a multitude of sonatas, concertos, and single pieces of singular grace and lyric elegance. This long line of composers included Archangelo Corelli (1653 – 1713), Tommaso Antonio Vitali (1665 – ?), Antonio Vivaldi (1680?_1743), Francesco Geminiani (1687 – 1762), Giuseppe Tartini (1692 – 1770), and Francesco Veracini (1685 – 1750). As can be seen, this line of composers spanned the better part of 100 years and included several pre-classical composers.

CORELLI AND VIVALDI

Perhaps the two outstanding figures in Italian baroque music were Corelli and Vivaldi.

Corelli, besides having systematized bowing on the violin, is said to have been the first to introduce double stops. But much more important than his fame as a player and innovator of violin technique is the nobility and profundity of his works. The solo violin pieces are still much esteemed by concert audiences, but it is with the concerto grosso and the trio sonata that Corelli's true greatness is apparent.

Vivaldi was an extremely colorful figure. Perhaps his music now is beginning to rival that of J. S. Bach and Handel in popularity with concert audiences. Called the "Red Priest" because of the color of his hair, Vivaldi was a clergyman whose pedagogical excellence matched his prowess with the violin and genius in composition. For 36 years Vivaldi directed a music school for indigent girls. One cannot better the quote from De Brosses in *Grove's Dictionary*: "Indeed they sing like angels, play the violin, flute, organ, oboe, cello, bassoon — in short no instrument. is large enough to frighten them. . . . I swear nothing is more charming than to see a young and pretty nun, dressed in white, a sprig of pomegranate blossom behind one ear, leading the orchestra and beating the time with all the grace and precision imaginable."*

His output was enormous: the 447 concertos for a wide range of instruments including guitar, mandolin, and piccolo represent a stupendous achievement. Particularly intriguing is the set of four violin concertos called *The Seasons*, each representing a different time of the year. They are studded with appealing moments of imagery, such as a summer storm and bird calls.

Not especially associated with the school of violinist-composers were two other masters, Alessandro Scarlatti (1659 – 1725) and Giuseppe Sammartini (1693 – 1770). Both wrote instrumental music that antici-

Grove's Dictionary of Music and Musicians, Vol. IX (New York: St. Martin's Press, Inc., 1960), p. 27.

"His temper was said to match the power of his music. He died through an infection of the foot caused by his striking his foot with his enormous baton while in a rage with his orchestra" (p. 379).

pated the classical symphony. In addition, Scarlatti was a great master of late baroque opera, and is credited with the perfection of the oratorio form.

LULLY

Underlining the influence of Italian masters in the early Baroque is the fact that the first truly great French composer of the Baroque, the founder of French opera, the creator of the disciplined court orchestra of Louis XIV, was a violinist from Florence by name of Jean Baptiste de Lully (1632–1687). He was a tremendous force in the music world of his time. Even the English acknowledged his luster. Roger North, a lawyer-turned-composer, in his *Memoires of Musick*, said, ". . . during the first years of Charles II all musick affected by the beau mond run in the French way; and the rather because at that time the master of the Court Musick in France, whose name was Baptista (an Italian frenchifyed) had influenced the French style by infusing a great portion of the Italian harmony into it, whereby the air was exceedingly improved."*

Lully's temper was said to match the power of his music. He died from an infection caused by striking his foot with his enormous baton while in a rage with his orchestra.

OTHER FRENCH MASTERS

Francois Couperin (Le Grand) (1668–1733), the most illustrious of a family of musicians rivaling the Bach family for longevity, wrote much charming music for the clavecin (harpsichord). His colorful pieces, replete with delightful titles, are still extremely popular with keyboard artists. Some of the finest of these are "Le Moucheron" (anticipating by two centuries the famous *Diary of a Fly* by Bartók), "Soeur Monique," and "L'Anguille," whose wiggling figurations charmingly suggest the slithering of the eel.

Jean Philippe Rameau (1683–1764), in addition to systematizing harmony, had a great influence on the theoretical thinking of composers after him. More important, however, is his music, especially the novel and majestic operas, such as *Castor et Pollux*. His pieces for clavecin rival those of Couperin for clarity, sophistication, and color.

Claude Daquin (1694–1772), the composer of the familiar keyboard piece, "Le Coucou," was a rival of Rameau's and famed for the clean articulation of his playing at the organ.

*David G. Weiss, *Samuel Pepys, Curioso* (Pittsburgh: University of Pittsburgh Press, 1957). p. 49.

Other important composers of French baroque music are Jean Baptiste Loeillet (1680–1730); Louis Marchand (1669–1732), the player who defaulted in the famous proposed organ playing bout with J. S. Bach; Marc Antoine Charpentier (1634–1730); and Jean Marie Leclair (1697–1764), a famous violin virtuoso.

THE ENGLISH

The English, after the luminosity of their many magnificent renaissance composers such as Byrd, Dowland, and Morley, produced only a few masters in the Baroque.

John Blow (1648–1708) was organist at Westminster Abbey before Purcell. John Christopher Pepusch (1667–1752), the collaborator with John Gay in the fabulously successful *Beggar's Opera*, was really a transplanted German. Dr. Thomas Arne (1710–1778) lived into the classical period.

Without question the leading personality of the English Baroque was Henry Purcell (1659–1695). In his short 36 years, he managed to produce a great many profound works. In the geniality of his melody, the copiousness of his output in so short a time, and the richness of his harmony, he is much like Schubert. Purcell's best known works are the operas *Dido and Aeneas* and *The Fairy Queen*, adapted from Shakespeare's *Midsummer Night's Dream*.

GERMAN MASTERS

Schütz.   Heinrich Schütz (1585–1672) is justly called the father of German music. He is a major figure in the early Baroque, occupying a position of equal importance to that of Monteverdi in Italy. His opera, *Daphne*, now lost, was the first in the German language. The many sacred choral works such as the *Seven Last Words of Christ*, the *Passions*, and the *Christmas Oratorio* show a Bach-like power and intensity. There can be no doubt that the sacred choral works of this master were the cornerstone and inspiration of much of the work of J. S. Bach and Handel.

If the favorite instrument of the Italian Baroque was the violin, that of the German Baroque was the organ. The violin was the perfect instrument for the transmission of Italian bel canto; the organ, with its power and diversity of tonal color, was the ideal instrument for German complexity of polyphony. Just as the violin, in the hands of the master craftsmen at Cremona, became highly perfected, so did the great baroque organs, especially in Germany.

These great organs, with their utter clarity and substantial body of tone, were the ideal instruments for the fugues, toccatas, passacaglias, and chorale preludes so intrinsic to German baroque music. There are many who feel that these great organs by Schnitger and others have never been surpassed.

An illustrious line of organist-composers accordingly arose beginning quite early in the seventeenth century. The student of Frescobaldi, Johann Jakob Froberger (1616–1667), was one of the first. Among many others were Johann Pachelbel (1653–1706) and Dietrich Buxtehude (1637–1707). Buxtehude's playing and compositions so attracted J. S. Bach that he walked 50 miles to hear him. Bach overstayed his leave from his church position by three months in order to hear and study the master's music.

George Philip Telemann (1681–1767), whose fame much eclipsed that of J. S. Bach in his day, wrote many facile and entertaining suites, concertos, trio sonatas, and vocal pieces. Such was his facile technique as a composer that he was said to be able to dash off an eight-part motet as easily as another would write a letter. Schumann quoted him as saying, ". . . a proper composer should be able to set a placard to music."

The Baroque culminated with two majestic names in music: Georg Friedrich Handel (1685–1759) and J. S. Bach (1685–1750).

Johann Sebastian Bach was a member of a distinguished family of composers and players that thrived in Germany for 200 years. Strong roots in the craft of his fathers and his own inclinations towards sober hard work kept him, perhaps, from wandering much in the world or from urgently seeking recognition. However, he did challenge the great French organist Marchand to a musical duel at the keyboard, and was happy enough late in his life to visit and play for Frederick the Great at Potsdam. He held posts as Kapellmeister at important churches, and as court composer.

Bach's musical style is matched by an interesting dichotomy. On the one hand it is super-sophisticated at almost every level. The polyphony is of such intricacy and such pervasive power of musical logic that it staggers the mind. The rhythms are more advanced by far than anything in Mozart or Haydn. His unique handling of dissonance anticipates the music of our times. In short, Bach's music is highly intellectual, showing the highest flights of which the musical mind is capable. On the other hand, his music is never dry. No matter how cerebral it may be, it always is suffused by a warmth, a uniquely human quality. For example, the "Crucifixus" from the Mass in B minor represents the highest kind of technical thinking in music. It is a chaconne, with utterly refined use of polyphonic variation over the repeated chromatic bass figure (Example 359). Yet, despite the formal intricacies, the effect is sublime. The sounds emanating from the voices are as rich and satisfying as anything from Beethoven or the Romantics.

Bach's best known works are the B minor Mass, the *St. Matthew*

Example 359   Mass in B minor, "Crucifixus," J. S. Bach

Passion, the *Well Tempered Clavier*, the Brandenburg Concertos, the concertos for single or multiple instruments, the chorale preludes for organ, and the cantatas.

Handel was much more volatile and enterprising than Bach. He once fought a duel with the organist-composer Johann Mattheson and survived to enter the lists later in England with his bitter rival for operatic supremacy, Bononcini (1670–1747). He traveled early to Italy, met both Scarlattis, and quickly ascertained that his fortune lay with the stage. In his later years in London, where he was much celebrated, he wrote a great many operas in the Italian style, and oratorios, including the famous *Messiah*. The effect of his music is much more immediate than that of Bach's. The texture is more open, with much less dissonance. Though counterpoint is the cornerstone of his style, it is much less compact than Bach's. The harmony, though occasionally astonishing in its chromaticism, usually is rather bland. The rhythms are seldom as intricate as those in Bach, and his melodic lines are more fluid and lyric.

Where Handel is supreme is in massed effects. Pieces such as the *Te Deum* are monumental in scope. In this respect Handel's music sounds rather good when sung by large choruses of 150 or so voices

"He once fought a duel with the organist-composer
Johann Mattheson . . ." (p. 382).

(though much of it was written for smaller groups), while that of Bach becomes almost unintelligible when done by anything larger than a chamber chorus.

Beethoven esteemed Handel above all others in the field of vocal music and asked for a complete Handel edition near the end of his life.

Handel, like Bach, was almost blind for his last few years, though he managed to play the organ in his own oratorios until his death in 1759.

The rococo

The next major period to be encountered after the Baroque will be the Classical, encompassing the lives of three giants: Mozart, Haydn, and Beethoven. The stylistic gulf that separates the densely intellectual, massively ornate Baroque from the directly expressive classical is huge.

The music that fills this gap is called **Rococo**. The word is derived from the French, *rocaille*, meaning "rockwork," and refers particularly to the ornate arrangements of rocks in the gardens at Versailles. As it applies to music it means an emphasis on the elegantly embroidered, graceful, and charming. Its purpose is simply to please. It is shallow on purpose, reflecting that hedonism so apparent in the court of Louis XV.

Rococo music frequently is saturated with melodic ornaments, called **agréments** by the French. Homophony predominates, with the harmonies simple and affecting. Frequently, as we saw earlier with Couperin, catchy titles were used.

The exquisite hedonism of the Rococo is reflected in the polished paintings of Watteau, where grace, sheen, and elegance reign supreme. The many scrolled mirrors at Versailles also reflect this accent on decoration, and the heightening of the pleasures of life. So does the exterior of the clavecin, the leading instrument of the gallant style.

We have already discussed Rameau, Couperin, and Telemann. Others, strongly associated with the gallant style are Domenico Scarlatti (1685–1757), the son of Alessandro Scarlatti, Johann Mattheson, who was involved in the celebrated duel with Handel, and the great sons of J. S. Bach: Carl Philipp Emanuel (1714–1788), Johann Christian (1735–1782), Johann Christoff (1732–1795), and Wilhelm Friedmann (1710–1784).

Domenico Scarlatti concerned himself much with music for the cembalo (harpsichord), on which he was as renowned a virtuoso as was Liszt on the piano in the nineteenth century. His sonatas, numbering approximately 500, are frothy, piquant, and elegant.

Analysis and commentary:
Wachet auf, ruft uns die Stimme
Chorale Prelude by J. S. Bach

This piece is particularly rewarding for analysis and study. It illustrates the highest kind of music by the master who is conceded to represent the very essence and culmination of the baroque style, Johann Sebastian Bach. It is rewarding from the historical point of view in that the form used, the chorale prelude, is of major significance, with a long line of ancestry in German music.

The Lutheran chorale, which is at the foundation of the form itself, was very important in the German Baroque. Also important is that this piece is found in two versions: as an organ piece (from the Schubler Chorale Preludes) and as the fifth number from Cantata 140. Thus, the music not only illustrates Bach's habit of setting the same music for different performance media, but offers an excellent opportunity to contrast the effect of the same music presented in different timbres. The chorale will already be familiar to many, for it is included in many modern Protestant hymn books.

Example 360   Chorale, "Wachet auf," third verse, J. S. Bach

This chorale illustrates another important facet of Bach's genius. The tune is actually by an earlier composer, Philipp Nicolai (1556–1608), but the beautiful harmonization by J. S. Bach only adds to the luster of his genius.

The form of the chorale prelude as used here by Bach is one of several possible. Bach creates soprano and bass lines of exquisite sensitivity. At certain points in the flow of these are heard successive phrases of the chorale itself. Thus, the whole consists of three-part counterpoint, the chorale acting as a cantus firmus somewhat in the fashion of music of the pre-Baroque. Each melodic part contrasts rhythmically with the others: the upper quite active, the lower more stately, using primarily quarter-notes and eighth-notes, while the chorale is quite plain.

It begins with an idea (Example 361), with the typical jagged inter-

Example 361

vals found in so much Bach. This rugged contour is explained by the
fact that not one but two melodic parts are suggested within one line
(Example 362). In measure 5 another, complementary, idea begins
(Example 363), which leads to an interesting syncopated figure (Example 364). At measure 13, on the third beat, the chorale enters

Example 362

Example 363

Example 364

(Example 365). The miracle of this moment is that it is so natural an

Example 365

entrance. The first 12 measures of two-part counterpoint are so
absolutely satisfying in themselves that one marvels at the arrival of a
third melodic part which suddenly seems an indispensable addition. We

wonder if Bach might very well have been able to add a fourth and a fifth part with perfect ease and natural effect.

The first phrase of the chorale is heard with its accompanying counterpoint. Then the music thins to a two-part texture again, where we hear a firm modulation to the dominant key, B-flat major (Example 366). After a repetition of this material a new phase begins and the

Example 366

music shifts to another tonal area, this time to the key of C minor (Example 367). The two-part counterpoint touches briefly on G minor, and

Example 367

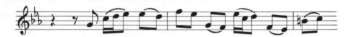

soon after sinks back into E-flat major, the home key. At this point the last phrase of the chorale is heard. After it is completed, the last part of the prelude is taken up by the final spinning out of the florid melody of the beginning, the whole gradually coming to a majestic repose with a cadence in E-flat major on a simple, reverent tonic octave (Example 368).

Example 368

12

Classicism

MONTAIGNE UNDOUBTEDLY EXAGGERATED when he said of man's progress in history: "We do not go; we rather run up and down and whirl this way and that; we turn back the way we came."* Certainly it is true that history repeats itself, at least in part. Nothing is all new. There simply does not exist a totally new style of painting or musical composition. This is particularly apparent in successive musical eras. A new period or style may well have evolved in an atmosphere of violent reaction to the "artistic establishment" immediately preceding it. The development of spare and simple monodic forms by the Italian Camerata near 1600 as a strong protest to the elaborate polyphony of renaissance music is a good example of this.

That which is new — and worthwhile — is always powerfully rooted in the past and especially in the near past. Classicism is no exception to this. Its energizing force was conditioned by a strong reaction to the Baroque. The sons of Johann Sebastian Bach considered the intricacies and complexity of their father's art old fashioned. The new, simpler style was more to their taste, and certainly more fashionable.

Yet Classicism sits squarely on the foundation built by baroque masters. In the field of harmony, Rameau and others had solidified

*Robert Maynard Hutchins, ed., *Great Books of the Western World*, Vol. 25, Montaigne (Chicago: University of Chicago Press), p. 439.

chord structure, chord progression, and major-minor tonality to such an extent that it sufficed basically unchanged for Haydn, Mozart, and Beethoven, and lasted until the twentieth century. Lyric homophony, which is the prevailing texture throughout the classical era, actually was fully developed in the Baroque, though it shared the attention of composers with polyphony. The masters of Classicism took full advantage of the enormous growth of instrumental music, as well as the refinement of the instruments themselves in the Baroque.

The music of the classical masters often shows strong atavistic traces. The slow introduction of Beethoven's last Piano Sonata, Opus 111, shows an unmistakable resemblance to the typically somber French overture of the Baroque (Example 369).

Example 369   Sonata, Opus 111, Introduction, Beethoven

Beethoven's predilection for the fugue in his later years is well known. Mozart, besides writing many sterling fugues himself, arranged five fugues from J. S. Bach's *Well Tempered Clavier.* His writing additional accompaniments to four choral works of Handel—including the *Messiah*—shows an involvement in the Baroque beyond simple homage to the past.

Yet, aside from these obvious and necessary connections with the Baroque, classical music is strikingly original in sound. We have seen in Chapter 11 what distinguishes baroque style. In it can be seen a splendid display of energy, drive, and passion tempered by utter dignity, and a luxuriance of detail made convincing by complete logic of structure. Briefly, baroque music can be said to display an intense but thoroughly ordered musical expression.

In contrast to this, typically classical music emphasizes symmetry, reserve, a profound simplicity. Emotion is present—indeed sometimes it seethes to the surface as in the Symphony No. 40 by Mozart—but it seldom is as obvious as in the Baroque. Its goal is balance: a Hellenistic blending of form with content.

In the music of the Classicists, symmetry, purity, and simplicity can be heard. One beautifully chiseled phrase will be answered and balanced by another very much like it. There is much expectedness. Nothing is done in excess. The music is seldom hotly passionate. Textures are open, simple, and pellucid. Everything is as functional, simple, and dignified as the Roman toga, woven of a single piece of undyed wool. Rather than the kingly dignity found in much baroque music, classical music shows controlled equanimity.

Though polyphonic forms continued to be used, especially in sacred music, cleanly chiseled, diaphanous single melody, supported by logically structured chords in various guises was predominant in the classical period. Lyric homophony was easier to understand, representing perhaps plainer, more direct expression. Therefore it was ideal for a serene, classical style.

Summing up, the transition from the Baroque was one from complexity to simplicity, from a luxuriant vivacity to a serene, generally buoyant simplicity. Rhythms became simpler, melodic contours smoother, textures more open, forms easier to perceive. Homophony largely replaced polyphony. In the Renaissance, music was apt to reflect the serenity and repose of an ideal world—another world accessible only through a churchly, pious life. Baroque music mirrored an expanding, vital, growing world on all levels. It is enormously energetic, the lavish sonorities of its secular music reflecting the high gloss of aristocratic life. Its sacred music mirrored the depth and passion of the Protestant Reformation, or the sincerity and brilliance of the Counter-Reformation. Rococo music, emphasizing expression, sensibility, and ultra-refinement of the sensual, reflected the jaded ennui of a fast decaying aristocratic society. In this process it strove for simplicity and directness. Here it began to approach what was to come in Classicism, Jean-Jacques Rousseau, who with his opera *Le Devin du Village* (1752), wrote in an extremely direct, simple homophonic style, said of polyphonic devices that they "reflect disgrace on those who had the patience to construct them." The very fact that Rousseau, the champion of "natural man" and of total democracy, propagandized and publicized the new gallant style is highly significant. It shows that the new, non-contrapuntal, melodic style dovetailed exactly with the revolutionary ideas about sentiment, importance of emotion, and the value of the individual.

The effect of this new, simple harmonic style on the sophisticated listening public must have been like the figure of Benjamin Franklin as an envoy to France during the American Revolution. His public appearances, in plain clothes and without ceremonial wig, did much to win French hearts to the Republican cause.

In sum, the atmosphere of the time was conducive to an establishment of a direct, more personal style of musical expression. Through

"*His public appearances, in plain clothes and without ceremonial wig, did much to win French hearts to the Republican cause*" (p. 390).

its emphasis on simplicity, reason, and directness of sentiment, it paved the way for a truly *personal music*. This subjective, intimate factor began to appear in late Mozart and Haydn and finally flowered with Beethoven. It was then—at the turn into the nineteenth century—that music became the magnificent medium for the expression of the essence and nobility of all men. Thus, Classicism is a most significant era in the history of music.

General characteristics

We have already touched on some of the basic characteristics of classical music, its perfect lucidity and ideal proportion. Content—melodic and harmonic ideas—is perfectly matched to structure. Though there are serious moments in the secular music, replete with tender pathos, the tendency is toward good humor, toward sparkle and zest. The classicists aimed to please. They had to, if they wished to retain their princely patrons.

Sometimes the humor achieved rather robust proportions, as in the *Musical Joke* by Mozart. Here the composer flashes one tonal jest after another. For example, after a perfectly innocuous beginning in the Menuetto, the horns are required to play the passage in Example 370.

Example 370   A Musical Joke, K.522, Movement 2, Mozart

MELODY

Mozart had declared, "I compare a good melodist to a fine racer, and counterpointists to hack post horses."

With the acceptance of homophony as the basis for much classical music, attention turned strongly toward melody, especially in its lyric aspect. Now that a single, predominating line received much of the compositional thrust, it had to be constructed so that it would instantly fix and hold the listener's attention. It therefore became simpler than either rococo or baroque melody. Though ornaments continued to grace classical melodies, they were used much more sparingly than before. Melodic contour was "smoothed out": intervals used caused the melodies to be less spiky and jagged than in the Baroque. Because of the tremendous emphasis of symmetrical phrase and period structure, melodies seemed neatly trimmed and tailored. They seemed blocked out more, segmented, conforming to the inner divisions and dimensions of balanced classical forms.

HARMONY

A powerful yet flexible system of major-minor tonality underlay the tunefulness, clarity, and elegance of classical music. Mozart and Haydn inherited a system of chord structures, consonance-dissonance, and chord progression that had been systematized by Rameau and refined by J. S. Bach. The Bach chorale is the paragon of harmonic usage. This the classical masters knew and enjoyed.

The prevailing key and scale was major. The minor was used for music in the *patetico* style, and with Haydn and Mozart it was quite subjective and personal. But though the usual overall key scheme tended to be major, episodes or secondary themes in minor could be striking in effect.

The Andante cantabile from the Sonata in C major by Mozart is a good example of this. The first section is dominated by a theme (Example 371) in luminous major. The second section, in F minor,

Example 371   Sonata in C, K.330, Movement 2, Mozart

begins as shown in Example 372. The sudden poignancy achieved through the intensity of the harmony is wonderful — especially after the serenity of the beginning.

RANGE

In one area, that of range and tessitura, Classicism was quite similar to the Baroque. Both favored the soprano. If one considers the string choir in Mozart symphonies, it becomes apparent that the

Example 372

violins consistently have the better of it melodically. Cello and contrabass are largely supportive.

The same can be said about the other forces of the classical symphony. The most important winds were flutes, oboes, and trumpets. Bassoons were the only winds to anchor the total sound in the bass. Trombones did not come into steady use until the nineteenth century. Neither did the tuba, bass clarinet, or the contrabassoon.

Of course, there are many striking pieces emphasizing bass instruments or voices. One thinks immediately of the Mozart bassoon concerto, or the buffo parts in classical opera such as that of Leporello in Mozart's *Don Giovanni*. But, perhaps, because of the classical masters' penchant for lucidity with brilliance, high registers were primary.

DYNAMICS AND TEMPO

We have already noted the tremendous stir caused by the systematic use of crescendo and diminuendo by the composers of the Mannheim School in the early classical period. Unquestionably, these surging dynamic effects stirred mightily the emotions of audiences of the day. Indeed, a well managed crescendo or diminuendo even today is a powerful tool for creating excitement and mood. In the time of Mozart and Haydn the resulting expressivity was precisely in line with the developing need for a more personal music. With Beethoven it became a major tool for achieving searing dramatic effects.

Along with the traditional use of *forte* and *piano* in juxtaposition, the *fp* and the *sf* attained some prominence. This last effect was especially useful in music for the pianoforte, which, in contrast to the harpsi-

"Mozart had his Leutgeb, sometime cheese monger and brilliant player of the horn, and four concertos were written for him" (p. 396).

chord, could effectively manage sudden louds followed by sudden softs within the body of a phrase or period.

However, a medium-loud forte and a gentle piano were the usual. It was not until Beethoven that *fortissimo* and its opposite, *pianissimo*, consistently came into use.

In a similar way, tempos were moderate. The plain truth is that the wealth of detail, marvelous juxtaposition and combination of ideas cannot be perceived adequately by the listener if tempos in this music are excessive.

PERFORMANCE AND INSTRUMENTS

Performance standards were quite high. With the development of many resident orchestras, at Mannheim, in Paris, at Esterhazy, and elsewhere, players took pride in their profession. Virtuosity became common. Mozart had his Leutgeb, sometime cheese monger and brilliant player of the horn, and four concertos were written for him.

And there was the brilliant Anton Stadler who did much to spur Mozart's interest in the clarinet. His playing was the inspiration for the Clarinet Concerto, the Clarinet Quintet, and many others.

The travels of the boy Mozart and his sister, Nannerl, throughout the continent as prodigies of the keyboard are well known. In maturity, Mozart was an incredible virtuoso at the keyboard. The performances of his own concertos were renowned. In like manner, young Beethoven was celebrated as a fiery, brilliant pianist; much more so than as a composer. His passionate improvisations affected audiences to such a degree that everyone in his audience wept.

Virtuosity on any of various instruments was much in vogue throughout the last half of the eighteenth century. Attesting to the public's hunger for any sort of instrumental virtuosity were the scintillating careers of two ladies, the English Marianne Davies and the German Marianne Kitchgessmer. Both were famed for their performances on the glass harmonica, an instrument perfected by Benjamin Franklin.

FORMS

The shift of emphasis from the polyphony of the Renaissance and the Baroque to the homophony of Classicism had many results: changes in melody, harmony, and rhythm were enormous. But most important of all was the new outlook on form. Obviously, the most important relationships in renaissance and baroque contrapuntal composition are parallel or oblique. The vital structural feature in an invention or a fugue is how the parts fit together on top of one another, how they invert and how imitation comes into play. Here energy, vital dynamism, come through the interplay of simultaneous melodic parts.

In contrast to this, because there is often only one leading melodic part in classical homophony supported by variously arranged chords, parallel considerations are not of primary importance.

To be sure, the way in which a melody is colored and enhanced by chords affects its style tremendously. But just as important as the way things *sound together* is the way things *sound side by side*. In other words, the horizontal connection of themes, parts, and sections is the most important principle in classical form.

Balance, symmetry, proportion become powerful factors in these forms: four measures balanced by four more; exposition matched by recapitulation; statement answered by restatement. The most important forms were those dependent on the Viennese sonata principle: the solo sonata, concerto, symphony, string quartet, and, in addition, opera. Sacred choral music continued to be prominent.

The composers

No other period in the history of music is represented by so few major composers as is that of Classicism. Beyond Joseph Haydn (1732–1809) Wolfgang Amadeus Mozart (1756–1791) and Ludwig Van Beethoven, composers of absolutely first rank, there is Christopher Willibald Gluck, who revolutionized opera but did not essay very much in other musical forms. But, though only few, these composers had tremendous impact. The essentials of their art — harmony, form, rhythm, melody — persisted as the foundation of music until the twentieth century.

Chronologically, the adult creative lives of the great triumvirate are separated by 20 years more or less. Thus, there occurred a rather neat line of descent, spanning the whole period. One generation separated each. Haydn came into his adult artistic powers in the early 1750's, shortly after the death of J. S. Bach, in the rococo period. Mozart matured as a creative artist at the apogee of the classical era, in 1776; while Beethoven reached adulthood in 1790. Beethoven's productive days paralleled the final ripening of Classicism, as well as its transition into the romantic century.

The content of their music reflects all of this quite faithfully. Though Haydn's music is sometimes quite passionate and stormy, it is conditioned somewhat by the pleasantries and mannerisms of the Rococo. It is likely to be level headed and good humored rather than hotly personal. The gallant style permeates much of his earlier work.

Mozart quite often is intensely subjective. It often seems that he deliberately plans for a special mood, for a certain melancholy atmosphere. A feeling of unrest, of spiritual travail and personal outpouring, saturates a great number of his mature works—especially the ones in the minor mode. What happens, of course, is that the composer cannot keep from exposing his deepest self. Mozart is very close to Romanticism here.

It is not surprising that Mozart's most mature years, 1776–1791, encompassed almost exactly both the American and French revolutions. It was at precisely these portentous years that the new world—built around the new premise of assertion of the self—was wrenching itself from the old. Mozart, the artist and professional, stood in the vortex of vast social dislocations. Small wonder that we feel a curious blend of poignant regret and new adventure in his most personal music.

Beethoven lived to epitomize the very thing that had been passionately sought and finally won—the dignity and unique value of all men. Though there is great tragedy and melancholy throughout Beethoven, there is, even more, exultation and victory. Beethoven, as an artist, symbolizes totally the spiritual charter newly won at the turn of the nineteenth century.

Curiously, little things in the daily lives of these masters corroborate the above. For example, Haydn, who as a young man had brushed the clothes and cleaned the shoes of the composer Nicola Porpora (1686–1766), and who was in the employ of the aristocracy most of his life, seldom, if ever, appeared publicly without donning the formal wig. Mozart often was wigged, but an unfinished portrait of the composer by his brother-in-law, Lange, done in 1791, and others earlier, show him unwigged. Of course, Beethoven, whose shaggy mane is well known, was wigged only in his youth.

HAYDN

Joseph Haydn lived a long, fruitful, methodical life. From humble beginnings in a peasant's hut in Austria, he became choir boy at St. Stephen's in Vienna and came under the influence of the poet, Metastasio, and the composer, Porpora. For 30 years he served as Kapellmeister for the noble house of Esterhazy in Hungary. Late in his life there were two trips to London, where he was acclaimed as composer and conductor. His last years were spent in the outskirts of Vienna, where he wrote the great oratorios, the *Creation* and the *Seasons*.

Haydn's output was truly voluminous, numbering many hundreds of compositions. He worked with all the major idioms of the day: opera, oratorio, mass, concerto, sonata, symphony, chamber music, song. But his major contribution was in the symphony and the string quartet. There were well over 100 symphonies and 83 quartets. He did not invent these forms, but he gave them the structure and scope that was to challenge most of the major composers after him for upwards of 100 years.

With Haydn, the symphony and its performance medium, the full orchestra, became truly modern, capable of expressing a wide gamut of emotion. The forms of the inner movements—sonata-allegro, theme and variation, rondo, song form, minuet with trio—became marvels of studied poise and balance. His development sections—intricate, coherent, logical all at once—were the models for Mozart and Beethoven. Anybody studying the brief development section from the rondo in Score Profile at the end of Chapter 5 will find an uncanny tightness and aptness of individual ideas wedded with an almost blithe naturalness.

MOZART

Mozart's life contrasts to that of Haydn in several important ways. For one, his background and education were completely different. Mozart's father, Leopold, was a respected and talented composer, the author of a well known method for the violin. Whereas Haydn progressed through life ever gaining reputation and material fortune, Mozart quite often suffered agonies of want and deprivation, and died at the age of 35. He died engrossed in the writing of his great Requiem, fully realizing that it was as much for himself as for the noble who commissioned it.

The catalogue of his works is very extensive. Köchel, who catalogued his music, gives over 600 works. In all major forms that he used, the music is unrivaled for purity, intellectual scope, and passion. Besides succeeding in Haydn's favorite forms, the symphony and quartet, he was the complete master of the concerto. There exist superb concertos for bassoon, horn, clarinet, flute, and violin, the whole collection crowned by upwards of two dozen for the keyboard. The analysis of the C minor Piano Concerto at the end of this chapter shows what unquestionable mastery he ultimately attained over the form. In it is represented the very essence of passion and tragedy tempered by nobility of design and purpose.

The operas of Mozart—*The Marriage of Figaro, Idomeneo,* the *Magic Flute, Don Giovanni*—are superb representations of his best work. *Don Giovanni,* to choose one example, was as fraught with implications for the music of the romantic century as was Beethoven's "Eroica" Symphony. The opera abounds in exquisite melody. There are moments of great pathos, as at the death of the commendatore in Act I. The comedy, of course, is superb, as when Leporello reads from the list of the Don's amorous adventures in the "Catalogue Aria." The flute clearly volunteers a kind of "wolf whistle" (Example 373).

Example 373   Don Giovanni, Act I, Mozart

When the frightened servant in Act II tells his master of the ghostly statue at the door, the music imitates the knocking in a delightful way (Example 374).

Example 374   Don Giovanni, Act II, Mozart

BEETHOVEN

Beethoven's early years and education form a kind of composite of those of Haydn and Mozart. His father was a musician, as was Mozart's, but he had little musical distinction. Beethoven, too, was a prodigy, but did not bud into greatness as easily or as early as had Mozart. Like Haydn, he worked very hard to achieve his style. Every new creative advance was marked by enormous labor and spiritual travail—the *Skizzenbuchen* attest to this.

The forms that challenged Beethoven were precisely those brought to such perfection by Haydn and Mozart: symphony, sonata, concerto, string quartet and chamber music, the mass, opera, song. From them, he gained a rigorous sense of the principles of classic form. Indeed, a great body of his early works point in essence and form back to earlier times.

Like Haydn and Mozart, Beethoven possessed a sense of humor that saturates much of his music. The scherzo from the "Spring" Sonata, Opus 24, for violin and piano, illustrates this perfectly. The piano begins with a saucy little tune (Example 375), which is full of bounce

Example 375   Violin Sonata ("Spring"), Opus 24, Movement 3, Beethoven

and snap. Then the violin joins in, supposedly doubling the melody. But, somehow, it is always one beat late, and never does catch up (Example 376). Apparently, Beethoven enjoyed musical frolic so much that he

Example 376

could not stop from repeating the whole "out of step" process in the Scherzo from his "Pastorale" Symphony—this time with the oboe out of step.

Though equanimity, grace, elegance, good humor, balanced structure, can be found throughout Beethoven, it is not in these areas that he was unique. Rather, it is the energy, dramatic power, exultant majesty, and intensity of mood and passion that distinguishes him from

"... *every new creative advance was marked
by enormous labor and spiritual travail—
the Skizzenbuchen attest to this*" (p. 400).

those before. Throughout his life, there were battles with the world and with himself. In his early thirties he found that he was doomed to deafness. The Heiligenstadt Testament, written in a moment of utter despair, shows the inner struggle that he underwent:

> Yes, the cherished hope—which I brought with me when I came here, of being healed at least to a certain degree, must now abandon me entirely. As the leaves of autumn fall and are withered, so, too—my hope has dried up. Almost as I was when I came here, I leave again—even the courage—which inspired me on lovely summer days—is vanished. O Providence—let a single day of untroubled joy be granted to me! For so long already the resonance of true joy be granted to me! O when—O when, Divine one—may I feel it once more in the temple of Nature and of mankind? Never?—no —that would be too hard!*

But despite constant physical afflictions, disappointments in love, gross misunderstanding by the public, his indomitable will and great faith in the dignity and greatness of the human spirit drove him on to achieve more with his music.

His work is generally divided into three periods. Roughly, the first period covers everything up to 1800, or the music up to the late Opus 40's. This music, though suffused by his peculiar dynamism, yet looks back to Haydn and Mozart. The early works, though often charged with passion and subjective power as in the "Pathetique" and "Moonlight" Sonatas, or the Quartet in C minor, Opus 18, did not really surpass certain items from Haydn or Mozart (Examples 377 and 378).

With the coming of the second period, inaugurated by works such as the Kreutzer Sonata, Opus 47, for violin and piano and the "Eroica" Symphony, Opus 55, Beethoven found his true artistic character. His apprenticeship had ended. The music of this period pulses with power and energy. In it can be heard everything from the agonized moans of the Funeral March of the Eroica to the philosophical detachment and serenity of the Scene at the Brook from the "Pastorale" Symphony, to the almost frenetic fury of the "Appassionata" Sonata.

The last period, beginning in the Opus 90's, also contains some marvelously exciting music: in the Gloria from the Missa Solemnis, for example, or the Scherzo and the Finale from the Ninth Symphony. But another dimension is present. There is withdrawal, a searching within. Forms become much freer, more fantasy-like, though solid principles

*Michael Hamburger, trans. and ed., *Beethoven, Letters, Journals and Conversations* (Garden City, N.Y.: Doubleday Anchor Book), p. 34.

Example 377   Sonata, K.457, Movement 2, Mozart

Example 378   Sonata ("Pathetique") Opus 13, Movement 2, Beethoven

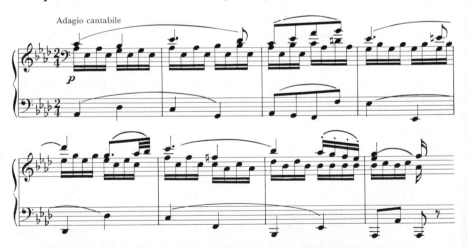

of structure are always present. There is a decided tendency to play down effect and dazzle. Harmony becomes much more refined, and a deep, searching polyphony often reigns. The Quartet in C-sharp minor illustrates this final renunciation and inner exploration perhaps better than any other late work. Its overall structure, as well as its content, are revolutionary. There are seven movements, forming a loose but highly cohesive fantasy-like structure.

GLUCK

Christopher Willibald Gluck (1714–1787) was an important transitional figure. As early as 1742, he was in London writing operas in opposition to Handel. Later, in Paris, he produced great master-works in the field, including *Iphiginie et Aulide* and *Orphée*. There was a fierce polemic with the followers of Piccini (1728–1800) and the Italian School of opera, including a bitter war of pamphlets. His operatic technique emphasized dramatic consistency and a psychologically true setting of music to text. This was in stark contrast to the Italian style, featuring rigid expected sequences of arias, duets, choruses, cadenzas, etc. The effect of his operatic reforms on Mozart, Weber, and later Romantics was profound and lasting.

OTHER COMPOSERS

Other important figures of the period are Muzio Clementi (1752–1832), fashionable concert pianist, composer and manufacturer of pianos; Luigi Boccherini (1743–1805), cellist and composer of elegant, sparkling music including 20 symphonies; Antonio Salieri (1750–1825), the rival of Mozart and sometime teacher of Beethoven, who was known primarily as a composer of opera.

Analysis and commentary: Mozart, Concerto for Piano and Orchestra in C minor, K. 491, Movement 3

This 24th piano concerto by Mozart is one of only two written by him in the minor mode. (The other is the 20th, in D minor.)

It was greatly admired by Beethoven, who patterned much of his own C minor Concerto, Opus 37, for piano after it. The Mozart concerto is replete with pathos and drama. It is a marvel of musical integration, the keyboard part blending naturally with the orchestra at all times. The virtuosity of the solo part never intrudes in the homogeneity and oneness of the whole. All of this Beethoven surely admired and emulated; his work in the concerto form constantly emphasized these virtues.

Opening themes in both works are similar (Examples 379 and 380).

Example 379   Piano Concerto, K.491, Movement 1, Mozart

Example 380   Piano Concerto, Opus 37, Movement 1, Beethoven

The final movement, an Allegretto in C minor, is cast by Mozart as a set of eight variations on an original theme. The theme itself (Example 381) is one of rare beauty. In a miraculous way Mozart managed

Example 381   Piano Concerto, K.491, Movement 3, Mozart

to capture within an impeccably patterned 16-measure frame a personal poignancy, perhaps tinged with regret. Its form is regular binary, both parts beginning with the same motive (Examples 382 and 383). The orchestra states it complete, without commentary by the piano. It is as if Mozart had wished his theme to be presented in all of its purity, without filigree or embroidery of any sort. The piano, however, quickly comes into its own. Variation 1 is entirely given over to embellishing material in the solo part with sparse chordal background in the

Example 382

Part A begins:

Example 383

Part B begins:

orchestra. Two important motives arise (Example 384). The second, an

Example 384

ascending, tripping figure (Example 385), will be used as the basis of

Example 385

Variation 6. The second variation is evenly divided between orchestra and soloist. The orchestra plays part A of the theme through once, after which the piano joins with brilliant scales for its repetition (Example 386). Part B is treated in the same manner. In Variation 3, things are

Example 386

reversed. The piano sallies forth with quite a stormy idea (Example 387). The *sturm und drang* character of this music surely must have thrilled

Example 387

Beethoven. The orchestra answers with fiery material of its own, and then they do it all over again. And then, a complete change of mood in Variation 4. The winds carry this idea, *p* (Example 388), a crisp little

Example 388

march in A-flat major, complete with saucy accents at unexpected places. The piano joins in later, featuring a bouncy rhythmic pattern of its own.

Variation 5 carries the music back to the original key—C minor. The piano is mostly in charge. It starts in a rather dense, contrapuntal manner (Example 389). Shortly afterwards, ascending scales in the left hand underline the motive heard at the beginning of Variation 3 (Example 390). The tumult of this variation ends with a solid cadence in the tonic minor (Example 391). Variation 6 enters, this time in the orchestra. Suddenly, it is in the warmth and geniality of the parallel key—C major (Example 392). Prominently featured is the tiny figure first encountered in Variation 1 (Example 393). Variation 7 reverts back to the tonic minor key. It is shorter than previous ones and is distinguished by flashing rising scales and glittering arpeggios. All of this leads to a cadenza that ushers in the last section, Variation 8 (Example 394). A very important change occurs in this variation: the meter,

Example 389

Example 390

Example 391

Example 392

Example 393

Example 394

instead of continuing in four beats, now is in two, in six-eight. At first the music shows a tripping, hesitant mien, but then skyrocketing scales lead to a brilliant, trenchant close (Example 395).

Example 395

13

Romanticism

"I UNDERSTAND that you are fond of music that does not distract your mind from affairs of state." This comment is said to have occurred during a conversation between the composer Luigi Cherubini and the first Napoleon. This obviously did not enamor the Corsican to the composer. But the veiled sarcasm of the remark helps us to understand the import and impact of romantic composers and their music. One cannot imagine Haydn, a few years before, addressing the nobility with anything but profound respect. The written terms to his appointment at Esterhazy attests to the menial position of composers and musicians in the centuries before the nineteenth. Haydn must ". . . be temperate; must abstain from vulgarity in eating and drinking and conversation; must take care of all the music and the musical instruments, and be answerable for any injury they may suffer from carelessness or neglect; . . . that when summoned to perform before company he shall take care that he and all members of his orchestra do follow the instructions given and appear in white stockings, white linen, powder, and with either a pig-tail or a tie-wig."*

Beethoven, giving lessons, rapped the knuckles of his aristocratic pupils. The nineteenth-century composer assumed a quite

*Thomas Paine and Klauser, eds., *Famous Composers and Their Works*, Vol. II (Boston: J. B. Millet Co., 1891), p. 252.

different role from his counterpart of the seventeenth and eighteenth centuries. The talents of Beethoven and those who followed were for hire—but now mostly on their own terms.

The early Romantics, Cherubini, Beethoven, Rossini, Berlioz, Mendelssohn, and Wagner, all had attained social position. Each man was independent in a way that his predecessors could only have envied, as can be plainly seen from Wagner's comments:

> . . . The world owes me what I require! I cannot live on a miserable post of organist like your master Bach! Is it such an unheard of demand when I ask that the little bit of luxury that I enjoy be given to me? I, who hold a thousand enjoyments in store for the world!*

Whereas the majority of the baroque and classical masters were directly dependent on either the church or aristocracy for their very bread, the Romantics frequently dealt with the public directly. They realized income from concerts and from the publications of their works. Now they were professionals with dignity and a clear, independent social position.

We do not mean to suggest that the path to material security for composers had become easy in the early 1800's. For many, it was still a very cruel fight for bare existence. But, despite this, the composer now had a voice. He was heard; the world noticed, took him into account, and was moved. Thus Cherubini could speak to Napoleon on somewhat equal terms. Napoleon had conquered his world, Cherubini his.

With the composer's new-found independence and dignity his music took on a new cast. It now became loosened, freer, expansive. Above all, it expressed deeply and tellingly the subjective state of the composer himself. The music unashamedly expressed *him* directly, and without reserve.

There were musical explorations into areas of human experience never before attempted. Berlioz produced a dazzling first symphony, the Symphonie Fantastique, in 1830; its intense passions and reveries we are told are those resulting from a young hero taking an overdose of opium. The symphony displays a great scenic panorama. In its five movements Berlioz joyfully leaps about from the yearnings of a young man in love, to an elegant ball, to a rustic scene in the country, to the guillotine, and finally, to a sulphuric scene somewhere near hell, replete with witches and the death bell.

In the piano works of Chopin we hear a refined, sensitive musical

*Reprinted from *Darwin, Marx, Wagner* by Jacques Barzun (1941) with permission of Atlantic-Little, Brown and Company.

language depicting in minute detail the composer's many fine shades of sentiment.

Program music — a major concern with the Romantics — not only represented various scenes and situations but lead to the depiction of the character of different countries and peoples. Mendelssohn traveled much and gave to the world musical "souvenirs" of great charm and polish: The Hebrides Overture, and the "Italian" and "Scotch" Symphonies. Nationalism became very important. Many composers occupied themselves primarily with trying to capture the spirit of their native lands.

Smetana wrote the first Czech nationalistic opera, *The Bartered Bride*. His compatriot Dvorak not only produced a great many Czech-oriented works, but during his stay in America in the 1890's was instrumental in making Americans aware of their native music. Later, Sibelius became a strong spiritual voice for Finland through his music. He said, "When we see those granite rocks we know why we are able to treat the orchestra as we do."

Thus, the Romantics constantly searched within and without themselves for new things to express. Because of this, new technical means had to be created in order to arrive at the desired musical ends. New forms evolved, and old ones were transformed. Melody, rhythm, harmony, orchestration, dynamics, performance: all were profoundly affected.

General characteristics

MELODY

Throughout the baroque and classical periods melodic elements were deemed worthy primarily for their potential in compositional development. Fugue subjects tended to be graphic, clear, and plain (Example 396). They usually became charged with emotional or intellec-

Example 396   Ariadne Musica, Fugue No. 10, J.K.F. Fischer

tual meaning after they were expanded, combined with other melodic elements. In short, they became interesting after they had undergone musical growth.

In the romantic period, melodies also were created for their utility. But more commonly, they were shaped for immediate, memorable tunefulness, for innate beauty. In other words, melody as such and for itself established a kind of structural hegemony over other elements such as rhythm and harmony (Example 397).

Example 397   Rigoletto, "Caro nome," Verdi

Romantic melody is striking and immediate, often extremely lyric and song-like. It tends also to span larger segments in composition than in previous periods. Because of the attention given to folk and dance music in general, romantic melody frequently takes on a nationalistic or regional tinge.

RHYTHM

Flexibility is a major characteristic of romantic rhythm. This shows itself strongly in tempo. In previous periods tempos tended to be uniform, the beat steady and unflagging. Restraint in tempo—as in nearly everything else—was primary. But the personal expressions of the Romanticists could not be stated within strict tempos. Rubato was used for emphasis and to intensify the emotional impact. Individual movements often exhibited major tempo changes. Tchaikovsky, in the finale of the Symphony No. 5, utilizes no fewer than nine tempos. They are: Andante maestoso, Allegro vivace, Poco piu animato, Tempo I, Poco meno mosso, Molto vivace, Moderato assai e molto maestoso, Presto, Molto meno mosso.

Nineteenth-century masters, besides allowing for fluctuation and change of tempo, wrote music in a tremendous range of tempos, from a crawl to a gallop. Rhythm, then, along with melody, became a means for broadened expression.

HARMONY

Vertical sonority particularly challenged and fascinated the romantic composer. It provided color and depth. He explored new sounds, vibrant chords, and striking instrumental textures—sounds that would touch and impress the listener and sounds that would delight the ear. Extended chords, their rich quality arresting the attention, were explored and consistently used from the time of Beethoven on.

DYNAMICS AND RANGE

Expansion is the keynote in both of these areas. Extreme louds and softs and sudden shifts from one to the other were common. The sudden explosion from a quintuple piano to a double forte in Example 398 is typical. In Tchaikovsky's Symphony No. 5, movement 2,

Example 398   Symphony No. 6, Opus 74, Movement 1, Tchaikovsky

the spectrum of dynamic color is very wide indeed: from *pppp* to *ffff*, with a great many levels in between. Berlioz, in his *Symphonie Fantastique*, movement 3, asks the strings to play *ppp*, the slightest musical whisper, and adds the words *"quasi niente"* (almost nothing).

In range, romantic music shows many extreme highs and lows. Each register is fully explored for its potential in sound. Leading melodic elements might be located in the lower abysses of the bass, then suddenly heard at the top of the soprano register.

INSTRUMENTS AND PERFORMANCE

The nineteenth-century concert artist, lionized by an adoring public, was a symbol of everything that is uniquely personal in romantic music. Through their magnetic presence on stage, Paganini and Liszt represented to the masses the quintessence of imagination and creative power.

As in previous centuries, many performing artists were also famous composers, including Paganini, Weber, Mendelssohn, Chopin, Brahms, and Liszt. Weber, Mendelssohn, and Wagner were famous as conductors. Sometimes, when native genius was immense, as with Mendelssohn or Liszt, the composer matched the performer. Other virtuosos on the piano such as Herz, Kalkbrenner, and Dreyschock spewed forth garish and tasteless compositions in the form of potpourris, variations on popular themes, and salon pieces.

Harold Schonberg in his book, *The Great Pianists*, tells about the herculean virtuosity of Dreyschock:

> "Dreyschock would practice sixteen hours a day with the left hand alone, and got to the point where he could play octaves as fast and as smoothly as single-note passages. Heine once said that 'when Dreyschock played in Munich and the wind was right, you could hear him in Paris'."*

Many instruments in use developed in quality, power, and flexibility. New ones, such as the saxophone, Wagner tuba, tuba, and celeste were invented. The orchestra expanded, both in size and in variety of instruments. English horn, bass clarinet, cornet, trombone, bass drum, and cymbals became increasingly common.

The concert artist and conductor became important members of society. Their skills were often prodigious, and the instruments that they played developed accordingly. Romantic music found adequate media for its expression.

FORMS

It would be an error to think that romantic forms were entirely new and unique. Though the fugue was a major compositional vehicle

*From *The Great Pianists* by Harold C. Schonberg. Copyright © by Harold C. Schonberg. Reprinted by permission of Simon and Schuster, Inc. and Littauer and Wilkinson.

in the Baroque, it continued to interest nineteenth-century masters. The symphony, concerto, opera, and sonata, magnificently developed in the classical period, continued to occupy a commanding position.

Among the many smaller forms that were particularly associated with the romantic century, the *lied* and the character piece for piano were prominent. The *lied* appealed especially to the romantic composer because of the opportunity to set to music poetry of the highest order. Since the time of Beethoven the romantic composer had considered himself a tone poet (*tondichter*). He felt that, like the poet, he could express definite things and feelings. The poems of Schiller, Goethe, Heine, Eichendorf, and Müller, accordingly, were matched by the superlative music of Schubert, Mendelssohn, Schumann, Brahms, Wolf, Mahler, and others. One need only listen to *lieder* cycles such as Schumann's *Dichterliebe* on poems of Heine to witness the very pinnacle of excellence in word-with-tone.

Nocturnes, intermezzi, ballads, novelettes, album leaves, etc., because of the possibility they held for intimate mood and atmosphere, were popular throughout the century. These occasionally appear alone but are more often grouped into suites like Schumann's *Carnaval*, Opus 9, or *Papillons,* Opus 2, for piano.

Of particular note among the larger forms was the tone poem, or symphonic poem. In these the composer attempted to depict poetic scenes or pictures with tone only. Typical of these are: *Battle of the Huns*, *Mazeppa*, and *Les Préludes*, by Liszt; *Manfred* and *Francesca da Rimini*, by Tchaikovsky; and *Don Juan*, by Richard Strauss.

The composers

WEBER AND SCHUBERT

Two important composers living and writing during Beethoven's lifetime were Carl Maria Weber (1786 – 1826) and Franz Schubert (1797 – 1828). Both can be thought of as pre-Romantics.

Weber and Schubert were composing music at a time when Classicism was still quite strong. Weber, writing as critic as late as 1809, severely castigated Beethoven's Third and Fourth Symphonies. Weber's ideal was still Mozart. Though Weber was a prolific composer of sonatas, concertos, occasional pieces, and the fine *Komzertstück* for the piano, his major contribution was in opera. He is considered to be the founder of German romantic opera. *Der Freischütz, Euryanthe,* and *Oberon,* through their beauty of characterization, great dramatic power, and superb orchestration, laid the foundation for Wagner and other operatic composers.

Franz Schubert is called by Alfred Einstein the "Romantic-Classicist." Listening to his Fifth Symphony, we feel that the music indeed is as lucid, and as symmetrical as that of Haydn or Mozart. In the short 31 years of his life Schubert wrote an astonishing number of compositions, including nearly 600 songs. The songs, as well as the chamber works, piano pieces, and larger works, all show one supreme quality — spontaneous lyricism.

Most of Schubert's works are saturated with memorable melody. It is as if the music's center of gravity were in the melody itself, with other musical elements — rhythm, harmony, and form — revolving around and existing for it. It was Felix Mendelssohn who invented the title "song without words" for some of his smaller piano pieces, but the term can apply to many of Schubert's instrumental compositions. With Schubert, the concept of song was never distant. Several of his instrumental works were based on his own *lieder:* the "Trout" Quintet; the quartet, *Death of a Maiden,* the *Wanderer Fantasy* for piano.

But though lyricism is the major characteristic in his music, Schubert cannot simply be considered a purveyor of astonishingly good tunes. Some of his works possess such dramatic force and piercing intensity of feeling that they truly would do justice to Beethoven. For example, the song, "Der Doppelgänger" ("The Double"), establishes an eerie mood: one that is so psychologically true that it is almost frightening.

MENDELSSOHN

Felix Mendelssohn (1809 – 1847) is a fascinating figure of early Romanticism, both for his music and for the influence of his personality. His life was completely opposite to the romantic image of the harried, starving composer in a garret, scratching out noble compositions with numb fingers by a flickering penny-candle. His family was as cultured and honored as it was affluent. The grandfather, Moses Mendelssohn, a German-Jewish philosopher, was called "the German Socrates." His father Abraham was a wealthy banker. From his mother he took his first music lessons and imbibed his early love of music.

His natural gifts were immense. Along with a fine appearance and evenness of temper was a natural aptitude for nearly everything he took interest in. He spoke several languages and was a brilliant conversationalist. His wit was remarkable. He was a classical scholar, could draw very well, and was attracted to chess. Swimming, riding, and dancing came naturally.

His influence in the world around him and after him was great. He revived and performed the works of J. S. Bach, including the *St. Matthew Passion*, which had lain fallow for many years. He helped to found the *Bach Gesellschaft*, a society for the publication of the entire works in authentic editions. Mendelssohn's gifts matched his material fortune and superior environment. But all of this was surpassed by his applica tion, good will, and modesty.

What, then, about his creative work: the concertos, sonatas, oratorios, and symphonies? As can be expected, the music is refined and polished. Orchestration is superb, with a transparency of texture reminiscent of Mozart's. The sunny, bright pieces, such as the Italian Symphony and the last movement of the Violin Concerto, or the G minor Piano Concerto, have rarely been surpassed for sparkle and luminosity.

Mendelssohn was always careful when it came to writing parts for others to play or sing. Ferdinand David was consulted about the Violin Concerto to ensure that the writing for violin was idiomatic and playable.

"Everything in good measure, nothing in excess," well describes Mendelssohn's music. Everything is clear, rational, and well mannered.

Mendelssohn's music makes good listening. The sounds are always pleasant. But one is seldom if ever shaken and stirred, as by Bach or Beethoven. Perhaps with Mendelssohn music came so easily that it could not become sublime. Perhaps Mendelssohn revered the great masters too much:

> Don't you agree with me, that the first condition for an artist is, that he have respect for the great ones, and do not try to blow out the great flames, in order that the petty tallow candle may shine a little brighter?*

CHOPIN

Frederic Chopin (1810–1844) did not possess the breadth of culture and universal interest of Mendelssohn. He wrote almost exclusively for the piano, on which he excelled. His father was a French tutor who had settled in Poland and married a Polish girl. Frederick Chopin himself was educated in Poland, but spent his mature life in Paris and other important cultural centers.

His music as a whole is a compelling composite of Slavic passion and French sophistication. Pieces such as the 'Minute" Waltz or the "Black Key" Etude show the utmost in refined grace and gentility. They

*Thomas Paine and Klauser, eds., *Famous Composers and Their Works*, Vol II (Boston: J. B. Millet Co., 1891), p. 422.

are salon pieces pure and simple, glib but impeccably crafted, and very sensitive.

Chopin contributed enormously to the development of piano idioms and of piano technique. In fact, the new role that he found for the piano set a precedent that was to remain until Debussy completely refashioned piano technique in the early twentieth century.

The 24 etudes of Chopin are amazing in that they provide the utmost challenges technically for the pianist: they are in fact a complete school of pianism. But while they serve as admirable instructional material, the music always transcends any utilitarian value it has.

SCHUMANN

Robert Schumann (1810–1856) was extremely emotional and passionate, and his music, like Chopin's, is always pervaded by his personality. The Appolonian reserve of Mendelssohn is seldom apparent with Schumann. The prevailing characteristics of his music are intense subjectivity and great diversity of mood. His harmonic vocabulary is much more original and daring than Mendelssohn's. The best work is in the smaller pieces, the short character pieces such as those in the *Carnaval*, Opus. 9, the *Kinderscenen*, Opus 15, for piano, or the individual *lieder* of the cycles, *Liederkreis*, and *Dichterliebe*. It was in these shorter pieces that the sudden flooding inspiration that seized Schumann could best be captured. The large musical canvasses, such as the four symphonies, the concertos, and the choral works, suffer somewhat from a certain lack of proportion and sustained intellectual interest. Unlike Mendelssohn, who was at his best in marshalling the components of large works into cohesive, balanced structures, Schumann frequently foundered in large works. Success in large works, where what is done to an idea is more important than the idea itself, requires detachment. This Schumann lacked. For him the ecstasy of the creative moment was supreme.

BERLIOZ

The comment about Delacroix, that he was "passionately in love with passion" applies as well to Hecter Berlioz (1803–1869). He was a man who could burst into tears at the beauty of a page of his own music, just finished. Here was a man who felt, felt, and felt some more, always with an ardor and vehemence that was controlled only by his superior intellectual gifts.

No effect was too sensational, no combination of instruments too unusual, if it served to express the volcanic musical ideas that were his.

For his Requiem he required not only a large symphony orchestra, and a full chorus with soloists, but four extra brass bands placed at the four points of the compass. Obvious in any of his music is the predominance of passion and color.

Berlioz was one of the few romantic composers who was not a virtuoso on any instrument. But he, like Mendelssohn before and Wagner after him, was one of the century's great conductors.

OTHER COMPOSERS

". . . William Tell is the work of an enormous talent, so much like genius that it might easily be mistaken for it." Thus did Berlioz, the critic, impale Giacomo Rossini (1792–1868) with his pen. We have already mentioned this enormously successful composer. His many operas are utterly winning, and the best of his comic operas, such as *The Barber of Seville* and *Cinderella*, have all the effervescence of champagne.

The fine *bel canto* operas of Vincenzo Bellini (1801–1835), including the perennial favorite, *Norma*, are distinguished for purity of melodic line and considerable power of characterization.

Gaetano Donizetti's (1797–1848) operas are similar to Bellini's. *Lucia di Lammermoor* is still very popular. The comic opera *Don Pasquale* is all froth, and compares very favorably with Rossini's work in a similar vein.

Before moving on to later developments in romantic music we will mention two other Italians and one Russian composer of considerable influence. Nicolo Paganini (1782–1849) was a concert violinist and competent composer of dazzling concertos for the violin. The high standards that he achieved as a player profoundly affected many Romantics, including Schumann, who, on hearing one of his concerts, resolved to become a virtuoso on the piano.

Luigi Cherubini (1760–1842) worked mostly in Paris, where he was much admired. Beethoven considered him the finest writer for the stage then living. Because his long life straddled rather neatly most of the classical period and nearly half of the romantic century, his music is particularly instructive. Basically, it is classical, with structure and balance primary. But there is also dramatic power and rich harmonic and orchestral color. Among his best works are the Requiem in C Minor, and the opera, *Medea*.

Mikhail Glinka (1804–1857) was the founder of the Russian Nationalist school that was to inspire the "Five." His opera, *A Life for the Tsar*, is beautifully written, containing many stunning choruses.

"He was as brilliant a virtuoso on the piano as was Paganini on the violin, and was as popular as Rossini" (p. 423).

The late romantics

LISZT

Franz Liszt (1811–1886) is a composer of great importance. He was present and active at the beginnings of Romanticism. At one of his concerts, when he was only 12 years old, he was kissed on the forehead by Beethoven. His first published piece was the "24th variation" from the collection of variations by eminent composers on a theme by Diabelli. This was the same theme that occasioned the masterly effort by Beethoven, *Variations on a Theme by Diabelli*, Opus 120. Liszt was also square in the middle of the exciting happenings in the time of Wagner, Brahms, and Tchaikovsky.

He was as brillant a virtuoso on the piano as Paganini was on the violin, and as popular as Rossini. His works number into the seven hundreds and are quite uneven in quality. Pieces of matchless beauty such as the "Faust" Symphony and the B minor Piano Sonata are joined by dozens of glittering, depthless potpourris and transcriptions.

Liszt's music had great significance for his day and for later developments. For one thing, his grasp of harmony and form was impressive. With him we find the same richness of modulation and chordal sound as in Wagner. But this is balanced by compression and unity. His large instrumental works often combined all movements into one, as in the Piano Concerto No. 1. Thematic transformation was tremendously effective in his hands. The tone poem was developed to perfection by Liszt. Pieces such as *Les Préludes* are highly original and point to Richard Strauss.

Also of importance was his work in national idioms such as the Hungarian Rhapsodies and the various pieces with Spanish, Italian, Polish, and Russian flavors. There are curious piano transcriptions of "God Save the Queen" and "La Marseillaise."

In addition to Liszt, there are four other masters of first importance in late Romanticism. They are Richard Wagner (1813–1883), Peter Tchaikovsky (1840–1893), Johannes Brahms (1833–1893), and Giuseppe Verdi (1813–1901).

In discussing the essence of late Romanticism, it is customary to contrast the work of Wagner and Brahms. And it is true that each represented an opposite point of view, the conservative Brahms espousing "Classicism," while Wagner championed the "music of the future." An imaginative juxtaposition of their lives and work is fruitful.

But even more fruitful is to compare Wagner and Verdi as composers of opera and Brahms and Tchaikovsky as symphonists.

*"But even more fruitful is to compare
Wagner and Verdi as composers of opera,
and Brahms and Tchaikovsky as symphonists" (p. 423).*

WAGNER AND VERDI

Wagner was a product of the great German operatic tradition by way of Gluck, Beethoven, and Weber. The Italian Verdi followed in the footsteps of Rossini, Bellini, and Donizetti. Both summed up and brought to maturity the respective operatic traditions of their land. Each was an innovator, Wagner especially scattering significant clues to be followed by Richard Strauss, Mahler, Bruckner, Franck, and the young Schoenberg.

Wagner's career was checkered by fantastic turbulence. He considered that it was the greatest of privileges for anybody to know him —and to aid him. He ran up huge debts, seldom if ever paying them back. He was eternally out of funds. He seduced many women, including Cosima, the wife of one of his strongest supporters, Hans Von Bülow. Cosima, whom he eventually married, revered him despite his constant unfaithfulness. He was exiled from Germany because of his overt anti-monarchist revolutionary actions. These included an essay, "The Revolution," an intimate acquaintance with the Russian nihilist revolutionary, Bakunin, and a public declaration asking the king to ". . . declare Saxony to be a free state." His personal and business relationships, in short, were odious, and he got himself constantly caught up in unpopular schemes and ventures. But despite this, such was the power of his personality and genius that many of his intimates stood behind him through every outrage. Ludwig II, king of Bavaria, subsidized him and especially helped in the great venture of the opera house at Bayreuth, all with full knowledge of Wagner's deficiencies. Cosima was so under his spell that she would not leave his body for 24 hours after his death.

Besides the magnetic appeal of this narcissist, and besides the immense power of his musical ideas, his idealism must have attracted many to him. His constant championing of better performance standards, especially in singing, his drive for the new opera house, his work with orchestras, and his constant aim to "reform" opera must have appealed greatly. For one performance of *Tannhäuser* he insisted on 164 rehearsals. Such was his perfection and idealism in performance.

Verdi's personal life contrasts vividly with Wagner's. Financial success came rather early, as did fame. There was not constant imbroglio, though his republican sympathies in Italy led him also to political action. After his first wife died, he found a lifemate in his beloved Giuseppina, whom he eventually married. She was a strong force in his life, contributing to the ever deepening current of his creative life. His whole life, though occasionally steeped in shadow, as when his first wife and two children died, was one of steady artistic growth.

What, then, about the music of these two giants, so dissimilar in personality but comparable in genius? Wagner's music clearly follows in the German tradition. The great German masters of the baroque, classical, and early romantic eras had always leaned towards "idea" music, to what could be done with a theme or a motive. With them, what happened to a melodic idea was more important than its own immediate appeal or innate beauty. In the operas of Wagner we see short, trenchant themes — *leitmotifs* — "treated" in the same way that they are in Beethoven symphonies. Tunefulness, of itself, is not the point. Harmony, both in beauty of individual chordal sounds and in scheme of modulation, is emphasized. The harmonic setting of the *leitmotif* is of paramount importance for the development of the character of the idea. The orchestra becomes symphonic, and is often entrusted with melodic elements as important as those heard in the voices. So vital and important is the orchestral part in some of Wagner's works that in concert it is sometimes played by itself, with the voice part left entirely out, as in the "Liebestod" from *Tristan and Isolde*.

The later operas become more and more homogeneous and organic. Continuous melody supersedes the old division of recitative and aria. The music never seems to end. Cadences do not lead to terminating tonics, but the music slips on and on. In this continuous, organic aspect of the operas after 1850, such as *Tristan*, the *Ring* Cycle, and *Parsifal*, we are reminded of the "unifying" theories of Darwin and Wallace, who in the 1850's were saying that all life is biologically related and stems from common origins. Jacques Barzun in his book, *Darwin, Marx, Wagner*, says:

> . . . Wagner's pretensions as a dramatist, his friendships with Nietzsche and Gobineau, place him at the heart of the biological and sociological theorizing which sprang from the idea of Evolution.*

In short, Wagner's music is as passionate as it is intellectual, reflecting perfectly Wagner the thinker and Wagner the poet.

Verdi was also a thinker. He also achieved magnificent drama through the force and sweep of his music. The power and dramatic unity of *Rigoletto*, *La Traviata*, *Aida*, and especially *Otello* certainly equal those of Wagner's operas, but are arrived at from another direction, that of lyric melody. Whereas Wagner completely transformed opera into music drama, Verdi still worked within the concept of the number opera and gave it new substance and meaning. It is Wagner's music,

*Reprinted from *Darwin, Marx, Wagner* by Jacques Barzun (1941) with permission of Atlantic-Little, Brown and Company.

not Verdi's, that was called the music of the future, "Zukunfts-musik."

Italian opera as Verdi found it consisted of a string of lyric numbers —arias, duets, and ensembles—connected by musically static recitatives. Emphasis was on tunefulness, and display of the bel canto voice. In the hands of masters like Rossini and Bellini, number opera was compelling despite the music's center of gravity unmistakably placed squarely in the vocal line. In the hands of lesser composers, number opera degenerated into showpieces for prominent singers of the time, full of high notes, fury, and spectacle, but signifying little. Verdi took the form as it was, and gradually enriched and ennobled it. His method was simple. Beautiful melody, display of voice, scintillating ensembles, spectacle —all were abundantly present—but the composer never used them at the expense of dramatic truth.

Verdi never abandoned his emphasis on melody, but the later operas, such as *Aida*, *Otello*, and *Falstaff* display a fuller use of the orchestra and an increase in dramatic power.

TCHAIKOVSKY AND BRAHMS

A comparison of the work of Brahms and Tchaikovsky is particularly rewarding, especially in the field of symphony. Both wrote only a few symphonies: Brahms, four (plus two "practice" symphonies, the Serenades); Tchaikovsky, six. (The Tchaikovsky Seventh is only a reconstruction from very incomplete sketches and should not be used for comparison.) Both lavished their most penetrating musical thoughts on these works. Both followed standard formal procedure, with very little exception. The orchestra used is very similar, though Tchaikovsky's is more colorful and sometimes larger.

The cello and the french horn figure prominently in the symphonies of both the German and the Russian. Both were strongly influenced by classical period composers. Beethoven cast his shadow on both, of course. But with Tchaikovsky, Mozart was of equal influence. A performance of Mozart's opera *Don Giovanni*, heard by the Russian when he was a young man, profoundly influenced him.

> . . . my worship for Mozart is quite contrary to my musical nature. But perhaps it is just because . . . I feel broken and spiritually out of joint, that I find consolation and rest in Mozart's music, wherein he gives expression to that joy of life which was part of his sane and wholesome temperament . . .*

*Catherine Drinker Bowen and Barbara Von Meck *Beloved Friend* (Boston, Toronto: Little, Brown and Co., 1937), p. 233.

Italian music moved him strongly, too. "There are melodies of Bellini which I can never hear without the tears rushing to my eyes."

Beyond a magnetic attraction to the music of Beethoven, Brahms was also influenced by the Great Cantor, J. S. Bach. The many glorious contrapuntal portions in most of the major works attest to this. One need only listen to the finale of the Fourth Symphony, the last portions of both sets of variations on themes of Handel and Haydn, and magnificent fugues in the *German Requiem* to see this at once.

The importance of the influence of early masters becomes clear when we see that both symphonists were concerned with preserving the essence and spirit of absolutism in their symphonies. Tchaikovsky did inject an element of Russian nationalism in his symphonies, and there is a suggested, but very tenuous program in No. 4. But all 10 symphonies — Russian and German — use strong classical forms. Occasionally, cyclic technique was used (Tchaikovsky, Nos. 4 and 5; Brahms, No. 3), but this was not entirely original; Beethoven had experimented with cyclic form in Nos. 5 and 9.

The basic problem that both masters faced was in keeping to the classical principles of form while taking advantage of new developments in harmony, instrumentation, rhythm, etc. Putting it in another way, they had to find new ways to breathe life into the old forms.

The Brahms symphonic style is really leagues away from that of Tchaikovsky, who preferred to dazzle his audience with an impressive array of instrumental color and orchestral gymnastics. Lyric melody, as such, often at the expense of other musical factors, is greatly emphasized. This last factor undoubtedly explains Tchaikovsky's great popularity with concert audiences and the ease with which his music wins new friends among the uninitiated. As mentioned above, Tchaikovsky took full advantage of the rising tide of Russian nationalism that occurred in the latter half of the nineteenth century and wrote into his symphonies either real folk songs and dances or simulated ones.

Brahms occasionally dazzles, but only incidentally. Whereas Tchaikovsky arouses emotions rather easily through the means mentioned above, Brahms seems to invite thought first, which then leads to emotional response. He therefore concerns himself very little with sheer sound for its own sake or with striking instrumental combinations. What he is interested in is musical idea, beauty of form, evolution of idea, depth and richness of textures. On first hearing a Brahms symphony, the neophyte often is puzzled; there is so much to hear all at once that he tends to hear little. Overall pattern is so masterfully woven on such a titanic scale that the beginning listener is lost. Brahms is the greatest master of musical understatement; Tchaikovsky appeals directly to the listener with either high rhetorical flourish or hyper-sensitive lyricism.

Brahms' music makes friends slowly but surely. His style is oblique, reserved, and thoughtful. The style of Brahms is like the discourse of a great philosopher-orator who rises to the heights of passion through the accumulating force of his ideas and the fervor of his idealism. Tchaikovksy's music wins rapport immediately. His symphonic style is brilliant, hotly emotional, passionate in the immediate sense. The sounds pour out of a Tchaikovsky symphony like lava spurting from a crater.

14

In transition: post-romantics, impressionists, pre-moderns

THE MUSIC PRODUCED in the waning years of the nineteenth century until the close of World War I is marked by diversity and flux. These few years linked two periods strongly contrasted in essence and manner—the Romantic and the Contemporary. In this time can be seen the dying yet still glowing embers of true Romanticism itself. Post-Romantics such as Mahler, Richard Strauss, the young Schoenberg, Sibelius, and Rachmaninoff gazed fondly back to an ebbing age and refused to let it die. Much of their music is possessed with a ripeness very near decay.

During these years Impressionism arrived on the musical scene. Its prime mover was a genuine master, Claude Debussy. But Impressionism as a movement was short lived. Its concern with and constant search for fresh sound was soon trampled under by the strident, urgent sounds of contemporary music.

All the while that the fruit of Romanticism was rotting on the bough and Impressionism was briefly flowering, contemporary music had actually germinated and new musical growth could plainly be seen.

Post-romanticism

Four post-romantic composers must be discussed when considering the transitional period from romantic music proper to contemporary music. They are Giacomo Puccini (1858–1924), Richard Strauss (1864–1949), Gustav Mahler (1860–1911), and Jan Sibelius (1865–1957). Each wrote important works in the late nineteenth century, yet lived well into the twentieth century. And though certain aspects in their music are contemporary, for example, the realism in the operas of Puccini and Strauss, their basic outlook is that of the nineteenth century. We find again the emphasis on beauty of melody and sound. We find also the grand, sometimes bombastic, gesture. We find the same concern for the subjective, personal, passionate, and intimate. Strauss and Puccini achieved notable success with opera; Mahler and Sibelius concerned themselves chiefly with symphony.

RICHARD STRAUSS

It was perfectly natural that Richard Strauss, the son of a leading horn player in the Munich opera, should have taken to opera. His father had known and worked with Wagner. It was inevitable that the creator of *Tristan and Isolde* and *Die Meistersinger* would cast his shadow over the young man. At any rate, his three best known operas, *Salome*, *Elektra*, and *Der Rosenkavalier* carry on the Wagnerian tradition through the dramatic use of voices, the large symphonic orchestra, and the use of the continuous style of melody.

An added element in these works, not usually found in Wagner, is the hyper-realism of the score. *Salome*, for example, originally a play by Oscar Wilde, is set with every detail of its gory plot minutely described by the music. When Salome offers the "Dance of the Seven Veils" for Herod, the music, while building in orgiastic frenzy, gives us a clue to what she is thinking. A theme associated with John the Baptist suddenly is heard. After the dance she asks for the head of John the Baptist on a silver platter. The orchestra suddenly shimmers and shines with a macabre silvery sheen.

Besides opera Strauss also wrote stunning, extravagantly detailed tone poems. *Till Eulenspiegel* is a humorous musical tale based on an early German fable. *Don Juan* and *Don Quixote*, though less uproarious, are similar in concept, while *Death and Transfiguration* and *Also Sprach Zarathustra* are deeply philosophical.

PUCCINI

While Strauss followed in the steps of Wagner, Puccini carried on in the tradition of Verdi. Unlike Wagner, who stressed the role of the orchestra in his operas, Verdi took the typically Italian view that voice and melody are primary. All of Verdi, then, is a glorious manifestation of how well the human voice can sound and how beautiful melody can be. Puccini, like his great predecessor, revered melody and the voice. His highly effective operas, including *La Bohème, Tosca,* and *Madama Butterfly,* are redolent with the melodic fragrance that has always permeated musical Italy. As in Strauss, there is great realism, a tremendous feeling for effective dramatic theater.

The Puccini orchestra is always colorful, full, luxuriant; though never impinging on the primacy of the voice parts. Puccini's harmony is highly refined, often suggesting French coloring and sensitivity.

MAHLER

In the nine titanic symphonies of Mahler can be seen the last fruit of the German symphonic tradition. This tradition began in the later 1700's and displayed such supreme masters of the form as Haydn, Mozart, Beethoven, Schubert, Mendelssohn, Schumann, Bruckner, and Brahms. Throughout this long development the symphony can be seen as a blending of profound musical thought with the utmost in refined expression.

A deep, soul-searing musical sentiment organized through grand, cohesive structural design permeates the Mahler symphony. The tonal canvas is almost always massive. Not only are these works very long, but the forces used are sometimes enormous. For example, the Symphony No. 8, the "Symphony of a Thousand," employed at its first performance a chorus of 850 voices, 8 soloists, and an orchestra of 146.

SIBELIUS

Jean Sibelius, another post-Romantic whose major contribution has been in the symphony, is quite different. Whereas Mahler is ultra-passionate, super-emotional, Sibelius is spare, incisive, granitic, frequently sober. His orchestra is not the juggernaut used by Mahler but one rather close to the modest one used by Brahms.

The prevailing spirit comes about through a blend of Finnish nationalism with powerful classical structures, the whole tempered by a Romantic sensitivity to sound and texture. Though Sibelius denied using actual folk songs in his symphonies, melodies such as the one in Example 399 strongly suggest the hardiness and sturdiness of north European folk song and dance.

OTHER POST-ROMANTICS

Of perhaps less stature, but of nevertheless considerable value are the works of several other post-Romantics: Elgar (1857–1934) in Vic-

Example 399   Symphony No. 2, Movement 1, Sibelius

torian England; Faure, d'Indy and Saint-Saens in France; Wolf in Germany; MacDowell in America; and Rachmaninoff in Russia and in the United States. Sir Edward Elgar, in the "Enigma" Variations and the fine oratorio, *The Dream of Gerontius,* is usually content to repeat harmonic and melodic formulas from the early eighteen-hundreds, though these are invested with great refinement and a certain elegant dignity.

The music of Fauré (1845–1924) and d'Indy (1851–1931) clearly points to Impressionism. It has little of the robust quality found in German and Italian Romanticism, but displays very subtle harmonic shading and effective orchestration. The Suite, *Pelléas et Mélisande,* by Fauré is well known.

Saint-Saëns (1835–1931) wrote polished, elegant works, often in classical forms. The five piano concertos reflect his own immense virtuosity at the keyboard. In this respect he resembles Liszt, whom he knew and admired. His four symphonic poems, including the well known *Danse Macabre* also point to Liszt. Among his best work is the massive "Organ Symphony," Opus 78, and the slight but charming "Carnival of the Animals: Zoological Fantasy."

Hugo Wolf (1860–1903) is best known for his *lieder*, many of which are equal in quality to the songs of Schubert, Schumann, and Brahms. Throughout the evolution of the nineteenth century *lied*, the piano part became more and more important. With Schumann and Brahms it frequently carries as much melodic interest as the voice part, in addition to setting the mood and atmosphere in general. With the *lieder* of Wolf, such as those in the *Goethe Lieder* and the *Michelangelo Lieder*, the piano part is not only equivalent to the voice but sometimes predominates.

The American composer Edward MacDowell (1861–1908) at one time was considered by many in the United States as a kind of musical Messiah, one who would kindle the flame of adventure and originality in young American composers while showing the way to a true school of American music. However, the effect of his music on our time has not been deep or lasting. Gilbert Chase, in *America's Music,* says:

> . . . MacDowell was not a great composer. At his best he
> was a gifted miniaturist with an individual manner. Cre-

atively, he looked toward the past, not toward the future.*

Serge Rachmaninoff's (1873 – 1943) work has had enormous success ever since the writing of his Second Piano Concerto in 1901. The public has always responded strongly to this composer's way with melody and to the smouldering, cresting passion of the music. Rachmaninoff was one of the world's great pianists, and his playing of his own compositions on the stages of many continents contributed to the enormous popularity of his music. Looked at objectively, the music is very solid: obvious Russian nationalistic elements are subtly blended with formal and melodic characteristics seen previously in Chopin, Schumann, and Liszt. The harmony is especially luxuriant and there is no little polyphonic ingenuity, especially in certain of the piano preludes.

Other important post-Romantics include Mascagni, Dukas, Glazounov, Pfitzner, Glière, Dohnanyi, and Reger.

In our discussion of the post-Romantics we have emphasized their *fin de siècle* orientation: each extended, stretched out, and ended an era that had run its course.

Because most of these masters lived well into the twentieth century, they must be considered as transitional. Though their musical aesthetics were derived from a past century, they continued to write and were themselves physically active and influential while newer musical styles were developing.

They affected a necessary overlap, stabilizing in effect, while newer musical attitudes were in the shaping.

Impressionism

Impressionism owed much to the romantic century. For one, it is in direct descent from nineteenth-century program music. But it emphasizes imagery of nature rather than the tonal representation of plot, drama, or personal characterization as in the typically romantic *Ein Heldenleben* by Richard Strauss, or *The Huns* by Liszt.

Second, Impressionism is firmly based on tonality, in spite of the new use of principles of key, relationships of consonance-dissonance, and modulation.

In a similar way, representation is present in the impressionistic painters Manet, Monet, and Renoir as it was in the romantic school of

*Gilbert Chase, *America's Music* (New York: McGraw-Hill Book Company, Inc., 1955), p. 364.

painters. We can plainly recognize the subject—a pretty girl, a field of flowers, a cathedral—in its everyday context with the Impressionists as we do with romantic painters, but there is no doubt that their treatment of the subject differs. So tonality, like representation in painting, is always present but subtly transformed. While Impressionism is clearly rooted in Romanticism, it also points to contemporary music. Its primary concern and search for unique, original sound as such is quite modern. Debussy always looked for *le ton juste*, the precise sound, that would make an original effect. This foreshadows the experimental approach of contemporary composers.

In their search for a fresh, unique sound, the Impressionists developed new instrumental techniques. Their orchestra became a highly flexible instrument, pregnant with coloristic potential. It still is the basis for much orchestral writing today. With Debussy and Ravel piano technique was so developed and transformed that very little has been added to it since.

Also strongly suggestive of contemporary music is the objective semi-detachment of Impressionism. In its shift away from the Romantic's tonal depiction of states of subjectivity, in its moving away from psychically generated emotion, it concerned itself almost exclusively with the world outside of man, the world of nature—of things. This very de-emphasis of the emotional, personal, subjective contributed greatly to the geometrical, cerebral element in contemporary music.

A particularly curious facet of Impressionism is its brief span: from about 1892 to perhaps 1918, a little over 25 years. After that there were no significant Impressionists, though impressionist techniques were often used in combination with others. This, of course, points to its transitory role: it unquestionably bridged the gap from the idealistic, subjective, powerfully humanistic music of Romanticism to the detached, "cooler," experimental realism of our time.

If, then, Impressionism contained within itself the seed and promise of the music of our day while resting solidly on the musical ground gained in the century before, the question may be asked: what gives it its unique character? Despite its dealing with objects and things in nature—rain drenched gardens, exotic temples in the light of the moon, footsteps in the snow, the sea in its myriad moods, girls with hair like silk, rag dolls, toy elephants, regal peacocks— it decidedly does not attempt to represent these objects directly in any way. Rather, the impressionist composer simply presents to us in musical terms sensations, moods, and emotional reactions that external·objects in nature have evoked from him. "Nuages," for example, is the musical response in the heart and soul of Debussy to his impressions of the particular

phenomenon in nature called a cloud. A different impressionist composer would undoubtedly produce a cloud piece with a completely
different sound.

Descriptive titles, of course, do head most impressionistic music.
But enjoyment of the music is not at all dependent on a pre-knowledge
of the title. Debussy, who insisted that his music was solid enough to be
enjoyed without knowing what it was about, inserted titles only at the
end of each of his 24 Preludes for Piano, and discreetly in parentheses.

Impressionism, in a way, is also a very simple kind of music. In
technical structure it is ultra-sophisticated, but in effect and in what it
tries to do for the listener it is plain and simple. Debussy said, "Music
should seek humbly to please . . . extreme complication is contrary
to art." A piece such as Ravel's "Rhapsodie espagnole," or Delius' "On
Hearing the First Cuckoo in Spring," appeals directly to our senses. It
aims to please, to entertain. It does not preach or try to stir us up. Of
paramount concern is the immediate beauty and effect of the sound.
Thus does the Impressionist combine his instrumental colors, with a
view to the utmost voluptuous quality.

Harmony is the area where this sensuous quality becomes most
obvious. In fact it can be said that much of the interest in impressionistic music is generated through novel chords, and especially in the
novel juxtaposition of chords. Sam Hunter, in his book, *Modern French
Painting*, says of the work of the impressionistic painter Monet ". . . he
had discovered that the most intense optical sensations were obtained
when colors were mixed by the eye."* In similar fashion, the novel effect
produced in musical Impressionism comes about when the ear mixes
adjacent chordal colors that in past periods did not "go well" together
(Example 400).

Another characteristic of impressionistic music is its scant use of
brio sound. Rather than overwhelm with an avalanche of sound, the
Impressionist insinuates and suggests. Much of his music begins with a
whisper and ends with the tiniest tremor of sound.

Marked. biting accents are also scantily used, though they will occasionally come, as in the "Dialogue of the wind and sea" portion of
Debussy's *La Mer*, or in the "General Dance" in Ravel's *Daphnis and
Chloé* Suite No. 2. Because of the lack of both rhythmic bite and obvious
melody, the music seems to some at first like an amorphous mixture of
musical tremors, trills, and gurgles. With the master Impressionists,
however, repeated listening reveals magnificent design and direction.

---

*Sam Hunter, *Modern French Painting, Fifty Artists From Manet to Picasso* (New York:
Dell Publishing Co., Inc., 1956), p. 91.

Example 400   Preludes, Book I, No. 1, Debussy

DEBUSSY

Without question, the two composers most successful in Impressionism are Claude Debussy (1862–1918) and Maurice Ravel (1875–1937). Though Debussy is credited with the first truly impressionist work, *Prelude to the Afternoon of a Faun* (1894), it should be remembered that Ravel composed the piano version of the "Rhapsodie espagnole" only one year later. It is true, however, that Debussy from 1894 wrote almost exclusively in the impressionistic manner, while Ravel frequently concerned himself with other styles and compositional techniques. Of the two, Debussy is the typically impressionistic composer and Ravel, the occasional one.

Debussy was born early enough (1862) to have been strongly influenced by Romanticism, and wrote several early works in the late romantic idiom. Music such as the "Deux Arabesques" and the "Reverie" for piano are suave, elegant, melodious, sentimental almost to excess — clearly in the romantic tradition. "Clair de Lune," from the *Suite Bergamasque,* is typical.

The later works of Debussy are typified by such works as the *Nocturnes, La Mer,* and *Iberia* for orchestra; *Chansons de Bilitis* for voice and piano; the *Images* and *24 Préludes* for piano; and the opera *Pelléas et Mélisande.* They are completely original and magnificent in conception. Their subject matter is far-ranging, geographically and pictorially.

The tendency of Debussy to communicate his aesthetic responses to outside scenes of nature is remarkably similar to the "plein air" school of painting typified by Manet. Here the painter strapped his easel to his shoulder, went out into the fields and woods to work, and captured an immediate impression. But, in addition to Debussy's obvious power to evoke atmosphere and mood, the music is saturated with mellow melancholy. In the phrase of Andre Suarès, it is "la douleur qui parle" (sorrow speaking). The music frequently is as warm as it is sensuous and colorful.

RAVEL

Ravel also possessed a gift for musical imagery. But he did not use it as often as Debussy. Nor is his Impressionism as sweet and warm. Stravinsky called Ravel the "Swiss watchmaker." Indeed, his music is fastidiously put together, as neat and ordered as a French formal garden.

To know the essential difference between the two Impressionists one need only compare Ravel's "Pavane pour une infante défunte" (Example 401) with Debussy's "Sarabande" from *Pour le piano* (Ex-

Example 401   Pavane pour une infante défunte, Ravel

ample 402), both written in the late 1890's and both re-creations of early court dances. The Ravel is tender, yet somehow cool and reserved.

Example 402   Pour le piano, Sarabande, Debussy

Its harmonies are sometimes frosty. The Debussy, on the other hand, pulses every moment with a warm, romantic glow. It is more relaxed, freer, less formal.

On listening to the music of Ravel, the listener is much more conscious of structure and a clear beat. His tempos generally are firmer. Typical are the *Valses nobles et sentimentales, Daphnis and Chloé,* and "La Valse." The "Bolero," of course, is well known. *Le Tombeau de Couperin* includes three dances from the Baroque, a "forlane," a "menuet," and a "rigaudon."

The opera *L'Enfant et les sortilèges* is remarkable. The "Duet of the Cats," for example, and the "Insect Music" are fantastically realistic. There is a clear use of polytonality, near the beginning of the piece (Example 403).

Example 403   L'Enfant et les sortilèges, Ravel

Autorisation Durand & Cie, Editeurs-propriétaire Paris.

OTHER IMPRESSIONISTS

Among several others writing with impressionistic techniques is the Russian Alexander Scriabin (1872–1915), whose exotic, almost mystic music is a curious blend of late romantic expressivity and French color. Among his best work is the *Poem of Ecstasy* for orchestra and the sonatas for piano—especially the Sonata No. 5 in F-sharp major.

Works such as *Nights in the Garden of Spain* for piano and orchestra by Manuel de Falla (1876–1949) show an interesting blend of Impressionism with indigenous Spanish musical elements. Falla was acquainted with Debussy in Paris. In fact, it was a postcard sent from Spain by Falla to Debussy picturing a gate of the Alhambra that inspired the piano prelude, "La puerta del Vino," by the Frenchman.

Frederick Delius (1862 – 1934), wrote many compositions in the impressionistic style. They are lusciously vaporous, sometimes overripe; but pieces such as "Brigg Fair" and "Walk to the Paradise Garden" are nevertheless charming.

Charles Griffes (1884 – 1920) was an American Impressionist whose untimely death at the age of 36 cut off a very promising career. His "Poem for Flute and Orchestra" is quite effective.

The pre-moderns

Two important figures were anticipating contemporary musical idioms and attitudes by at least 20 years. They are the great French iconoclast, Erik Satie (1866 – 1925), and the American iconoclast, Charles Ives (1874 – 1954).

Satie was perhaps the first to revolt against romantic "expressivity" and bombast. His music is rather ascetic, often mordantly witty. The well known *Gymnopédies* are chaste, objective, and detached. Titles of many of his works are highly ironic, meant to arrest the attention and to pique the curiosity: for example, "Dessicated Embryos," and "Cold Pieces," both for piano. Satie's playing directions are outrageously humorous: "Play like a nightingale with a toothache," or, for the "Tango" in his *Sports and Diversions for Piano*, "Play in moderate tempo and very bored."

Satie's attitude affected Debussy, who himself had a rather caustic sense of humor. It also influenced later French composers such as Poulenc, Milhaud, and Auric. His non-sentimental approach is similar to that of Stravinsky, who in the twenties and thirties ruthlessly resisted all "expression" in music. "For I consider that music is, by its very nature, essentially powerless to express anything at all. . . . " These words by Stravinsky could well have been uttered by Satie, who resisted all expressionistic or impressionistic suggestions in his own music. *Socrate*, a symphonic drama based on Plato for soprano with chamber orchestra, is considered to be Satie's most important work. In its pale simplicity and homely, non-coloristic mien, it symbolizes the anti-romantic outlook of many twentieth-century composers.

In contrast to Satie, who was at the center of the fluid, exciting developments in Paris at the turn of the century, Charles Ives was a lonely, isolated figure whose originality has been recognized only recently. He was little touched by European artistic currents, but was saturated with folk, popular, and church music of his own land. The New England

Transcendentalists, especially Emerson, influenced him. These, added to a natural inclination for experiment in tone, strongly encouraged by his band master father, led to some incredibly prophetic work.

One of the masterpieces of Ives is the orchestral work, *Three Places in New England.* This is the work of an ecstatic visionary with musical roots deep in his land, who perhaps set the stage for many of the younger men of contemporary music.

Analysis and commentary: Debussy: "Fêtes"

"Fêtes" ("Holidays") is the second of three *Nocturnes* for orchestra written by Debussy in the late 1890's. The translation given here, "Holidays" rather than the usual "Festivals," is given because of Debussy's own description of the piece as given in *Achille-Claude Debussy* by Vallas.

Swirling, sweeping music illustrates that Debussy was not all vapour and mist. Indeed, some of his more rhythmic pieces are as springy as the luminous ballerinas in the paintings of Degas. Besides the rhythmic vitality and drive in "Fêtes," there is a stunning use of climax. The fantastic, almost orgiastic climax achieved by the fanfare-march in the middle section shows that Debussy sometimes loved the great splashes of sound as well as the delicate nuances.

The orchestra is large: 3 flutes, 2 oboes, english horn, 2 clarinets, 3 bassoons, 4 horns, 3 trumpets, 3 trombones, tuba, 2 harps, timpani, cymbals, snare drum, and strings.

The piece's form is very simple: Ternary, ABA. The first section, A, is characterized primarily by the swirling figure in Example 404, with a dancing background figure consisting of repeated notes (Example 405). The B section is procession-like in its steady, repeated accents with

Example 404   Fêtes, Debussy

Example 405

a fanfare theme first heard in the trumpets (Example 406). In its grad-

Example 406

ual, massive buildup to a soaring climax just before the return of the A section, the B section anticipates the "Bolero" by Ravel. A returns but considerably modified with occasional flashes of the fanfare theme from the previous section.

The piece begins with a brusque figure, in open intervals for the divided violins played *ff*. This serves to introduce a first theme (Example 404), played by the clarinets and english horn. All of this is *ff*. Suddenly the dynamic level drops to a hushed *pp* and the accompaniment figure now appears fleshed out in parallel ninth chords (Example 407). Above this, the first theme (Example 408) is handed down

Example 407

from treble to bass in crescendo leading to a brilliant, but brief heraldic statement in the brass, *ff* (Example 409). Note the 3rd measure in Example 410, which is now quite different from Example 404. This comes

Example 408

Example 409

Example 410

twice. Then, a rough figure in the horns backed by bassoons (Example 411) is answered by a blithe idea, *piano* and staccato, in the clarinets and

Example 411

english horn (Example 412). Both Examples 410 and 411 are heard

Example 412

again. Then the first truly lyric theme of the piece occurs, in the solo oboe (Example 413). Example 405 is always heard in a background that is electric, and rhythmically vital. Example 413 soon is heard again, but

Example 413

this time with flutes added, the whole higher in the soprano, and again crescendo. Ultimately, the oboe and flutes joined by the clarinet give out a new idea (Example 414), which is accompanied by the strings play-

Example 414

Example 415

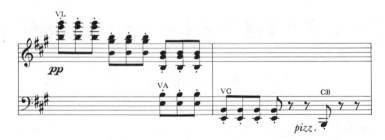

ing a figure derived from earlier materials. A portion of Example 413 re-enters in the clarinet and horns, surrounded by echoes of Example 405 fluttering about in the divided strings. For the remainder of the A section, Examples 413 and 414 alternate, the whole finally building to a crashing climax which, just before cresting (Example 416), drops

Example 416

suddenly to the hypnotic, eerie march rhythm, ultra-soft (Example 417).

Example 417

This signals the beginning of the B section. Above the shuffling march rhythm and above an *A*-flat in the bass that remains throughout the section, as if out of nowhere, three muted trumpets give out a fanfare theme, *pp* (Example 418). Later the woodwinds take up the fanfare. The

Example 418

horns sally forth with the basic motive of the fanfare rising (Example 419) to be answered by the winds falling (Example 420). When the

Example 419

Example 420

trumpets, buttressed by trombones, reiterate the complete fanfare theme (Example 418), the strings play a version of the first theme (Example 404). Thus the leading melodic idea from A joins with the theme of B to provide unity and homogeneity. The A section returns, with most of the melodic materials also returning but with many changes of orchestration.

Instead of the original heraldic statement of Example 409 followed closely by the harp glissandi, the composer writes a broad figure in the strings (Example 421), followed immediately by Example 422 in the

Example 421

Example 422

trumpets. The other themes—except for Example 414—come back in order and the music gradually becomes more and more quiet, terminating in the pianissimo tremors of the last measure. But before the music fades away, echoes of the fanfare theme of the B section (Example 423)

Example 423

and a strange, new melodic fragment (Example 424) glow quietly through the gathering stillness.

Example 424

15

The twentieth century

Any tone can succeed any other tone, any tone can
sound simultaneously with any other tone or tones, and
any group of tones can be followed by any other group
of tones, just as any degree of tension or nuance can
occur in any medium under any kind of stress or duration. Successful projection will depend upon the con-
textual and formal conditions that prevail, and upon the
skill and the soul of the composer*.

THE CONTEMPORARY COMPOSER has complete freedom of
choice. As a result of this freedom, however, he is much more
responsible for his choice. The independence of the individual in
his thought and in his action is predominant in the world today as
in no other time.

This has been reflected in the arts as well. Andy Warhol's
painting of a can of soup—whatever it is of itself—is a statement
against all preconceived ideas of what art should be. Experiments
in music that deny the use of regular vibrations of sound and
emphasize noise are statements against all former concepts of
music. The emphasis on the random expression, the interest in a

*Vincent Persichetti, *Twentieth Century Harmony* (New York: W. W. Norton and
Co., Inc., 1961, p. 13; and London: Faber and Faber Ltd) Copyright 1961 by Vincent Persichetti.

"happening," is exactly opposed to the conception that a work of art is a *selection* of materials in an ordered form. All of these experiments are a symbol of the search for new stimuli that is prevalent in our society today.

These rejections of previous concepts raise an important point that has been stated very clearly in the writings of Jean-Paul Sartre. Rejection of authority and tradition is not enough. Something must take their place. The establishment of meaning now rests with each individual.

"The existentialist . . . finds it extremely embarrassing that God does not exist, for there disappears with Him all possibility of finding values in an intelligible heaven."* Sartre also says ". . . the first effect of existentialism is that it puts every man in possession of himself as he is, and places the entire responsibility for his existence squarely upon his own shoulders."† And this is the dilemma of the twentieth-century composer. The entire responsibility for a new composition is his. And since every door is open to him, his decision is the more difficult.

There are no rules of composition, but there are principles of organization. Each composer must find these for himself. We have seen, in the evolution of music, in each period, constant searching and constant change. What was accepted at one time is no longer true in a later time. What was true in a later time became superseded itself by a new expression. Each age must find its own expression. This expression — when it is true — does not result from formulas that already exist, but from an inner need to express, and from a seeking of the way to make this expression meaningful.

Major influences

STRAVINSKY

The work of the twentieth century that had perhaps the most far-reaching, as well as the most immediate effect, was *Le Sacre du Printemps (The Rite of Spring)*. Igor Stravinsky, born in Russia in 1882, was brought up in musical surroundings, began piano lessons at the age of nine, and thereafter began to compose. He was self-taught with the exception of two years of study in orchestration with Rimsky-Korsakov.

Before *Le Sacre*, however, Stravinsky already had two large works

*Jean-Paul Sartre, *Existentialism and Humanism,* translation and introduction by Philip Mairet (London: Methuen & Co, Ltd., 1946, 1948, reprinted 1960), p. 33.
†*Ibid.,* p. 29.

to his credit, which had achieved success. He had already written *The Firebird*, and *Petrouchka* for Diaghilev's Ballets Russes in Paris. But where "*Petrouchka* had shaken the musical art of the period," according to Alexandre Tansman, "*The Rite of Spring* delivered a blow from which it was never again to recover. . . ." Stravinsky's concept of rhythm seemed to the audience barbaric and relentless, after the "lovelinesses" of most romantic and impressionistic music. Stravinsky's tonal concepts were basically those of the impressionist school. But whereas Debussy had been criticized for the vagueness in his melody, Stravinsky was attacked for its absence. It was even said by some musical reactionaries that Stravinsky was incapable of writing a melody. Where Debussy had alternated chord structures to blur the tonality, Stravinsky combined them. What the critics could not comprehend in the music of Stravinsky was only what they had not comprehended in the music of Debussy: originality. They constantly tried to assess the new by what they were familiar with in the old.

Stravinsky was to influence two generations of composers with his harmonic procedure and his exposure of the "raw nerve" of rhythm.

EXPRESSIONISM

Stravinsky was heir to the musical legacy of Debussy. Romanticism was dying, and the new Expressionism was beginning to manifest itself in the arts.

One definition of Expressionism* speaks of it as a "revolution from the 'superficial' . . . to a style directly expressive of the artist's soul in all its hidden depth and with as little interference as possible from formal and compositional elements." In further explanation, in one kind of Expressionism, "The artist paints the expressive character of the object. Instead of painting a tree, he paints its convulsiveness or its strength."

The term "Expressionism" did not come into use until 1911, but we see convulsiveness in the late paintings of Van Gogh, who was a forerunner of both the expressionist and Fauvist movements. In 1900 Sigmund Freud published *Interpretation of Dreams*, the first public statement of his theories. Met at first by incredulity and scorn, during the first decade of the twentieth century his doctrine gained wider and wider acceptance. The theories of Freud were not without their effect in contributing to the dominant thought of the time. The exploration of the subconscious helped to lay bare man's inner nature. The probing into the innermost thoughts was equated with a removal of the mask desired

*Runes and Schrickel (eds), *Encyclopedia of the Arts* (New York: Philosophical Library, 1946), p. 340.

by the Expressionists. It may not be too far-fetched to say that the original shock that met the exposures of the inner self in Freud's writings was not too different from the shock that the audience felt at the first performance of *Le Sacre*. At any rate, something aroused them to the point of hissing and booing.

SCHOENBERG

Arnold Schoenberg, even more than Stravinsky, shows the influence of the expressionist movement. An early work, *Pierrot Lunaire*, reflects this in its choice of subject and the treatment of that subject. Although· the impact of his music was less immediate than that of Stravinsky's, his ultimate rejection of the old was even more complete than that of Stravinsky. His search for a new means of expression finally turned him completely away from tonality.

Schoenberg (1874–1951) was born in Vienna. In addition to his studies, which included violin, cello, and counterpoint, he gained some practical experience in orchestration through the commercial avenue of arranging music for popular consumption.

In view of his later rejection of nineteenth-century Romanticism and its tonal system, it is somewhat ironic that his first successful work, written in 1899, is probably one of his best known, and certainly the most played of his entire output. This is *Verklärte Nacht (Transfigured Night)*, written originally as a string sextet. Its later arrangement for string orchestra is the version that is usually heard, and it is this arrangement also that provided the music for the ballet, *The Pillar of Fire*. The work is in the full romantic tradition.

Soon after this he abandoned the romantic concept and began experimenting with new ways of constructing chords and using dissonance. He further searched for new methods of organization of materials. As a modernist he attracted many students and young composers, among them Berg and Webern, who were to follow him into *serial* writing. His *Pierrot Lunaire* came out in 1912, a year before Stravinsky's *Sacre*. In this he introduced "*Sprechstimme*," which is a kind of half-singing, half-speech.

In 1933, as a result of the rise of Nazism, he left Germany, going to Paris and then to the United States, where he ultimately became a citizen and remained until his death in 1951.

His constant search for new methods of expression gradually turned him away from all previous methods of composition, and in 1924 he initiated the serial technique of composing with 12 tones. In this system the tones represented by the 7 white notes and the 5 black notes of the piano keyboard are completely equal. The idea of diatonic scales with "coloring" chromatic tones, the concept of tonal center and keys, the idea of tendencies of tones inherent in all preceding scale patterns, and the idea of tonality affirmed by the root progressions of chords are all abandoned. The basic concept of twelve-tone writing is the establishment of a "row." This row is the placement of all of the 12 different tones in an order that uses each and all of them in series as set up by the composer. Both the melody and the chords arise out of the order of the tones. When the tones are used melodically, the approach is in a way similar to the statement of a subject in contrapuntal writing, and thus it is natural to the system to use the devices of counterpoint: imitation, transposition, retrograde motion, inversion, and so on. When the row is used chordally, dissonance and spacing are completely at the discretion of the composer. Writing in the system of 12 tones does not *necessarily* abrogate the use of tonality, but Schoenberg's use of it was a rejection of tonality in the traditional sense. Although Schoenberg disliked the use of the term *atonal*, it has been consistently applied to his twelve-tone method of composition.

The possibilities inherent in serial writing attracted wide attention and influenced composers throughout most of the Western world. The system of writing with 12 tones can be at once the most abstract and yet the most personal. That it yet leaves the rhythmic aspect, chordal spacing, orchestral color, and all the other aspects of composition to the composer still puts the burden of choice on the shoulders of the composer. This is as it should be.

WEBERN

Anton von Webern (1883–1945), born in Vienna, studied at the University of Vienna. He conducted theater orchestras, taught composition and became actively involved in a series of performances organized by Schoenberg for the purpose of presenting new musical works without the "benefits" of press coverage. In his adoption of the twelve-tone method he extended the idea of non-repetition of tones into the area of tone color, so that there is a constantly changing "wheel of color," as it were. His output was not large and, at first, acceptance of his work was tentative, but since his death the circle of appreciation has been growing larger and larger. His *Five Pieces for Orchestra* is an example of intense concentration of materials.

BERG

Alban Berg (1885–1935) was also born in Vienna. After some untutored music study he began the study of composition with Schoenberg, who became not only teacher but friend. Berg aligned himself with the private performances of new music that had been organized by Schoenberg and supervised by Webern. He taught, lectured, and wrote articles on new music for magazines.

His adoption of Schoenberg's twelve-tone method, in contrast to that of Webern's, allowed for a freer use of the disciplines of serial technique. Whereas the writing of both Schoenberg and Webern has been considered pointillistic, or dry and acerbic, Berg did not deny himself a lyricism that many listeners readily identify with. This lyricism, as well as the use of tonality when he chooses, have allowed for a readier acceptance of his music than is true in the case of both Schoenberg and Webern.

Analysis and commentary: Berg, Violin Concerto

One of the most felicitous works written in the twelve-tone system is the Violin Concerto of Alban Berg. It is this work that we shall look at in some detail. We shall examine Berg's use of the twelve-tone system, and concurrently it will become evident that Berg was not willing to abandon all implications of tonality.

Dem Andenken eines Engels — thus is the Violin Concerto of Alban Berg dedicated: "In remembrance of one of the angels." Berg had been approached in 1934 by the American violinist Louis Krasner to write a violin concerto. The project of the concerto lay dormant in Berg's mind until, in the spring of 1935, a close friend, an *intime* in Berg's circle, died. This was Manon Gropius, the 18-year-old daughter of the widow of Gustav Mahler. Berg decided that the concerto would be a memorial to her memory. It was his last work.

Although a memorial, the Violin Concerto is not a brooding work, nor does it depict an attitude of resignation. It has rather an aura of quiet reflection, an intellectual contemplation, as it were, on the mystery of life and death. Though we shall discuss the work with this in mind, the listener should seek his own personal relation to the work.

The Violin Concerto is in two movements. The movements are further divided as shown in the table (page 454).

In the Violin Concerto there are tonal implications both within and without the twelve-tone row. In the opening measure of the work (Example 425) we hear pyramiding perfect fifths over a pedal B ♭ sus-

1st Movement

TIME SIGNATURE		MEASURES
$\frac{4}{4}$	Introduction: Andante	1–10
$\frac{2}{4}$	Section I	11–103
	Improvisatory style (ruminative)	
$\frac{6}{8}$	Section II	
	Scherzando: Allegretto	104–136
	Trio I	137–154
	Trio II	155–175
$\frac{3}{8}$	Scherzando (like a waltz)	176–213
	Folksong	213

2nd Movement

TIME SIGNATURE		MEASURES
	Section I	
$\frac{3}{4}$	Allegro (like a cadenza)	1–62
$\frac{4}{4}$	Written cadenza	63–96
	Pedal point on F	97–135
	Section II	
$\frac{4}{4}$	Adagio (chorale)	136–200
$\frac{3}{4}$	Folksong	201–213
$\frac{4}{4}$	Coda (chorale)	214–230

Example 425   Violin Concerto, Berg

Used by permission of the Theodore Presser Company and Universal Edition A. G. Vienna.

tained by the bass clarinet, which is an implication of a tonality that is later clarified in the setting of the chorale in the final pages of the work. The solo violin enters in the second measure, imitating the bare fifths of the first measure, and establishing *G* as a second important tonal "root." The bass clarinet B♭ continues during this measure (Example 426). We first see the tone row that is basic to the work dispersed

Example 426

Used by permission of the Theodore Presser Company and Universal Edition A. G. Vienna.

throughout the harmony in measures 11 to 15 (Example 427). The row

Example 427   Violin Concerto, Berg

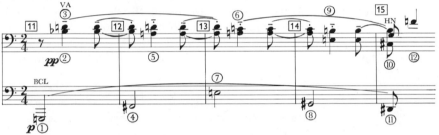

Used by permission of the Theodore Presser Company and Universal Edition A. G. Vienna.

is then clearly seen in melodic order in the solo violin entrance which begins in measure 15 (Example 428). While the row is being played

Example 428   Violin Concerto, Berg

Used by permission of the Theodore Presser Company and Universal Edition A. G. Vienna.

en toto by the solo violin the row is also being played simultaneously by the accompanying instruments but scattered through the harmony to form chordal structures. You can see from measures 11–14, shown above, that the composer has considerable freedom—even within the row—in choosing the notes to form a chord and in choosing their specific position within a chord.

Let us "step aside" for a moment to emphasize that the twelve-tone row is only a method of organization of sound. Whether the basis of a piece of music is pentatonic, modal, tonal, twelve-tone, or otherwise, the basis and the resulting consonance or dissonance possible within the system is but the means to the end. What is important is the composer's ability to handle his materials within the all-encompassing concept of music as existing in time. It is the rhythmic movement of the work that is the deciding factor. The rhythmic movement—in all its diversity of tension and release, climax and calm, ebb and the flow—is the essential, the *sine qua non*. The melody and the harmony may seem more interesting at times, and they are easier to discuss; the orchestration adds the piquancy of color; but these are, and can only be, a part of the time concept.

There are several ways in which this row may be grouped. It may be thought of primarily as a series of ascending thirds from (1) through (9) and of major seconds from (9) through (12) (Example 429). It may

Example 429   Violin Concerto, Berg

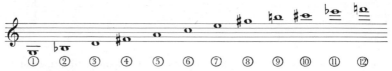

Used by permission of the Theodore Presser Company and Universal Edition A. G. Vienna.

also be considered for its possibilities of forming triads (Example 430).

Example 430   Violin Concerto, Berg

Used by permission of the Theodore Presser Company and Universal Edition A. G. Vienna.

It may also be considered as three four-note groupings, in which the first two groups form identical chord structures, with the third group being the whole-tone tetrachord that is the hallmark of the Bach chorale, *Es ist Genug*, which concludes the work (Example 431).

But note that the Bach chorale, *Es ist Genug*, is not only the goal of the entire work. It is at the very heart of it. The twelve-tone row that is

Example 431

Example 432

Es ist Genug, J. S. Bach

the basis of the work is so designed that the end of the row and the opening of the chorale will "mesh."

Before continuing with Berg's concerto, it is wise to become familiar with Bach's chorale. The chorale is given in Example 432 in the key of Berg's presentation. The particular sections that he uses to alternate with the solo violin are bracketed.

Berg divides the first movement into two main sections, the first ruminative, or reflecting, in its quasi-improvisatory style. The contrasting second section, beginning at measure 104, marked *Allegretto*, is freely based upon the traditional *dance form with trio* (Example 433).

Example 433   Violin Concerto, (Section II), Scherzando, Berg

Used by permission of the Theodore Presser Company and Universal Edition A. G. Vienna.

Berg marks the sections: Scherzando, Trio I, Trio II, Scherzando (like a waltz), and towards the end introduces a Carpathian folk-song. At measure 137, which begins Trio I, the Viennese waltz flavor is introduced by the use of broadly lyric major sixths in the strings (Example 434).

Example 434   Violin Concerto, Movement 1, Quasi Trio I, Berg

Used by permission of the Theodore Presser Company and Universal Edition A. G. Vienna.

Shortly after the beginning of the second Scherzando the solo violin plays, beginning at measure 182, a theme which, by virtue of the parallel thirds and the melodic contour is suggestive of a Viennese Waltz. This is immediately echoed in the woodwinds (Example 435). Shortly thereafter, at measure 208, Berg brings back the theme of the first Scherzando, measure 104 (Example 436), leading directly to the introduction by the horn, in measure 213, of the folk song (Example 437), which may be thought of as representing the simple joys of every-

Example 435   Violin Concerto, Movement 1, Scherzando, Berg

Used by permission of the Theodore Presser Company and Universal Edition
A. G. Vienna.

Example 436

Used by permission of the Theodore Presser Company and Universal Edition
A. G. Vienna.

day life. This is to appear again in the second movement in a different
guise. The last 12 measures show the presentation of the row in the solo
violin and the closing harmonies reminiscent of the opening measures
of Section I, ending on a G minor M^7 structure (G minor triad with
major seventh), clearly defining G as the second important tone of the
work.

The second movement may be divided into two sections, the first
of which is in the manner of an accompanied cadenza. The improvisa-
tory style of the first section leads to the crystallization that is the Bach
chorale. Out of the randomness that often seems to be true of everyday
existence emerges the clarity of thought and the peace of mind that
Es ist Genug exemplifies.

In the second measure of the second movement the solo violin
enters in an arpeggiation of the first four notes of the row and establishes G as the axis tone during the next few measures. During this
section the four notes of the tritone tetrachord, and the logical extension of this, the whole-tone scales, are explored in the devices of
inversion, retrograde motion, and so on. At measure 97 Berg establishes
a pedal-point on F that lasts for 39 measures. At measure 136, the
chorale, which has been alluded to in fragments, emerges in the solo
violin part. It is alternately stated by the solo violin and the woodwind
section. The woodwind section plays the Bach harmonization. The
chorale becomes the summation of the work, and although it is briefly
transformed and overshadowed by the Ländler folk song in measures
196–213, it reassumes its rock-like symbolization of stability at the coda,

Example 437   Violin Concerto, Movement 1, Folk Song, Berg

Used by permission of the Theodore Presser Company and Universal Edition A. G. Vienna.

measure 214, and concludes the work. The final chord, a B♭ major triad with added major sixth, reaffirms B♭ as the central tone of the work.

HINDEMITH

Paul Hindemith (1895–1963), born in Germany, attained proficiency early on several musical instruments. His main instrument was the violin, and his ability was such that he became concertmaster of the Frankfort Opera. His interest then turned to the viola, and it is this instrument that he played in quartet tours of Europe. He later maintained that a composer should be able to play, at least a little, any instrument that he wrote for. This is an interesting ideal, and there is certainly nothing that can be said against it. But it has not, by any means, been effectively demonstrated in practice.

Hindemith, along with Stravinsky, Schoenberg, and Bartók, was one of the most dominant forces in musical thought in the United States until at least the middle of the twentieth century. Hindemith contributed to this influence further through several books that he wrote. *The Craft of Musical Composition* was a standard work used in many colleges across the country, in addition to his *Elementary Training for Musicians. A Composer's World* was a collection of essays delivered at Harvard University in 1949.

His style was his own, as expounded in *The Craft of Musical Composition*, and was a careful construction that included a contemporary way of approaching music, which, nevertheless, had its roots in tradition. His melodies, which often seem both to evade and to suggest tonality, are sometimes modal in flavor but spiked with jagged contours that temporarily disguise the mode. His harmonies are based upon a system of comparative tension of vertical structures.

An early short opera, *Hin und Zurück,* showed the use of a basic contrapuntal retrograde device applied to a total work. The story and the music having proceeded about half way, each thereupon goes backward until the end, which was the beginning. Hindemith also believed, contrary to most contemporary composers, in practical music, *Gebrauchsmusik*—music that may be performed by amateur groups. A concert of his music at Harvard University in 1949 was an example of this. The concert was on the occasion of the birthday of Mrs. Coolidge, sponsor of the Coolidge Quartet. For the occasion Hindemith had written a round, which he taught to the audience so that they could sing it to Mrs. Coolidge.

BARTOK

Béla Bartók was born in Hungary in 1881. His father died when he was seven, and there developed between mother and son a close bond. It was she who gave him his first piano lessons when he was five, and it was she who discovered that he not only had perfect pitch, but a Mozartean faculty for remembering a tune he had composed, not needing to write it down until some time later. At the age of 11, Bartók made his first public appearance as both pianist and composer, a dual role he was to maintain throughout his life. Perhaps the most important phase of his career was entered when he notated a Hungarian peasant song, taking it down from the singing of a young peasant girl. This brought him to the realization that there was a vast native music of which he was unaware. He began a study of peasant music, and with Zoltán Kodály he spent about two years recording the native music not only of Hungary, but also of the Rumanians, Slovakians, Walachians, Turks, and Arabs. The peasant folk song became central to Bartók's compositional style, and examples of this influence may be found on many pages of his work. To it, however, Bartók applied a constantly fresh, imaginative, highly original technique.

Whereas Hindemith had a system that encompassed all of his writings, Bartók had no general system, but rather approached each work anew. The system for that work would arise out of the composition itself. Thus, if Bartók is harmonizing a Hungarian folk song, he may find the harmony from the melody itself, by "verticalizing" the melody.

Bartók's manner of approaching each work may be seen most conveniently in his six volumes for piano, *Mikrokosmos*. The title is indicative of his intent. Within a specific small world of a certain number of tones Bartók will explore and probe every corner. This small world is sufficient unto itself. It desires no other world, nor does it need one. What this technique does require, however, is a certain kind of composer, because this kind of writing can lead the composer into the trap of monotony. For each piece Bartók sets the problem, and he finds the solution. But the solution is unique for each piece. This approach may be seen in Bartók's last large work, the Concerto for Orchestra, written for a commission by Serge Koussevitzky. The entire first movement has as its seed and its defining feature the interval of a perfect fourth.

PROKOFIEV AND SHOSTAKOVICH

Sergei Prokofiev (1891 – 1953) began composing at the age of nine, and before he graduated from the St. Petersburg Conservatory he had become an excellent pianist and was performing his own works. He later traveled extensively as a concert pianist, including trips to America. His biting, ironic style of writing produced *Diabolical Suggestion* and *Sarcasms* for piano and earned him a reputation as a "futurist." *Scythian Suite* was his first important orchestral composition, and is an example of his barbaric, primitive style. Its approach is somewhat similar to that of Stravinsky in the *Rite of Spring*.

He also wrote music that is simple, charming, and naive. *Peter and the Wolf* was written for a children's theater and has since attained great popularity. Although Prokofiev's music contains sudden juxtapositions of keys, polytonality, and other contemporary practices, it is rooted in the tonal system. In his music may be found a mixture of Russian nationalism, neo-Classicism and French colorism. He was a prolific composer and wrote in all idioms, including music for a film, *Alexander Nevsky*. His "Classical" Symphony is a superb example of sophisticated wit, concise form, and clear, sparkling orchestration.

Dimitri Shostakovich, who was born in 1906, is best known in this country for his symphonies. His First Symphony, composed when he was 18, is still one of the most popular. The Fifth Symphony is also often performed. His "Polka" from *The Golden Age*, a ballet, is exceedingly well-known. After World War II he was in great favor in both his own country and the United States, and the completion of his new symphony in 1942, the Seventh, set off a flurry in the world press. Known popularly as the "Leningrad" Symphony, it was widely hailed. As the representative composer of Russia, Shostakovich often found himself in a precarious position. He was often denounced by the Russian government as leaning towards the "decadence" of capitalism and would as often admit his "fault." During a visit to New York in 1949 he tried to expound—somewhat unsuccessfully—to the press why a composer must be guided by his political and national ties.

Other important composers

LES SIX

In the Paris of post-World War I, the names of six composers were grouped together by Henri Collet in a newspaper article as representative of the new expression in French music. Known as Les Six, and with Satie as their "spiritual" leader, they made a strong impact. Only three of these six composers moved forward in the twentieth century to take their places in the main stream of music.

Arthur Honegger (1892–1955) symbolized the machine age with *Pacific 231*, a musical "imitation" of a locomotive. This attracted much attention, but Honegger moved away from this "representational tone-painting." A prolific composer, he wrote five symphonies, as well as operas, choral works, ballets, chamber music, piano music, and songs. He also composed for film and radio. His large choral work, *King David*, is representative. His chamber work, *Sonatine*, shows the influence of jazz. Although he used devices such as polytonality and suggestions of atonality, his music was tonally based and lyrically melodic.

Darius Milhaud (1892–1963) wrote a steady stream of music from his student days in Paris. The first to exploit polytonality; a pianist, conductor, and teacher; an experimenter in forms as well as means, he wrote in every important genre in interesting styles that encompassed the lyrical and the rhythmical, the dramatic and the playful. He exerted a great influence on young American composers through his teaching in the United States. One of his earliest works is still the best known: the ballet, *La Création du Monde.* Written for a small orchestra, the musical idiom suggests not so much jazz, as is often stated, as the music of the night-club of the 1920's.

Francis Poulenc (1899 – 1963), of the three composers discussed here, is the most representative in his music of a certain delightful kind of Gallic wit and charm. His style is eclectic, but a certain tongue-in-cheek approach often adds a distinct individuality to his scores. His work covers satirical chamber works, concertos and ballets, large choral works both secular and sacred, and opera. The opera, *La Voix Humaine,* is a splendid example of his ability to impart an immediacy to his work that is compelling in its portrayal of a woman at the telephone.

COPLAND

Aaron Copland, born in 1900 in Brooklyn, New York, was one of the first American composers to study in Paris with Nadia Boulanger. The "trek" had begun, and many young American composers after Copland were to come under her wing. Growing up in an America that was seeking to find itself musically, Copland was influenced in Paris by the frenzied search for expression. He was energized by the cosmopolitan exchange of ideas of the artists there. He purposely sought to become an "American composer," and in so doing we find for awhile the influence of jazz in some of his works. His Piano Concerto (1927) reflects this. He then turned to the music of an earlier America, and the barn dance and the hoe down became prominent parts of his style. In *Rodeo, Billy the Kid, Appalachian Spring,* all ballets, we find the "prairie" style in the homely dance rhythms.

Copland has sometimes been referred to as the dean of American composers, not so much for an Americanism that is found in his music, but for his constantly active life in all phases of American music: as composer, conductor, author, lecturer, and teacher. In addition, he has constantly proselytized the young American composer.

He wrote several books, which have had wide dissemination, one of these being *Our New Music.* He has always pleaded the work of the American composer — calling attention to it, discussing it, analyzing it, performing it, conducting it. For many years his influence was strong in his position as head of the Composition Department at Tanglewood.

OTHER AMERICANS

Roger Sessions, born in 1896 in Brooklyn, New York, was influenced early by Ernst Bloch, with whom he studied, and later to some extent by Stravinsky. His writing is highly individual, with emphasis on a tight contrapuntal style and uncompromising dissonance, with the result that his work has not gained wide acceptance by the public. A thoughtful, probing approach has not resulted in a large number of works, but there are four symphonies, a variety of chamber works, some concertos and choral works, and an opera among his output. As a teacher at Smith College, Princeton University and other institutions, he has had widespread influence. This influence was extended by a text on harmony, as well as other writings.

Walter Piston, born in 1894, was handily served during 36 years of teaching at Harvard University by the proximity of the Boston Symphony Orchestra, for which he wrote many commissioned works. In his personality are still discerned traces of his Maine heritage. We find a workmanlike approach, a sense of craftsmanship, and a careful concern for design. There are six symphonies to his credit, and much delightful chamber music, but his most played work has been the ballet, *The Incredible Flutist,* introduced by Arthur Fiedler and the Boston Pops Orchestra in 1938. His teaching resulted in three important texts, each of which is widely known and widely used: *Harmony, Counterpoint,* and *Orchestration.*

Samuel Barber has been the recipient of many commissions and many honors. Born in 1910, and considered to be American to the core by some, his work nevertheless has its roots in Europe. His diatonic style is easy to listen to. His *Essay for Orchestra* is one of his most played works, and his *Overture to the School for Scandal* is also well known.

Elliott Carter studied with Piston and Nadia Boulanger. He was born in 1908 into a well-to-do family in New York, and acquired a leisurely, thorough education. Some of his early works show influences of Stravinsky and Copland, but his style was constantly developing towards a rhythmic — or time — concept that was to be unique. His Piano Sonata of 1945 – 46 is considered his first outstanding work. Others are the Sonata for Cello, the String Quartet, and the Variations for Orchestra. Although his work was largely unknown before 1950, it has been gaining much more notice and far wider acceptance in the last few years. Perhaps Carter's most important achievement has been what he calls "metrical modulation," in which the speed is carefully adjusted by special metronomic designations for successive note values.

Underlining the strong Americanism of William Schuman (born

1910) is his *Chester Overture* for band, based upon the hymn tune by William Billings, a composer of American Revolutionary times. Among others writing in this pleasing, colloquial style are Douglas Moore (1893 –   ), Howard Hanson (1896 –   ), Virgil Thompson (1896 –   ), Roy Harris (1898 –   ), Paul Creston (1906 –   ), and Randall Thompson (1899 –   ).

Gunther Schuller (1925 –   ), another New York composer, is one of the most recent leading lights on the musical scene in America. His activities are many and varied, and in this respect he may be considered a latter-day Aaron Copland. He has written much for small groups; and also has to his credit a Symphony for Brass and Percussion, which is an exceedingly well wrought piece. It is one of the few works written for brass by a composer who knows how to handle these instruments well, from practical experience. (See Example 331, Chapter 9.) His best known work is *Seven Studies of Paul Klee*, and it takes its place beside a work written well over a half-century before – Moussorgsky's *Pictures at an Exhibition* – as a composer's reaction to a graphic expression. Schuller has not only been active in the music of the concert hall, but has concerned himself with the most serious personal expression of the times – jazz. Originator of the phrase, "Third Stream," which refers to the blending of jazz and art music, he has been intimately involved as composer, conductor, and promulgator of these apparently opposite expressions in an attempt to find a new expression of our times, to see if there can be a fusion of these two opposed forms of expression, combining the emotional and cerebral.

MUSIC FOR THE THEATER

Two composers, some distance apart, and of rather opposite backgrounds, met, as it were, in midstream to produce two of the most important works in musical theater. They were George Gershwin and Leonard Bernstein. They had been preceded by Kurt Weill, who in 1933 brought over from Germany *The Threepenny Opera*, a modern adaptation of *The Beggar's Opera*. In its social satire the popular song style is purposely used to illustrate social decadence. It is used so well that one of the songs, "Mack the Knife," has *become* an American popular song. Weill settled in America in 1935 and thereafter produced several successful musical plays, among them *Knickerbocker Holiday*, *Lost in the Stars*, and a folk opera, *Down in the Valley*.

Gershwin grew up in the world of popular music. Born in Brooklyn in 1898, he began playing piano in music stores at the age of 16 to demonstrate the current songs for buyers of sheet music. Gershwin was not a jazz musician, as has been so often claimed. This confusion on the part of many writers was caused by the fact that the twenties were referred to as "The Jazz Age," and the popular music of the time and all orchestras of the time that played for dancing were referred to as "jazz" orchestras. He was, however, a highly gifted composer of popular songs, and in turning his talents to works in larger forms successfully synthesized the popular music element with the aims of these large dramatic forms. This is apparent in his *Rhapsody in Blue*, the Piano Concerto, and *An American in Paris*. His supreme achievement, however, was his folk opera, *Porgy and Bess*.

Porgy and Bess was written for a completely Negro cast. Gershwin had already become extremely familiar with the multitudinous problems of producing successful musical theater in the writing of many musical comedies. To this work Gershwin brought his unique approach to writing popular music.

Popular music is, in certain ways, a folk music. It is not written for the concert hall, and it is not usually written for instruments; it is written to be sung. It is similiar to true folk music in that it is for an individual singer with or without accompaniment. That it is often trite or insipid is true, but unimportant. And the fact that jazz has often used popular materials in its art expression has no bearing except perhaps to show how much difference there is between popular music and jazz. Gershwin's contributions to popular music were of the highest order.

Besides this, Gershwin brought his experience in writing his orchestral works in the larger forms. In addition, *Porgy and Bess* exhibits influences of the blues and of the Negro spiritual. The opening song, "Summertime," in its almost totally pentatonic usage, is reminiscent of the spiritual. None of these elements make a successful work, but in *Porgy and Bess* they are a part of its importance.

Leonard Bernstein's musical background was the antithesis of George Gershwin's. Born in Lawrence, Massachusetts, he studied music at Harvard University and went on to study further at the Curtis Institute in Philadelphia. Here, in addition to piano, he studied orchestration and conducting. At the Berkshire Music Center he became at first a protégé of and then an assistant to Serge Koussevitsky, director of the school and conductor of the Boston Symphony Orchestra. In 1943 Bruno Walter, who was to conduct the New York Philharmonic, fell ill, and on short notice Bernstein filled in. His achievement was noted in the press and he went on to conducting engagements with major symphony orchestras throughout the world.

He wrote symphonies and chamber works, ballets and vocal works. More important to his ultimate contribution to the theater were *On the Town* in 1944 and *Wonderful Town* in 1952, both extremely successful musical comedies. In *Trouble in Tahiti*, a one-act opera, and *Candide*, a rather "serious" musical comedy, he received further experience in the theater, which was to culminate in 1957 in *West Side Story*, which successfully reflects the issues of contemporary America.

Gershwin began as a composer of popular music and finally broadened his talents through constant study so that his scope finally embraced the larger forms. Bernstein learned the formal aspects of music first, and thoroughly, and then allowed the popular music idiom to permeate his work for the theater.

It is important to stress that in each of these composers the ultimate expression, which embraced both popular music and the larger dramatic concept, was not a forced expression. The fusion was the natural result of an honest appreciation of both types of expression. Neither had to search to *be* an "American composer." Each was.

Experimental composers

Henry Cowell (1897–1965) was one of the early experimental composers. He was at first self-taught, and when 15 years of age he came upon the idea of playing upon the piano keyboard with his forearm or fist, thereby producing large clusters of sound. This technique may be used to produce percussive sounds or soft "multiple vibrations." This, and a procedure of plucking the piano strings as if it were a harp, opened the way for many younger composers into experiments with sound. Cowell also, with Leon Theremin, produced a Rhythmicon, an electronic instrument that could produce multiple rhythms concurrently. Composer of over 1,000 works, he was constantly active in championing new music. His experiments—including others not mentioned—have been perhaps his outstanding contribution to contemporary music.

John Cage (1912–   ), as the innovator of various "techniques" and "non-techniques" of composition, has been a rather constant influence on young American composers. His studies with Schoenberg, but more especially Varese and Henry Cowell, turned him in a new direction. The first experiments to attract attention were with a "prepared piano." The piano strings are "prepared" by changing their pitch or their sound. The latter may be achieved by inserting upon or between the strings various foreign objects such as pieces of metal or paper. Other experiments include "random composition," which may consist of setting the dials of various radios at different wave-lengths. The result is the composition. His well known attempt to negate the very foundations of composition and performance is a piece called *4 minutes and 33 seconds*. During this length of time a pianist (although it is not necessary for him to be one) sits at the piano, but does not play. This particular work has had its influence. Discussion continues as to its merit. In the case of such a work as this, there is no need to await the verdict of posterity. There can be no verdict; there is no evidence.

Olivier Messiaen (1908 –   ), through his treatise on methods of composition, as a teacher at the Paris Conservatoire, as well as through his association with the group, *La Jeune France*, has had considerable influence on younger composers. Some of his works are massive in scope and contain elements of mysticism and oriental influences, using various modes. To enhance his expression he has used unusual percussion instruments, as well as the electronic instrument, the *Ondes Martenot* (named after its inventor), which produces a sound not unlike a female voice with a tremendous range. *Turangalila*, his 10-movement work for orchestra, exhibits his full technique, and in spite of its length is a masterful expression, almost hypnotic in its profound probing. Messiaen, with Pierre Boulez, was a leader in France in experiments in electronic music.

Musique concrete consists of recording musical and natural sounds on tape. The speed of the tape may be adjusted so that totally new sounds may be achieved. The composer, or controller of the tape, splices and edits to achieve his results. The musician, as performer, is no longer involved. Composition by electronic means currently is the object of much interest, and certainly new doors to the uses of sound as a means of expression will be opened. Some American composers have involved themselves in the possibilities inherent in the uses of tape, and centers for experiment have been established, such as that at Columbia University. The composition may be complete on tape, or may be used in combination with instrumental groups. As has been true in all periods throughout the history of music, critical criteria must be carefully applied to the merits of each work.

Other experiments in random composition have included what may be termed a "musical mobile." The mobile effect is achieved through assigning to each performer a certain number of "examples." Each example will contain a certain amount of notated music, from one note to perhaps several measures. Each performer chooses the order in which he will play these examples. In the next performance, either immediately or at some later time, the order is again chosen by the performer. In other words, the particular "viewing" depends upon the way "the wind blows," as with a mobile.

Random composition would most certainly include improvisation, and while this had once been a vital force in music, especially in the Baroque, and also during the classical period, it waned during the nineteenth century. The spirit of improvisation has never died out in folk expression, nor in the great tradition of organ extemporization. Until the advent of jazz, however, it did not contribute again to any growing cultural body of music.

Improvisation, dead in the concert-hall, was brought to life again by jazz as jazz ushered in the twentieth century. Through the entire history of jazz, improvisation has been its life-blood, constantly nurturing it and revitalizing it. Improvisation has always been understood by the jazz musician. It is seriously open to question whether the non-jazz oriented composer has known how to handle it.

Aleatory, or chance, music may include improvisation, but as this includes the possibilities of selection by the performer, there are many experiments that emphasize the aleatory aspect—that of "gambling" with the results—even more. Such experiments include the throwing of dice to decide the order of tones, or sections of music.

Jazz

The seeming paradox of jazz is that it is both a personal expression and a group expression. On the one hand, it is the highly subjective, spontaneous personal expression of the jazz soloist; on the other, it is the constant group expression of the other players, which seeks to align itself with the soloist and support him. There is ever-present, in good jazz, an "electric current" connecting the soloist and the group. Each of these two expressions—that of the soloist and that of the group—is sparked by, and sparks, the other. Thus there is a constant cross-reaction. To put it another way, the soloist is part of a "performing collective."

The performance of symphonic music, to take one kind of art-music, seems to be a large group effort. But each does not so much seek to spark and be sparked by his fellow player as to play his individual part as well as possible. The playing of a symphonic composition is in reality a one-man operation in spite of all the words that have been written to the contrary. The one man is the composer. And everyone from the conductor to every single player is intent on one thing: to carry out the composer's wish—whether the composer is dead or alive. And this is as it should be. Unless the composer himself is the conductor, this kind of performance can be an exceedingly impersonal project. An analogy may make this clear. The composer is like the president of a large corporation. From the president's office comes the overall policy (the composer's score); directives and orders and sextuplicate copies are processed (the score is copied into parts); the man out in the field is told to put the policy into action (the conductor receives the score and studies it); he contacts his subordinates and they are given a specific job to do (the players receive their parts and the rehearsals begin). You can see how far it is from writing the music to having it performed.

The important thing about jazz is its immediacy. The composing soloist, the improviser, is there, on the spot. It happens here and now. This is the excitement of it. Whether jazz was born in New Orleans is not pertinent to our discussion here, but New Orleans certainly nurtured it through its first years and sent it out into the world. Jazz at various times has been described as an unhealthy, and even wicked, offspring, but it has shown an amazing vitality through the years, and the diatribes against it have abated to the extent that it is now invited into the church (e.g., Ellington's *A Concert of Sacred Music*). The result of a fusion of the culture of the African Negro, European harmonies, and some American folk idioms, early jazz also contains traces of Creole French and West Indian. It has always borrowed and absorbed whatever seemed interesting or pertinent to its expression, but it has never lost its own individual personality. It is recognized throughout the world as America's unique contribution to music. But the critical and academic recognition has come slowly in America.

Epilogue

It has yet to be established whether happenings, third stream, chance music, random treatments of material in either jazz or art music can be meaningful experiences as art forms. The artist in each of the arts will —and must—constantly search for new means of expression. It is not within the province of this book to discuss a matter that properly belongs to aesthetics. The aesthetics of music has been a vexing philosophical problem for some time, and we can do no more here than make a suggestion. This book has been about the appreciation of music, and about the understanding of music. You may already have found that more understanding can sometimes result in *less* appreciation. Certain works that were once favorites have lost their luster. Like a first love, they are remembered with some nostalgia, but as understanding develops tastes broaden. Your taste must continue to broaden and you should not only go back further in time, and dig deeper into certain areas, but keep your eyes—and especially your ears—towards the future.

Whether a new work becomes a part of the literature of the twentieth century only the future can tell. Rebellion is not enough. The rebellion must be successful. Its success depends not only upon the overthrow of the old regime, which is certainly the first step, but most especially in putting in the place of the old authority a new authority. The standards of judging the worth of a work of art in any field have never been set to the satisfaction of the majority. These words of Aldous Huxley are to the point.

> The traditional distinction between the crafts and the fine arts is based among other things, on degrees of complexity. A good picture is a greater work of art than a good bowl or a good vase. Why? Because it unifies in one harmonious whole more, and more diverse, elements of human experience than are or can be unified and harmonized in the pot. Some of the non-representational pictures painted in the course of the last fifty years are very beautiful; but even the best of them are minor works, inasmuch as the number of elements of human experience which they combine and harmonize is pitifully small. In them we look in vain for that ordered profusion, that lavish and yet perfectly controlled display of intellectual wealth, which we discover in the best works of the "literary" painters of the past.*

Whether Huxley's view is valid is something that must be considered seriously. Whether you ultimately accept or reject his premise must be your decision. But let us make a final statement to the listener.

With regard to contemporary music, as with all contemporary art: (1) You must have an absolutely open mind. But at the same time: (2) You must not allow yourself to be "taken in." With reference to the first statement, do not judge new music by the values you have set on the old. And with reference to the second, do not conclude, as some extremists do, that because music is new and daring, it is good. One of the tests of a work is whether you can go back to it again and again. You do not have to be a musician or a critic or a philosopher to make this test. What you must do is listen.

*Aldous Huxley, *On Art and Artists* (New York: Harper & Row, Publishers, 1960), pp. 301 and 302.

Index of musical examples

473

Glossary-index

A 440, *21*
a cappella, *274*
accelerando, *109*
accent, 6, *85,* 87–89
   agogic, *85,* 88–90, 94
   dynamic, *85,* 88
   intervallic: emphasis achieved by note or
         notes approached by a leap. *85*
   mark, 32
   melodic, *85*
   metric: emphasis occurring through the
         successive, regular alternation of
         strong and weak beats. *85,* 93
   nature of, 89
accented offbeats, *105*
accidental, *48*
accidentals in chords, 152–153
accompaniment patterns, *91*–93
acoustics, *283*
Adagio, *107*
Adagio molto, 5
additive forms, *228*
Aeolian mode, 372
aesthetics, music and, 471
aggregate structures, *235*
aggregate vocal forms, *243*
Agnus Dei, 244
agogic accent, *85,* 88–90, 94
agréments, *384*
album leaf, *239,* 417
Allegro, 5, *107*
Allegro con brio, 5
alto (instrument), *286*
alto clarinet, 289, *299*
alto flute, *294*
alto horn, *310*
alto trombone, *312*
alto voice, *262,* 268
Amati, Nicolo, 374, 376–377
Ambrose, Bishop of Milan, 356
Ambrosian Chant, 356
Andante, 5
answer, *196*
anthem, *242*
antecedent, *225*

antiphony, *274*
aria, *92, 242*
   Baroque origins, 375
   concert, *242*
   da capo, *242*
arioso, *242*
Arne, Thomas, 380
arpa. See harp
Ars Nova, 363
articulation: the manner in which tones are
          performed with respect to clarity;
          also relating to staccato, legato, etc.
art song, *242*
a tempo, *109*
arpeggio, *154*

B-flat clarinet, 289
Bach, Carl Philipp Emanuel, 384
Bach, Johann Christian, 323, 384
Bach, Johann Christoff, 384
Bach, Johann Sebastian, 381
   as culmination of Baroque, 375
   as performer, 374
Bach, Wilhelm Friedmann, 384
Bach Gesellschaft, 419
Bach trumpet, *307*
Bacon, Roger, 362
ballad, *239,* 417
ballet, *240*
ballet suite, *239*
band, concert. *See* concert band
bar or bar-line, 6, *31, 95*
Barber, Samuel, 465
Bardi, Count Giovanni. *See* Camerata
baritone horn, *312*–313
baritone voice, *262,* 270–271
Bartók, Béla, 461–462
basic unit beat, *28*
bass, *288,* 289
bass-baritone, *271*
bass of chord, *152*
bass clarinet, 289, *300*
bass drum, *318*
bass fiddle, *288*
bass trombone, *312*